Yorkshire Stories Re-told

James Burnley

Yorkshire Stories Re-told.

Yorkshire Stories Re-told.

BY

JAMES BURNLEY,

AUTHOR OF

"FORTUNES MADE IN BUSINESS;" "WEST-RIDING SKETCHES;"
"TWO SIDES OF THE ATLANTIC," &c., &c.

LEEDS: RICHARD JACKSON.

LONDON: SIMPKIN, MARSHALL & CO.,
AND WHITAKER & CO.

I Dedicate this Book

TO

THE MEMORY OF

A NOTABLE YORKSHIREMAN,

THE LATE

William Foster, Esq., J.P., D.L.,

OF HORNBY CASTLE, AND QUEENSBURY;

IN GRATEFUL REMEMBRANCE OF THE KINDLY

INTEREST HE TOOK IN MY WORK, AND

IN RESPECTFUL RECOGNITION OF

HIS MANY NOBLE QUALITIES

OF HEART AND MIND.

Jas. Burnley.

PREFACE.

THE author has endeavoured in the following pages to invest a number of old Yorkshire Stories with such fresh interest as could be imparted to them by a careful examination of their circumstances and surroundings, and by personal visits to the scenes of many of the Stories. In some instances the narratives are altogether new, and in others, special investigation has led to the bringing to light of facts which had previously escaped notice. The Stories in themselves are, for the most part, of peculiar interest to Yorkshire readers; and if, in the handling of them, the author has succeeded in putting them into acceptable literary shape, he will have achieved all that he set himself to accomplish.

J. B.

CONTENTS.

NO.		PAGE
1.	The Story of Eugene Aram	1
2.	The Holmfirth Flood	20
3.	The Clockhouse and the Jowett Family	39
4.	The Luddite Riots	55
5.	Mary Bateman, the Yorkshire Witch	70
6.	The Hermit of Rombalds Moor	81
7.	Jonathan Martin and York Minster	89
8.	The Calverley Tragedy	105
9.	A Yorkshire Stable Boy	127
10.	The Hebden Valley Murder	141
11.	The Bishop Blaize Festivals	159
12.	The Halifax Gibbet	179
13.	Robin Hood and Little John	192
14.	The Elland Tragedy	213
15.	The Story of the Prophet Wroe	223
16.	William Nevison, the Highwayman	243
	Yorkshire Ghost Stories :—	
	17. The Bierley Ghost	255
	18. The Scottish Pedlar	257
	18. Fair Rebecca	260
20.	A Yorkshire Stroller—" Old Wild's "	268
21.	The Grass Wood Murder	300

Yorkshire Stories Re-Told.

THE STORY OF EUGENE ARAM.

IT was a cold, wintry night; the snow was on the ground, and the air was keen and piercing. The date was the 7th of February, 1744; and as the darkness closed in over the picturesque town of Knaresborough, a tall, straight-limbed man, about forty years of age, attired in a long blue coat, was seen to turn the key in the door of a little building used as a school, in the White Horse Inn yard. When he had locked the door and put the key in his pocket, this man, with his precise dress and moody brow, went up the yard and looked in at a flax-dressing shop, and had a word or two with the proprietor. The name of the man who had come from the school was Eugene Aram; the master flax-dresser's name was Richard Houseman. The ordinary observer would have found it difficult to account for the fact that between these two men there existed the closest ties either of friendship or interest. In appearance and character they were utterly different. Aram was a man of great learning, of refined and scholarly aspect, and respected by every one: while Houseman was rough, uncultured, heavy-jawed, and repulsive of countenance, with a mind incapable of understanding or appreciating the finer nature of the schoolmaster. The flax-dresser, who was about the same age as Aram, had for

B

his daily companion a large domesticated raven, which usually perched on the top of his shop steps ; and on this particular night, if the " grim, ungainly, ghastly, gaunt, and ominous bird of yore" possessed any of that prophetic insight which it has been credited with, it must have croaked most dismally while Aram and its master conversed together in subdued and mysterious tones.

Two other men were probably seen by Aram before he went home that evening, and these were Henry Terry, the landlord of the Barrel Inn, and Daniel Clark, a shoemaker, with both of whom he was on closely intimate terms.

It was about six o'clock when Aram reached his own house, which was situate up a passage in Church Lane. His wife was washing the kitchen floor as he went in, and he requested her to put out the fire there and make one in the room above stairs. She did as he desired, and Aram then had his tea and went out again.

Aram and his wife did not live happily together. They had been married when very young, and there seems to have been little harmony of taste between them. Aram himself was a strange being ; his habits of meditation and solitary wandering would be little calculated to agree with the desires of a spirited, active, cheerfully-disposed woman, and therefore it is not surprising that they frequently had their matrimonial existence marred by domestic differences.

Aram was a native of Ramsgill, a little village in Netherdale, and had been born in 1704. His father was a Nottinghamshire man, and a gardener of great ability, who served in turn Dr. Compton (Bishop of London), Sir Edward Blackett, and Sir John Ingilby. Aram claimed some celebrity for his ancestors, asserting that they were formerly Lords of Eryam, or Aryam, now called Eryholme, on the southern banks of the Tees, in Yorkshire, and that they subsequently removed from those parts and settled at

Aram or Averam Park, in Nottinghamshire, where they were possessed of no less than three knights' fees in the reign of Edward III. Be this as it may, there is no doubt Eugene Aram was very respectably connected. At the age of thirteen or fourteen he joined his father at Newby, and remained there till the death of Sir Edward Blackett, occupying himself with great assiduity in the study of mathematics. At the age of sixteen, Mr. Christopher Blackett, the fourth son of Sir Edward Blackett, engaged him as "bookkeeper in his accompting-house" in London, and here Aram continued for a year or two, when an attack of smallpox caused him to return home to Newby. At Newby, with leisure on his hands and an abundant supply of books at his command, he renewed his mathematical studies, and prosecuted others, with great avidity. Then, after a time, he was invited to take a school at Ramsgill, his native place; and it was during his residence there that he married his wife, Anna Spence, who lived at Lofthouse. For several years he now appears to have devoted himself heart and soul to the acquirement of learning, gaining a very extensive knowledge of the Greek and Latin classics. "In the midst of these literary pursuits," wrote Aram afterwards, "a man and horse from my good friend William Norton, Esq., came for me from Knaresborough, along with that gentleman's letter inviting me thither; and accordingly I repaired thither, in some part of the year 1734, and was, I believe, well accepted and esteemed there."

On the memorable evening to which we have previously referred—the 7th of February, 1744—Aram would have been resident at Knaresborough ten years. How he came to associate himself during that time with such men as Houseman, Clark, and Terry is a mystery, for it is known that while carrying on the little school in the White Horse Inn yard he added a knowledge of Hebrew to his other attainments. "When not in his school," says Scatcherd, the historian of Morley, who interested himself greatly in the unhappy career of Aram, "he was a complete recluse, and if seen abroad on an evening he was always alone, and appeared lost in meditation. The company and busy haunts of men he invariably avoided. He was a man of few words, and seldom deigned to converse except with very sensible or literary characters. He was, in fact, a sublime visionary, who held chief converse with the ancients or with the stars, and followed nature to her inmost recesses." The late Lord Lytton, despite the halo of romance which he has thrown round the life of the Knaresborough schoolmaster, and despite the perversions of fact in which he indulged in the exercise of his function as a novelist, formed a very correct idea of the character of Aram, into which he inquired more fully and particularly even than Scatcherd. " Eugene Aram," says Lord Lytton, "was a man whose whole life seemed to have been one sacrifice to knowledge—a man who had taught himself, under singular difficulties, nearly all the languages of the civilised earth ; the profound mathematician, the elaborate antiquarian, the abstruse philologist, uniting with his graver lores the more florid accomplishments of science, from the scholastic trifling of heraldry to the gentle learning of herbs and flowers."

Imagine a man of this mental calibre lowering himself to the vulgar plottings and schemings of such rogues and ruffians as Houseman, Terry, and Clark ! Some very strong disturbing influence must have been at work to cause such a falling away from the better feelings of his nature. Aram himself alleged the misconduct of his wife as the reason of his disgrace, and suspected her of being too friendly with Clark. It is easy to imagine that, preyed upon by such feelings as these, Aram might at times be driven to seek the solace of the public-house ; that there would be times even when his beloved studies would not serve to afford relief to his unsettled mind. In this manner he might occasionally find his way to the house of Terry, the Barrel Inn, and make the companionship of Houseman and Clark, who would doubtless be regular frequenters.

A week or two previous to the 7th of February, 1744, Clark had married a woman who possessed a fortune of some £200, which in those days would be considered a rather large sum. This event was much talked of in the town, and the shoemaker was congratulated upon his good luck. The knowledge that he had come into a nice sum of money was calculated to place him in good credit, and he and his associates resolved to take advantage of this circumstance to effect a series of frauds. Clark was prevailed upon to order considerable quantities of linen and woollen drapery, table and bed linen, of a number of tradesmen in the town ; and in addition to this, he borrowed from innkeepers and others a number of silver tankards, watches, rings, &c. : the pretext being that he was going to entertain a number of friends to supper, and wished to feast them sumptuously. The better to deceive those from whom he borrowed, he ordered large quantities of ale and other liquors for the supposed supper. Amongst other things that Clark thus fraudulently obtained may be mentioned a dictionary, in two folio volumes, and an edition of Pope's translation of the Iliad of Homer, in six volumes. Aram, in all probability, would have suggested the procuring of these, and, had all things turned out as desired, would have taken them as part of his share of the plunder. This was the position of affairs on the night of the 7th February, 1744. The various articles which Clark had obtained were to be distributed or converted, and the plotters were to make fair division of the spoil. Between six o'clock that night and five next morning, Aram, Houseman, Clark, and probably Terry, were engaged in some dark and mysterious deeds, regarding which the full truth was never to be revealed. Aram's wife, fourteen years afterwards, stated that early on in the evening of this 7th of February, her husband went out and did not return until two o'clock in the morning. He was then accompanied, she said, by Clark and Houseman, and they came upstairs into the room where she was, and remained about an hour. She says her husband asked her for a handkerchief for Dickey (meaning Houseman) to tie about his head, and she lent him one; after which Clark said, "It'll soon be morning, we must be off." Then, she says, they all went out together, Clark having a wallet or sack upon his back, and where they went to she could not tell. About five o'clock the same morning, she states, her husband and Houseman returned, without Clark, and Aram came upstairs and asked for a candle so that he might make a fire in the room below, to which she objected, saying that there was no occasion for a fire there, seeing that there was already a good one in the room where she was. Aram then said, "Dickey is below, and he doesn't choose to come upstairs." She then said, "What have you done with Daniel?" and her husband gave her no answer, but requested her to go to bed, which she refused to do. Aram now went downstairs with the candle, she says, and she listened to the conversation, and overheard them planning to shoot her "when her passion was off," to prevent her telling. On hearing this, she remained quiet until seven o'clock, when Aram and Houseman went out of the house a second time. She then went downstairs, and amongst the ashes in the grate found several bits of wearing apparel, and upon the handkerchief which she had lent Houseman discovered a spot of blood. On seeing this she went to Houseman, showed him the blood-mark on the handkerchief, and said she was afraid they had done something bad to Clark. Houseman protested that he had no idea what she meant.

How far this story of Mrs. Aram's was true, it is

impossible to say. Generally speaking, she was not a woman whose word was to be relied upon, and the fact that her husband separated from her and left her behind him at Knaresborough, is not to be forgotten. If Aram had been in the power of this woman—which he must have been if her story was true—it is hardly credible that he would have left her at Knaresborough, with the full knowledge that she might at any time, by letting fall a single word, bring him to the gallows.

After Clark's disappearance there was naturally a great commotion in the neighbourhood of Knaresborough, and the people from whom he had procured goods soon saw that they had been the victims of a cruel fraud. It was imagined that Clark had absconded ; and Aram, Houseman, and Terry were suspected of being his accomplices. Search was made, and a portion of the goods—some velvets and drapery goods—were dug up in Aram's garden, and other articles were traced to the possession of Houseman. Aram was at the time understood to be in pecuniary difficulties, and owed a certain sum to a Mr. Norton—in all probability the Mr. Norton upon whose invitation Aram had originally come to Knaresborough. Mr. Norton was prevailed upon to arrest Aram for this debt, in order that the schoolmaster might be detained until the proper legal process for charging him with being concerned in the Clark frauds was completed. To everybody's astonishment, however, Aram discharged the debt for which he was arrested, and shortly afterwards paid off a considerable mortgage on a house which had been left him by his father, in Bondgate, Ripon. The intended prosecution was abandoned, and in a short time Aram took his departure from Knaresborough, and nothing was heard of him there again for many years.

According to Aram's own statement, he proceeded in April, 1744, to London. "Here," he says, "I agreed to teach Latin and writing for the Rev. Mr. Painblane, in

Piccadilly, which he, along with a salary, returned by teaching me French, where I observed the pronunciation the most formidable part, at least to me, who had never before known a word of it. But this, my continued application, every night or other opportunity, overcame, and I soon became a tolerable master of French. I remained in this situation two years and above. Some time after this I went to Hays, in Middlesex, in the capacity of a writing master, and served a gentleman there, since dead; and stayed after that with a worthy and reverend gentleman. I continued here between three and four years. I succeeded to several other places in the South of England, and all that while used every occasion of improvement. I then transcribed the Acts of Parliament, to be registered in Chancery, and afterwards went down to the Free School at Lynn." All this time he was studying the Chaldic, Arabic, and Celtic languages, and advanced a considerable way with a comparative polyglot lexicon, upon a new and, for that age, improved plan.

In such pursuits as these he passed his days and nights, living a secluded and perhaps melancholy life. His favourite daughter Sally came to reside with him at Lynn, and very great affection subsisted between them. Whether, as the poet has written,—

> " Much study had made him very lean,
>   And pale and leaden-eyed,"

or whether it was his custom to sit " remote from all, a melancholy man," we have only the somewhat doubtful evidence of the poet and the novelist (both of whom have dealt powerfully with the poor usher's story) to advance. In any event, however, Aram could hardly be a happy man. His domestic troubles were in themselves sufficient to cause him endless sorrow.

A very serious circumstance occurred on the 1st of August, 1758, while Aram was quietly pursuing his scholastic duties at Lynn. A labourer, while digging for stone at a place called Thistle Hill, near Knaresborough, came upon a wooden chest which was found to contain a human skeleton. Murder was at once suspected, and many people were bold enough to make known their belief that the bones were those of Daniel Clark, the shoemaker, who had disappeared so mysteriously fourteen years previously. An inquest was held, and Aram's wife, who had frequently let fall hints of her suspicion that Clark had been murdered, was had up and examined, when she made the statement before alluded to. Houseman was then brought before the coroner and the jury. He was very much agitated and confused, and on the skeleton being shown to him, took up one of the bones and said, "This is no more Dan Clark's bone than it is mine!" The man who could speak so positively as to what were *not* Clark's bones was presumed to know something about Clark, so Houseman was arrested.

On being examined, Houseman made a statement, in which he acknowledged that he had been with Aram and Clark the night before the latter "went off," but denied any knowledge of his murder. He declined to sign his deposition, however, and it was presumed, therefore, that he had not spoken the full truth. He was then committed to York Castle, and on his way thither declared himself ready to make an additional confession.

He then stated that "Daniel Clark was murdered by Eugene Aram, late of Knaresborough, a schoolmaster, and, as he believes, on Friday, the 8th of February, 1744–5, for that Eugene Aram and Daniel Clark were together at Aram's house early that morning (being moonlight and snow upon the ground), and that he (Houseman) left the house and went up the street a little before, and they called to him desiring he would go a short way with them, and he accordingly went along with them to a place called St. Robert's Cave, near Grimbald Bridge, where Aram and

Clark stopped. There he saw Aram strike Clark several times over the breast and head, and saw him fall as if he was dead; upon which he came away and left them. But whether Aram used any weapon or not to kill Clark he could not tell; nor does he know what he did with the body afterwards, but believes that Aram left it at the mouth of the cave; for that, seeing Aram do this, lest he might share the same fate, he made the best of his way from him, and got to the bridge end, where, looking back, he saw Aram coming from the cave side (which is in a private rock adjoining the river), and could discern a bundle in his hand, but did not know what it was. Upon this he hastened away to the town, without either joining Aram or seeing him again till the next day, and from that time to this he had never had any private discourse with him.

The picture which Houseman thus drew, representing himself as in abject fear of Aram, could hardly be a truthful one, and his declaration that he hastened away to the town alone could not be accepted by any dispassionate person. He tried to screen himself from being regarded as an actual accomplice in the murder, but did it so clumsily as to disentitle him to credit.

In a subsequent examination Houseman said that Clark's body was buried in St. Robert's Cave, and that his head lay to the right in the turn at the entrance to the cave. Proper persons were thereupon appointed to examine the cave, and a human skeleton was found in the exact position indicated by Houseman.

A warrant was now issued for the apprehension of Aram, but it was not known where he was. A horse-dealer who had been travelling the country came forward, however, and said he had seen Aram at Lynn, and added, "but he was too proud to speak to me." The constables were accordingly despatched to Lynn, with orders to call at every post-office on the road and inquire for letters directed to

Aram, but they only found one, in which was written, "Fly for your life; you are pursued."

The officers had no difficulty in carrying out their instructions. Aram was found at the Free School at Lynn, and was at once arrested and brought down into Yorkshire. He denied any knowledge of Clark's death, and made a statement which threw strong suspicion upon Houseman and Terry. Terry also was arrested now.

On the 3rd of August, 1759, Houseman and Aram were brought to the bar and arraigned for the murder of Daniel Clark. Houseman was first tried, and acquitted for want of sufficient evidence against him. He was then admitted King's evidence, and repeated his former evidence. The skull was produced in court. There was a fracture on the left side which from the nature of it could only have been made by a blunt instrument, and it seemed to be a fracture of many years' standing.

After this and other evidence had been given, Aram read a written defence, in which he endeavoured, very ingeniously and by the display of much curious learning, to weaken the case against him.

"First, my Lord," he said, "the whole tenour of my conduct in life contradicts every particular of this indictment; yet I had never said this, did not my present circumstances extort it from me, and seem to make it necessary. Permit me here, my Lord, to call upon malignity itself, so long and cruelly busied in this prosecution, to charge upon me any immorality of which prejudice was not the author. No, my Lord, I concerted no schemes of fraud, projected no violence, injured no man's person or property. My days were honestly laborious, my nights intensely studious; and I humbly conceive my notice of this, especially at this time, will not be thought impertinent or unseasonable, but at least deserving some attention;

because, my Lord, that any person, after a temperate use of life, a series of thinking and acting regularly, and without one single deviation from sobriety, should plunge into the very depth of profligacy precipitately and at once, is altogether improbable and unprecedented, and absolutely inconsistent with the course of things. Mankind is never corrupted at once; villany is always progressive, and declines from right step by step, till every regard of probity is lost, and every sense of moral obligation totally perishes.

"Again, my Lord, a suspicion of this kind, which nothing but malevolence could entertain and ignorance propagate, is violently opposed by my very situation at that time with respect to health; for but a little space before I had been confined to my bed, and suffered under a very long and severe disorder, and was not able for half a year together so much as to walk. The distemper left me indeed, yet slowly and in part; but so macerated, so enfeebled, that I was reduced to crutches, and was so far from being well about the time I am charged with this fact, that I never till this day perfectly recovered. Could, then, a person in this condition take anything into his head so unlikely, so extravagant? I, past the vigour of my age, feeble and valetudinary, with no inducement to engage, no ability to accomplish, no weapon wherewith to perpetrate such a fact—without interest, without power, without motive, without means.

"Besides, it must needs occur to every one that an action of this atrocious nature is never heard of but when its springs are laid open it appears that it was to support some indolence or supply some luxury, to satisfy some avarice or oblige some malice, to prevent some real or some imaginary want; yet I lay not under the influence of any one of these. Surely, my Lord, I may, consistent with both truth and modesty, affirm this much; and none who have any veracity, and knew me, will even question this.

"In the second place, the disappearance of Clark is

suggested as an argument of his being dead. But, my Lord, the uncertainty of such an inference from that, and indeed the fallibility of all conclusions of such a sort from such a circumstance, are too obvious and too notorious to require instances; yet, superseding many, permit me to produce a very recent one, and that afforded by this castle.

"In June, 1757, William Thompson, amidst all the vigilance of this place, in open daylight, and double-ironed, made his escape; and notwithstanding an immediate inquiry set on foot, the strictest search, and all advertisements, has never been seen or heard of since. If, then, Thompson got off unseen, through all these difficulties, how very easy was it for Clark, when none of them opposed him! But what would be thought of a prosecution commenced against anyone seen last with Thompson?

"Permit me next, my Lord, to observe a little upon the bones which have been discovered. It is said—which is perhaps saying very far—that these are the bones of a man. It is possible, indeed, they may; but is there any certain known criterion which incontestably distinguishes the sex in human bones? Let it be considered, my Lord, whether the ascertaining of this point ought not to precede any attempt to identify them.

"The place of their *depositum*, too, claims much more attention than is commonly bestowed upon it; for of all places in the world none could have mentioned any one wherein there was greater certainty of finding human bones than a hermitage, except he should point out a churchyard; hermitages, in times past, being not only places of religious retirement, but of burial too. And it has scarcely ever been heard of, but that every cell now known contains, or contained, these relics of humanity—some mutilated and some entire. I do not inform, but give me leave to remind your Lordship, that here sat solitary sanctity, and here the hermit, or the anchoress, hoped that repose for their bones, when dead, they here enjoyed when living. . . . Suffer me then, my Lord, to produce a few out of many evidences, that these cells were used as repositories of the dead, and to enumerate a few in which human bones have been found, as it happened in this in question, lest to some that accident might seem extraordinary, and consequently occasion prejudice.

"1. The bones, as it was supposed, of the Saxon St. Dubritius, were discovered buried in his cell at Guy's Cliff, near Warwick: as appears from the authority of Sir William Dugdale.

"2. The bones, thought to be those of the anchoress Rosia, were but lately discovered in a cell at Royston, entire, fair, and undecayed, though they must have lain interred for several centuries, as is proved by Dr. Stukeley.

"3. But our own county, nay, almost this neighbourhood, supplies another instance ; for in January, 1747, were found by Mr. Stovin, accompanied by a reverend gentleman, the bones, in part, of some recluse in the cell at Lindholme, near Hatfield. They were believed to be those of William of Lindholme, a hermit who had long made this cave his habitation.

"4. In February, 1749, part of Woburn Abbey being pulled down, a large portion of a corpse appeared, even with the flesh on, and which bore cutting with a knife, though it is certain this had laid above 200 years, and how much longer is doubtful, for this Abbey was founded in 1145, and dissolved in 1538 or 1539.

"What would have been said, what believed, if this had been an accident to the bones in question?

"Further, my Lord, it is not yet out of living memory, that at a little distance from Knaresborough, in a field, part of the manor of the worthy and patriotic baronet who does that borough the honour to represent it in Parliament, were found, in digging for gravel, not one human skeleton only, but five or six, deposited side by side, with each an urn placed on its head, as your Lordship knows was usual in ancient interments.

"About the same time, and in another field almost close to this borough, was discovered also, in searching for gravel, another human skeleton; but the piety of the same worthy gentleman ordered both the pits to be filled up again, commendably unwilling to disturb the dead.

"Is the invention of these bones forgotten, then, or industriously concealed, that the discovery of those in question may appear the more singular and extraordinary? Whereas, in fact, there is nothing extraordinary in it. My Lord, almost every place conceals such remains. In fields, in hills, in highway sides, and on commons, lie frequent and unsuspected bones; and our present allotments for rest for the departed are but of some centuries.

"Another particular seems not to claim a little of your Lordship's notice, and that of the gentlemen of the jury,— which is, that perhaps no example occurs of more than one skeleton being found in one cell; and in the cell in question was found but one, agreeable in this to the peculiarity of every other known cell in Britain. Not the invention of one skeleton, then, but of two, would have appeared suspicious and uncommon. . . .

"But it seems another skeleton has been discovered by some labourer, which was full as confidently averred to be Clark's as this. My Lord, must some of the living, if it promotes some interest, be made answerable for all the bones that earth has concealed, or chance exposed? And might not a place where bones lay be mentioned by a person by chance, as well as found by a labourer by chance? Or is it more criminal accidentally to name where bones lie than accidentally to find where they lie?

[He then adverts to the damage found to have been inflicted upon the skull, which he shows might have been occasioned in the course of the ravages committed at the Reformation.]

" Moreover, what gentleman here is ignorant that Knaresborough had a castle, which, though now run to ruin, was once considerable both for its strength and garrison ? All know it was vigorously besieged by the arms of the Parliament; at which siege, in sallies, conflicts, flights, pursuits, many fell in all the places round it, and where they fell were buried ; for every place, my Lord, is burial-earth in war, and many, questionless, of these rest yet unknown, whose bones futurity shall discover.

" I hope, with all imaginable submission, that what has been said will not be thought impertinent to this indictment, and that it will be far from the wisdom, the learning, and the integrity of this place, to impute to the living what zeal in its fury may have done ; what nature may have taken off and piety interred ; or what war alone may have destroyed, alone deposited.

" As to the circumstances that have been raked together, I have nothing to observe but that all circumstances whatsoever are precarious, and have been but too frequently found lamentably fallible ; even the strongest have failed. They may rise to the utmost degree of probability, yet are they but probability still. Why need I name to your Lordship the extraordinary case of Joan Perry and her sons, recorded by Dr. Howell, who all suffered upon circumstances, because of the sudden disappearance of Mr. Harrison, their lodger, who was in credit, had contracted debts, borrowed money, and went off unseen ; and returned again a great many years after their execution ? Why name the intricate affair of Jaques de Moulin, under King Charles II., related by a gentleman who was counsel for the crown ? And why the unhappy Coleman, who suffered innocently, though convicted upon positive evidence, and whose children perished for want, because the world uncharitably believed the father guilty? Why mention the perjury of Smith, incautiously admitted King's evidence, who, to screen himself, equally accused Faircloth and Loveday of the murder of Dunn; the first of whom, in March, 1749, was executed at Winchester; and Loveday was about to suffer at Reading, had not Smith been proved perjured, to the satisfaction of the Court, by the surgeon of the Gosport Hospital.

"And now, my Lord, having endeavoured to show that the whole of this process is altogether repugnant to every part of my life—that it is inconsistent with my condition of health about that time—that no rational inference can be drawn that a person is dead who suddenly disappears —that hermitages were the constant repositories of the bones of the recluse—that the proofs of these are well authenticated—that the revolutions in religion, and the fortune of war, have mangled or burned the dead—that the strongest circumstantial evidence is often lamentably fallacious: the conclusion remains, perhaps, no less reasonably than impatiently wished for. I, at last, after a year's confinement, equal to either fortune, put myself upon the candour, the justice, and the humanity of your Lordship— and upon yours, my countrymen, gentlemen of the jury."

In spite of this elaborate and ingenious defence, the evidence was considered strong enough to prove Aram's guilt, and sentence of death was passed upon him in the usual form.

On the morning of the execution he was found almost dead in bed, having attempted to commit suicide by inflicting wounds upon his arm with a razor. On the table in the cell he had placed a paper justifying his attempt upon his life. It was as follows:—

"What am I better than my fathers? To die is natural and necessary. Perfectly sensible of this, I fear no more to die than I did to be born. But the manner of it is something which should, in my opinion, be decent and

C

manly.   I think I have regarded both these points.
Certainly nobody has a better right to dispose of a man's
life than himself; and he, not others, should determine how.
As for any indignities offered to my body, or silly reflec-
tions on my faith and morals, they are—as they always
were—things indifferent to me.   I think—(though contrary
to the common way of thinking)—I wrong no man by this,
and I hope it is not offensive to that Eternal Being that
formed me and the world : and, as by this I injure no man,
no man can be reasonably offended.   I solicitously recom-
mend myself to the Eternal and Almighty Being, the God
of Nature, if I have done amiss.   But perhaps I have not;
and I hope this thing will never be imputed to me.
Though I am now stained by malevolence, and suffer by
prejudice, I hope to rise fair and unblemished.   My life
was not polluted, my morals were irreproachable, and my
opinions were orthodox."

Aram also composed the following lines shortly before
attempting to commit suicide :—

"Come, pleasing rest ! Eternal slumber, fall !
Seal mine, that once must seal the eyes of all ;
Calm and composed, my soul her journey takes,
No guilt that troubles, and no heart that aches.
Adieu, thou sun ! all bright, like her arise ;
Adieu, fair friends ! and all that's good and wise."

He was conveyed to the place of execution in a very
weak condition.   On arriving there he was asked if he had
anything to say, and he answered "No."   He was then
hanged, and his body was afterwards conveyed to Knaresborough, and there hung in chains pursuant to the
sentence.

Aram's widow continued to live at Knaresborough,
residing during her later years in a house near the Low
Bridge, where her husband's gibbet was in full view.   As
his body tumbled piecemeal down, she is said to have

collected the fragments and buried them. She obtained her livelihood by selling bread, pies, &c. She died in 1774.

Aram had three daughters and two sons. Sally, his eldest daughter, married an innkeeper at Westminster; and one of the sons, Joseph, settled at Green Hammerton, and acquired property there.

As for Houseman, on his return to Knaresborough from York, he was received with great disapprobation. His effigy was burned in the public streets, and he was hooted and mobbed wherever he appeared. The remainder of his life was spent in misery and terror, and when he died at length, in 1777, eighteen years after the execution of Aram, his body had to be carried away for burial in the nighttime for fear of the popular indignation.

Although two human skeletons were found, one at Thistle Hill, and the other in St. Robert's Cave, it was only the remains found in the latter place that were associated with the murder of Clark. Some have suspected, however, that the bones found at Thistle Hill were those of the Jew with whom it was thought Aram, Houseman, and Clark had dealings in regard to the conversion of the stolen plate, and that he was put out of the way for fear he should betray them.

Had Eugene Aram been tried in our own time the probability is that he would have got off. There was a very strong element of doubt in the case, and a modern jury would have given the prisoner the benefit of it. The late Lord Lytton has placed it on record that after going, with mature judgment, over all the evidence on which Aram was condemned, he had convinced himself that, though an accomplice in the murder of Clark, Aram was free both from the meditated design and the actual deed of murder.

THE STORY OF THE HOLMFIRTH FLOOD.

WHEN the sun went down over the picturesque and romantic village of Holmfirth, on the night of the 4th of February, 1852, a scene of comparative stillness and repose was presented to the industrious community which tenanted the deep valley and craggy acclivities around. Heavy rains had prevailed in the district for some days. On this one day there had been a long and steady downpour, but before nightfall the rain-clouds had moved away, and although the swollen waters came tumbling down with somewhat unusual force from the mountainous range of hills and bleak stretch of moorland above, a certain calmness seemed to follow the cessation of the rain, and, when the moon rose over the rugged landscape, a soothing influence took possession of the hearts of the people, and, as they betook themselves to their homes after the labours of the day were over, little thought of impending disaster disturbed their hours of rest. As the night advanced, the lights began to disappear one by one from the cottage windows on the hill sides, and long before midnight the village and the straggling hamlets by which it was surrounded were wrapt in slumber.

Some fourteen or fifteen years previously, an Act of Parliament had been obtained, by Commissioners appointed for that purpose, authorising the making of a certain reservoir at the confluence of two streams, which ran at the foot of the brown moorland bluff known as the Good Bent. The reservoir in question was called the Bilberry Reservoir, being situated just above Bilberry Mill. This reservoir had been constructed by erecting a wall across the valley, damming up the two streams, and thereby enclosing some twelve acres of surface. Situated, as it was, at the top of a narrow gorge or glen, it presented engineering difficulties of an uncommon character. These difficulties were taken into consideration to begin with, and Mr. George Leather, C.E., was engaged to prepare plans and specifications. This having been done, the contract for the work was let to Messrs. Sharp, of Dewsbury, for £9,324, and the construction of the reservoir was proceeded with. Mr. Leather was not able to give much direct personal supervision to the undertaking, still he paid occasional visits to the place, and to a certain extent endeavoured to get the work done according to his original plans. But, after a time, he found not only that the contractors were neglecting to carry out the specifications, but that direct orders given by him for the remedying of defects had been countermanded by the Commissioners. Mr. Leather thereupon ceased to be connected with the work, and he afterwards refused to certify that the reservoir had been properly constructed. During the progress of the works a spring of water had been met with. It rushed out in a stream the thickness of a man's arm, and was in the very centre of the puddle bed. Various attempts were made to stop this spring, but the funds at the disposal of the Commissioners were small, and they objected to the laying-out of any great additional sum. So the contractors went on with the work, and the spring was constantly letting down the puddle and washing it away down the mountain torrent. As time went on, the leakage became more serious, and the mill-owners in the valley, for whose use the water in the Bilberry Reservoir was conserved, began to be alarmed, and insisted upon something being done. Another contractor was then engaged—in 1848—to repair the embankment, and he opened it and put in a great amount of material with the view of preventing a rupture. When he had been at work some time, he informed the Commissioners that he had not got down low enough, and that a further opening would have to be made, and more puddle put in, if the evil were to be remedied. But the Commissioners declined to go to any further expense, and the work of repair was discontinued. There was a waste-pit, but it was not sufficiently low to admit of flood waters passing away, and when the heavy rains came down at the beginning of February, 1852, the waste-pit became utterly useless, and the water in the reservoir rose and began to overflow the embankment. Mr. Leather said if he had been consulted he should have recommended the lowering of the pit to the depth of seven or eight feet below the top of the embankment, and if this had been done, he was of opinion no accident would have occurred. An expenditure of some £12 10s. would have sufficed to have carried out this precautionary measure, but the Commissioners were so blind to their duty that they refused even to incur this small cost.

This was the condition of the Bilberry Reservoir on the eventful night of the 4th of February, 1852. It was calculated that that night the quantity of water in the reservoir would not be less than 86,248,000 gallons, of the enormous weight of 300,000 tons. In the immediate neighbourhood of the reservoir many people realised the danger they were in by the deluge of rain which had fallen, causing the reservoir to overflow, and they betook themselves to the heights above and looked down with awe upon the vast accumulation of waters. The village of Holmfirth, however, was three and a half miles down the valley, and the alarm does not appear to have spread so far. It was

known for miles round that the Bilberry Reservoir was not
as safe as it ought to be, but it had withstood the force
of floods before, and it was not imagined that it would
fail to do so on this particular night.

Soon after ten o'clock, the engineer residing at Bilberry
Mill, which was situated immediately below the base of
the embankment, observed that the water began to overflow
the bank. The reservoir had been rising at the rate of
eighteen inches an hour during the greater part of the
day, and there was now a strong wind blowing, which
impelled the water with great force against the inner face
of the embankment. The position of affairs was growing
more and more alarming, and as the few scattered figures
who stood on the heights in the moonlight and watched
the wind-beaten waters rush over the top of the reservoir,
their terror rapidly increased, and their concern for the
slumbering thousands in the valley below was very great.
A considerable portion of the outer embankment was swept
away with the first overflow of water, and large fissures
were immediately made down the grass-covered sides of
the embankment, tons of loose earth and rubbish being
carried away. It was now too late for those above to give
the alarm to the unfortunate creatures who were wrapped
in peaceful repose below. The outer bank was soon washed
away. The puddle bank next gave way ; and then, shortly
after midnight, as if a thunderbolt had pierced the immense
wall, the whole mass of earthwork constituting the inner
embankment rolled over with a crash that reverberated
like the boom of death far down the moonlit valley, and
instantly the pent-up waters which had formed this gigantic
reservoir rushed in one mighty devastating flood into the
sleeping valley below. The immense reservoir was emptied
in twenty minutes, and as the awful and stupendous volume
of water sped with relentless fury through gorge and glen,
and rugged hollow, sweeping down each successive obstruc-

tion, and carrying with it the struggling forms of men, women, and children, who, without a moment's warning, had been startled from their sleep and borne onward by the flood, the air was filled with death-shrieks ; and the sound of falling buildings, the crash of machinery, the upheaval of rocks, and, above all, the rush and roar of the escaped waters, converted the valley into a wailing wilderness of water. Desolation and death overspread the Holme valley for miles ; mills were swept down, trees were uprooted, steam-engine boilers were carried away ; and amongst the struggling masses of wreck the moonlight revealed bags of wool, carding machines, dye-pans, looms, furniture, and the dead carcases of cows, horses, pigs, dogs, and other animals, borne hither and thither upon the flood. The whole accumulation of water seemed to tumble down into the valley in one great mass, and in consequence of the narrowness between the mountain bluffs an immense weight of water was kept together until it descended like an avalanche upon Holmfirth, where the crowd of houses, shops, mills, warehouses and other buildings for a moment seemed to present a barrier to the progress of the flood, and then the next moment suddenly gave way, and such a scene of horrifying wreck and destruction of property and life succeeded as has seldom been witnessed. It would be impossible to realise the despair and terror of that hour. Surprised in their sleep, in the middle of the night, some washed away without a second's warning, some buried in the ruins of falling buildings, and others clinging half-naked to floating bits of wreck ; mothers calling on their children, children piteously crying for their parents, wives clinging despairingly to their husbands. On the waters rushed beyond this dreadful prospect, soon finding a further outlet, and passing forward by Thongs Bridge, Honley, and Armitage Bridge, and then making their way into a more open part of the country and spreading themselves out into a great watery expanse over the low-lying fields and rivers below Huddersfield.

When the engineer at Bilberry Mill saw that the embankment was likely to give way, he rushed to the mill and just managed to get a few articles out of the premises, when the flood broke upon him and it was with difficulty that he escaped with his life. This mill was tenanted by Messrs. Broadbent and Whiteley, and was used as a fulling and scribbling mill. It was entirely gutted. A house close by, occupied by Mr. John Furness, was partly destroyed, and an adjoining barn and stable were completely swept away, along with three cows and a horse and a valuable stack of hay. The family, fortunately, had been warned of their danger, and had removed out of the house when the catastrophe happened. The next object of destruction was the Middle Digley Mill, occupied by Mr. Furniss as a woollen mill. This mill stood broadway across the valley, and there was a dwelling-house adjoining it. The house was nearly swept away, but the walls of the mill were left standing. Almost the whole of the machinery was washed out of the windows and doors, and a large number of pieces were also carried away. Between this mill and Digley Mill a scene of great devastation was presented. The previous day had seen it a picturesque bit of green pasture-land; when the flood had spent its fury upon it it was one mass of sand and loose stones. Some of these would weigh four or five tons, and they had been tumbled forward by the flood like so many bits of wood. Digley Mill, a little lower down, was situated at a point where the valley becomes contracted into a narrow gorge. These premises were of considerable extent, comprising, on the left bank of the river, some extensive dyeworks and a large weaving-shed. A wright's shop, a mistal, a barn, two cottages, and other buildings stood between the shed and the dyeworks, and on the opposite side of the river there were five cottages and a large woollen mill. The whole of this property, with the exception of the mill chimney, was swept away. The boiler had been floated down the stream, and the bed of the river thereabouts was strewn with heavy fragments of machinery. The occupier of the mill, Mr. George Hirst, and his family, had been warned of the possibility of the reservoir bursting, and had made their escape before the flood descended. A man named Peter Webster, who lived at one of the cottages, had been apprised of the dangerous condition of the reservoir, and had given timely warning to his master and neighbours, and to this fact the inhabitants at Digley Mill no doubt owed their lives. Peter was one of those who were watching on the heights at midnight, and about that time he could not resist the temptation of visiting the mill again. But on his way thither he was met by a neighbour, who in breathless excitement exclaimed, "Peter, it's coming; run back!" Peter immediately returned, and soon afterwards the whole valley was inundated. In one of the cottages at Digley Mill there was a young man confined to his bed by an attack of rheumatism. A man named James Armitage, along with three other men, wrapped the sickly man in blankets, and carried him out of the house to the residence of a person who lived higher up the hill side. They had only just got him out of the house when the flood swept past. One minute later and the whole five would have perished.

At Bank End Mill, occupied by Messrs. Roebuck as a woollen manufactory, a great portion of the building was forced in and much of the machinery was washed away. The embankment of the mill dam was also broken down, and thus a fresh body of water was added to the furious current. At Holme Bridge the valley widens, and the flood was able to spread itself over a wider surface; still it did much damage in that locality. It rushed against Holme Church, stove the doors in, lifted the pews from their places; and the cushions, prayer-books, &c., were set floating about in all directions. The churchyard walls were tumbled down, nearly all the tombstones overturned, and several bodies were washed out of their graves. A goat, which had last been seen feeding in the graveyard, was found dead in the middle aisle of the church, having been washed there by the flood. The battlements and one of the arches of the bridge were washed away, and the gates of the toll-bar were lifted from their position, and borne away on the bosom of the torrent. The bar-house itself escaped.

Further down the river stood the woollen mill and hamlet called Hinchliffe Mill. The mill was occupied by Messrs. Butterworth and Co. A large dam was situated on the easterly side of the mill, and on the opposite side of the river were six cottages. There was a large mistal on the easterly side of these cottages, and above that another long row of cottages closely adjoining the river. This last-named block of houses was known as Water Street. Hinchliffe Mill is some two miles below the reservoir, and although the inhabitants had been warned that the reservoir was not considered safe they did not apprehend any immediate danger. The cry of "wolf" had been raised so often without any "wolf" appearing, that they heeded not the warnings that were given this time. The six cottages which constituted Water Street faced sideways to the river, and the head of the mill dam was immediately opposite. The cottages were tenanted respectively by Eliza Marsden, Joseph Dodd, Jonathan Crossland, John Charlesworth, James Metterick, and Joshua Earnshaw, with their families, comprising in all forty-four persons. A man who happened to be within sight of these houses when the flood came rushing down upon them, said he saw the water coming rolling down the valley ; in a minute after he saw the cottages tremble, as it were, on the top of the water, and the next moment they were clean gone. Houses, furniture, beds, inmates, were all swept away, and thirty-six persons out of that little community of forty-four perished. The Marsdens, consisting of Eliza and Nancy Marsden and two sons ; the Dodds, man, wife, and two daughters ; the Crosslands, comprising father and seven children ; and the Earnshaws, father, son, grandson, and granddaughter, were lost utterly, not one of them being saved. Three of Charlesworth's children ran to the door of a neighbour named Ellis, and were taken in by him just in time to make their escape out of the top of the house. Other two children belonging to the same family had escaped as far as the top of the fold leading into the turnpike road, but returning to save two favourite hens were overtaken by the flood and drowned. A rather remarkable incident occurred in regard to one of the Mettericks. The eldest son, William, who did not live with his father, had been for a warp to the mill, but the evening being wild and stormy, he decided to stay all night at his father's house, and was drowned. A second son, twenty-four years of age, was washed out of his bedroom, but contrived to get astride a small beam, on which he succeeded in balancing himself. He was carried with impetuous force down the rushing waters, and must inevitably have perished but for a rather singular circumstance. The end of the beam got turned in the direction of Mr. Harpen's mill dam, and into this harbour of refuge the young man was rapidly impelled, and there he remained until friendly hands rescued him. The cottages which stood in the rear of the six which were swept away, were flooded to a great height, but managed to resist the force of the water. The lowermost house in the row was occupied by Robert Ellis. It was to this house that three of Charlesworth's children ran when the flood first approached. The moment after he had admitted them and closed the door the waters were upon them, and it was only by running upstairs with his own and Charlesworth's children, fourteen of them in all, and getting on to the roof, that they escaped.

There was another row of cottages in continuation of Water Street, higher up than the six which were destroyed. Several remarkable escapes took place in this row. One of the cottages, occupied by Joseph Brook, his wife, and child, was perfectly inundated. He and his wife slept downstairs, and his little daughter upstairs. Sometime after midnight the child came downstairs crying, " Father, father, I am frightened by the wind ! " Brook started up and listened, and a strange, unearthly noise filled his ears. He ran to the window and looked out. " It's not the wind," he exclaimed, " it's the water ; it's up to the door stones ; run upstairs." He then made for the stairs himself and clambered into the chamber, and to his dismay, he found himself alone. The next moment he heard the house-door give way, and heard the rush of water below him. A shriek and a few muffled sobs told him but too plainly that his wife and daughter had met their death. He rushed to the window and called for help, and some men brought a ladder, and he escaped in nothing but his shirt. When the water subsided his wife and daughter were found lying in the bed together dead, the child clasped in the mother's arms.

Brook's next-door neighbour, George Crossland, had a marvellous escape. His family had managed to get away, but before he could join them the water, which rose to the height of seven feet in a few minutes, had caught him. Crossland, fortunately, was able to swim, and for a while was able to keep his head above the water. Ultimately, however, he became exhausted, and having such little space left to breathe in, was almost suffocated. He was just on the point of giving way when he clutched at a "sampler" that was enclosed in a frame and hung to the wall, and luckily the nail proved strong enough to bear him up, and there he stuck until the flood passed away, and he was saved. In an adjoining house, three persons—James Booth, his wife, and a lodger named William Heeley—were drowned. The family of Jonas Wimpenny, consisting of eight persons, living in a house in the same street, were saved by the presence of mind of one of the inmates, who prevented the eldest son from opening the door. The door withstood the pressure of the water until the whole family had had time to escape, and the next minute it was burst open and the house was flooded almost to the ceiling. Forty-one persons in all were drowned at Hinchliffe Mill.

Below Hinchliffe Mill the valley opens out considerably, and in a central situation stands a factory known as Bottoms Mill. The waters being able to spread themselves in this locality, this mill sustained but little damage. From Bottoms Mill the flood rushed onward towards the machine shops and works of Messrs. Pogson and Co., and the Harpen and Victoria Mills, where machinery was broken, out-houses and cottages carried away, and much other property destroyed. When the catastrophe happened, there were twenty persons in the cottages near Victoria Mill, and they were only rescued by a communication being opened up through the walls with the end house, which was rather higher up away from the flood. Here, in one chamber, the poor creatures were huddled together in momentary expectation of death. After the water had subsided sufficiently to admit of their removal, they were rescued, and they had hardly got clear of the building when, with a loud crash, it fell in.

Not far from Victoria Mill stood another factory, called

Dyson's Mill, occupied by Messrs. Sandford and Company. Mr. Sandford, jun., lived in a house near the mill with his two daughters and a servant. The previous evening Mr. Sandford had been informed of the unsafe condition of the reservoir, and advised not to sleep at home, but he disregarded what was said, and retired to rest without any feeling of danger. The house was entirely swept away, however, and the whole of the inmates perished. Mr. Sandford was a gentleman of considerable means, and, it was said, had £3,000 or £4,000 in the house when the calamity occurred. He had just been in treaty for the purchase of a large estate at Penistone, and that very week had given instructions to a Huddersfield sharebroker to buy for him a large amount of London and North-Western stock. His life was insured for a large sum, and for some time it was feared that this would be lost to his relatives, his body not having been found. A reward of £10 was offered for the recovery of the body, and the sum was afterwards increased to £100, but it was not until the 20th of February that the corpse of the unfortunate manufacturer was found. The bodies of his daughters and servant had been discovered a few days after the flood.

The next obstruction that the furious waters met with was at Upper Mill, occupied by Mr. J. Farrar. The large dyehouse at this place was destroyed, with its huge pans and fixtures, and one of the boilers, weighing six tons, was carried by the force of the water to Berry Brow, a distance of three miles. The factory called Lower Mill, a little below, was built across the stream, but when the flood came upon it a great portion of the building was swept away, the two ends being almost all that was left standing. The mill dam was also burst. A bed with two little children upon it was swept out of one of the houses, and the poor creatures were drowned in the factory yard. A little further down a third child was discovered dead.

At Scarr Fold a house occupied by John Charlesworth, his wife, and two children, was swept away, but the occupants made their escape up some steps which led out of the fold. The next house was occupied by Richard Woodcock, who, with his wife and two of his children got away, but other two children were drowned. In a row of houses just below this place all the inhabitants escaped except the occupants of one house, in which a weaver named Joseph Helliwell, his wife, and five children resided. They all slept in the room on the ground floor, and when the water burst upon them they were overwhelmed. The affrighted wife and children were drowned in their beds. Helliwell himself had just time to run upstairs, and was only rescued by being dragged through the floor of the house above.

The flood was now dashing impetuously upon Holmfirth. A young man was heard rushing down the valley crying, "Flood! Flood!" and here and there a few sleepers were awakened by the ominous sound, but at last this precursor of woe fell to the ground exhausted, and others had to take up the alarm. Mr. Lomas, surgeon, was one of the first to be aroused, and leaping out of bed and running to his window he saw the water surging in the road beneath, and looking across the valley saw the toll-bar house carried clean away before his eyes. He alarmed the house, and he and his wife and family escaped by a back window to one of the neighbouring heights. A house adjoining the Upper Bridge, occupied by Enos Bailey, was swept away, and his wife and children were carried down the flood. Bailey himself grasped hold of a beam which was floating down the stream, and by a sudden sweep he was brought to the left bank of the river, and scrambled out and got into the turnpike road. The Upper Bridge was dismantled and soon overflowed, and the whole of the houses in Hallowgate, a long street on the right bank of the river, were inundated. The bed of the stream at this point was completely choked with the accumulated ruins of mills and houses, and the current was diverted from its usual course. The toll-bar previously mentioned was situated in Hallowgate, and the inmates, Samuel Greenwood, his wife and child, perished. Greenwood had been seen to come to the door with a lighted candle in his hand to ascertain what was the matter, and he had hardly closed the door upon the flood when the house was swept out of existence. A little lower down, on the same side of the street, an extensive warehouse, occupied by Messrs. Crawshaw, curriers, was completely destroyed, and the same fate befel two cottages a little lower down, one of which was tenanted by a man named Ashall, his wife and child, and the other by a labouring man named John Kaye, with whom resided his daughter and her husband, and their child. All these persons were carried away—the Ashalls and the Kayes—with the exception of John Kaye, who was driven by the force of the current into Victoria Square, on the opposite side, and a little lower down the street. The landlord of the Rose and Crown seeing Kaye floating on the water, stretched out a pole to him, and by this means saved his life.

In Victoria Street every building was deluged with water; and grocers, drapers, and others had their stocks entirely carried away or rendered unsaleable. Two houses in this street were partially destroyed, and the inmates, ten in number, escaped through a skylight on to the roof, and were rescued by means of ladders.

The premises occupied by Mr. T. Ellis, plumber, were inundated, and the lives of the persons sleeping in the upper storey were placed in great jeopardy. Mr. Ellis escaped by forcing open a small portion of the ceiling of the workshop with a crowbar, by which means he got into one of the houses on the hill side. Richard Tolson, one

D

of Ellis's workmen, who lived on the premises, with his wife and four children, and a lodger named James Roberts, seeing the water already up to the lower ledge of their bedroom, and having witnessed the destruction of three houses opposite, made their way up the narrow bedroom chimney, and got into another house higher up.

At Rochet, a continuation of Hallowgate, a tailor named James Lee, and his grandson Job, were engaged downstairs making some clothes for a funeral when the waters descended upon them. The flood burst open the door, and Lee, being an old man, was unable to help himself, and was drowned. Job, however, managed to swim about the house, and fortunately his cries were heard by a man and his wife who lodged in the house, and were in bed upstairs. They ran to his assistance, but were unable to open the chamber door. With their feet, however, they managed to force out one of the panels, and the lad was dragged through a small aperture only five inches square, and thus was saved.

"The Holmfirth mill sustained very serious damage," wrote one who visited the scene on the day of the flood. "On the opposite side stood the Wesleyan Chapel, with part of the graveyard washed away. Although the chapel stood very firm, the earth was washed away to the depth of several feet very near one corner. The chapel was flooded to within a foot of the tops of the pews. The preachers' houses were elevated a few yards higher up, but the cellars were filled, and terror-stricken by the awful calamity, the Rev. B. Firth and the Rev. T. Garbutt, with their wives and children, ran out of their houses in their night-dresses, and sought shelter on the hill side. Several strange sights were presented in the graveyard, and perhaps the most singular was that occasioned by the whirling flood having scooped out the slumbering occupant of one of the graves, leaving a yawning gulf. To the left were some extensive blue dyeworks; the destruction of these premises was most complete. A little above the mill, and between that building and a stable, stood two small cottages, one occupied by Sidney Hartley and his family, and the other by Richard Shackleton and his family." Both these families, except three members thereof, and the cottages also, were swept away. Mrs. Hartley had heard that the Bilberry Reservoir might burst, and she put her eight children to bed, and waited up in the hope that if the catastrophe did occur she would receive sufficient warning to ensure the escape of her family and herself. She sat up until one o'clock, then becoming more hopeful, went to bed, and soon afterwards the flood was upon them, and all were drowned except three of her children and an apprentice boy. When the devoted mother found that they could not escape she held her infant child above the water outside the window, hoping to save it, but finding the front of the house giving way she bade her family farewell, and was swept away with the babe down the foaming torrent. Three of her little daughters and the apprentice lad caught hold of the rafters in the roof and clung to them, and when the flood began to abate the lad got out upon the roof and helped the girls out also, and there they remained for twenty minutes. He afterwards carried them one by one into the portion of Holmfirth Mill which had escaped destruction, where in their night-clothes, standing up to their knees in mud, they were exposed to the inclemency of the night air and to the falling rain. Ultimately, however, they discovered their way into a room nearly full of wool, and burying themselves amongst it obtained the warmth they so much needed, and remained there till morning.

Victoria Bridge was dismantled, and the shops in the vicinity were all flooded and suffered much damage. Many of the gas mains were washed up, and the county bridge was greatly injured. When the flood had spent itself upon Holmfirth it passed forward and was enabled to spread itself rather more. It did much damage to Mytholm Bridge Mill, and at Smithy Place a number of people only just escaped with their lives. From Honley to Armitage Bridge the wreck was fearful. Two children were found dead above the Golden Fleece Inn, and a woman was discovered dead and naked in a field near the Armitage Fold. The mill belonging to Messrs. J. and T. C. Wrigley, Dungeon, also sustained much damage. Beyond this point the waters dispersed themselves over the widening plain, and the injury that was done was comparatively slight.

When the sun rose on the morning of Thursday, the 5th of February, the scene of devastation and ruin, from Bilberry Mill to Armitage Bridge, was something terrible to behold. Dead bodies were lying about in all directions, and the river was choked with *débris*. A force of special constables was at once formed, and everything was done that possibly could be done to assist the sufferers, and to recover the dead. From all parts of the country people flocked in thousands to view the scene of the disaster, and the greatest sympathy was expressed in all parts of the kingdom on behalf of the sufferers. Subscriptions to the amount of £68,000 were raised, and a considerable surplus that was left after supplying the needs of the sufferers was devoted towards the erection of five alms-houses in commemoration of the flood.

Over eighty persons perished by this terrible calamity ; 42 of them were adults, and 43 were children. The estimated damage was as follows :—*Buildings destroyed :* 4 mills, 10 dyehouses, 3 stoves, 27 cottages, 7 tradesmen's houses, 7 shops, 7 bridges, 10 warehouses, 8 barns and stables. *Buildings, &c., seriously injured :* 5 dyehouses and stock, 17 mills, 3 stores, 129 cottages, 7 tradesmen's houses, 44 large shops, 11 public-houses, 5 bridges, 1 county bridge,

200 acres of land, 4 warehouses, 13 barns, 3 places of worship, and 2 iron-foundries. *Hands thrown out of employment :* Adults, 4,896 ; children, 2,142 ; total, 7,083. The total loss of property was estimated at £250,000.

The coroner's jury returned a verdict of " Found drowned," and added a statement that the Holme Reservoir Commissioners had been guilty of culpable negligence in allowing the reservoir to remain for many years in a dangerous state, with a full knowledge thereof ; and that had they been in the position of a private individual or firm, they would have subjected themselves to a verdict of manslaughter.

The memory of this great flood will remain for ever impressed upon the valley of the Holme. The evidences of the disaster are yet thickly scattered about, after a lapse of thirty-two years. There is an aspect of rugged grandeur about the reservoir itself, which in its reconstructed condition seems as safe as it is possible to be. The embankment which now holds the water in its mountain-hollow is an immense wall of earth and stone, capable of withstanding the severest strain. On either side of the reservoir rise high natural banks of rock, with here and there a massive wall built up as a support, while at the head of the far-stretching basin rises the great frowning moorland bluff called Good Bent. A mountain stream runs down each side of this immense mound, and uniting they form the reservoir. Sloping walls of great rugged stones constitute the inner sides of the reservoir, and fit in well with the bleakness of the scene. At the side of the embankment the water is fifty feet deep. High above Good Bent stretch those giant moorlands from which so many towns receive their supplies of water. A strong wind is almost always blowing up in this region, and as one stands on the edge of the reservoir and views the scene, one must needs have his coat well buttoned round him and keep his hand to his hat. The old useless bye-wash is still to be seen, and on the opposite side is now the new culvert, by which the water, by a succession of leaps over strongly-built masses of stonework, makes its way into the valley below. Bilberry Mill, twice rebuilt and once burned down since the flood, is now deserted and empty, as are many other mills in the picturesque valley to-day. At Digley Mill there still stands the tall, square chimney, which was all that resisted the fury of the flood in that little hollow. It stands in its solitude to-day, like a monumental column amidst an unremoved heap of ruins. It bears upon its face the date 1821. Lower down are many other tokens of the awful event—cottages untenanted and half broken down, piles of stones which once formed the walls of mills or houses, and stumpy factory chimneys which seem to belong to nothing, and from which no smoke has issued probably since the 4th of February, 1852. At Holmfirth there is an obelisk just below the bridge, which is made to commemorate two very different events. It was erected to celebrate the Peace of Amiens in 1802, and stood as a monument of a fruitless treaty until the flood came in 1852, when it was honoured with a metal plate upon which an inscription is wrought, and this serves to mark the height which the waters reached at that point. The column, which is not remarkable for its architectural beauty, may be fairly considered to have been—and with good reason—diverted from its original purpose. A tablet has also been inserted in the wall of the shop which borders on the bridge, to show the height to which the flood attained there. The people of Holmfirth still talk of the great calamity which cast such a gloom over their beautiful dale in the early part of 1852, and the story will remain a fireside tale for generations yet unborn.

THE STORY OF THE CLOCKHOUSE.

ON the highroad from Bradford to Shipley, opposite Lister Park wall, there stands another wall which stretches from a point nearly opposite the old Jumbles to the road leading down to Frizinghall. It is a very long wall, and a very high wall. The building of it must have been a really important contract for the builder who erected it. This gigantic wall was put up to hide a mansion called the Clockhouse from the gaze of the vulgar. It was the custom of rich people in those days to fence their habitations round with unclimbable stone walls.

There has been a mansion at Clockhouse from the seventeenth century, and from the year 1743 the Clockhouse estate has been held by the Jowett family. It used to be a local tradition that the first clock that was brought to this part of the country was put up at Clockhouse. Be that as it may, there is no doubt that it gained its name from the fact that a clock formerly occupied a place on the southern front of the mansion, and was visible to the public in the early days of its existence, when the highroad ran close to the house. At that early period Bradford was a picturesque little town of hill, and dale, and woodland, and was far removed from Clockhouse. There would be the mansion of the Listers in the park opposite, and there would be the Spotted House, where the magistrates used to hold their little court and try prisoners, but all the space between there and the top of Cheapside, a distance of more than a mile, would be comparatively houseless, the road being bordered by meadows, and gardens, and cornfields. The mail coach was then one of the daily sights on this road, and long factory chimneys and a smoky atmosphere were unknown. Pleasant enough it would be for the Yorkshire yeoman who lived in happy seclusion at Clockhouse in those days. The estate was then entirely rural, "smelling of Flora and the country green," and the prospect around would be one of great beauty.

In the year 1743 Samuel Jowett, the son of William Jowett, of Idle Thorpe, in the parish of Calverley, clothier, purchased the Clockhouse estate. Samuel Jowett, who had lost a leg by an accident in the twenty-third year of his age, died in 1774, aged eighty-one, a bachelor, at Clockhouse, and by his will, dated the 26th May, 1768, bequeathed certain legacies to his near relatives, and the estate devolved upon his nephew and heir, Nathan Jowett. This same Nathan Jowett, who has been described as "weak in body, but blessed with the soundest understanding and the strongest integrity, which he daily exerted for the benefit of his fellow-creatures," a few days after his uncle's death wrote as follows to his cousin, Nathan Atkinson, of Bolton :—

Couzn Nathan,—I have looked over my Unkl'es Will and finds you have a Legacy of £40 to be paid 12 months after his death, yr Bror Saml £20, John Crummack £20, George Childn. do., and if you chuse to reed the Will which has been made some years may at any time see it if you call. My wife has a Wig of her fathers which she could like you to wear if the color is not disagreeable, it is a Grey and if will fit may have it when you call.—And am yrs. to comd.

To Mr. Nathn. Atkinson,   NATN. JOWETT.
         of Bolton.

Whether the offer of the grey wig was accepted or not, history sayeth not, but it is safe to presume that the legacy of £40 would not be rejected. On the 9th of November, 1760, fourteen years before he came into possession of the Clockhouse estate, Nathan Jowett had married his quarter-cousin, Mary Jowett, of Knaresborough : a young lady of whom it was said "her good temper and beauty may be equalled but not surpassed." They had four children—Samuel, born in 1761 ; Sarah, born 1766 ; Mary Ann, born 1773 ; and Nathan, born 1776. Samuel is said to have "inherited his father's good sense and weak constitution ;" and after staying his terms at Trinity College, Cambridge, he died at Edinburgh, where he was studying medicine, in January, 1785, in the 23rd year of his age. Sarah married George Baron, of Leeds, draper and merchant. Mary Ann suffered from a cancerous complaint, and was "seldom a day well for many years," and on the 16th of January, 1813, she died, aged forty. Nathan, the youngest son, married his cousin, Sarah Hodgson, of Whetley, on the 31st of August, 1801, "with a prospect of all the happiness that wealth and beauty could secure." Two years previous to this auspicious event Nathan Jowett, the father, had died. The death occurred on the 13th of December, 1799, and by its happening Nathan Jowett the younger, the husband of Sarah Hodgson, became the inheritor of the Clockhouse estate. Their married life was but of brief duration, however, for on the 22nd of July, 1805, the young wife died of consumption, leaving one child, "a beautiful and good-tempered girl," born February 13th, 1803, and christened Sarah. This "beautiful and good-tempered girl" subsequently, on the death of her father in 1816, became entitled to the Clockhouse estate, which had by this time been greatly extended and had much improved in value. She became "tenant in fee simple in possession," thus holding the fullest possible title in the estate.

Miss Jowett, who never married, when she grew up to womanhood settled down to the management of her large property in a very intelligent fashion. She was often to be seen, attended by her groom, riding through the streets of Bradford, and was a lady who was in every sense equal to the position in society that she occupied. The town gossips used to couple her name with one of the Listers of Manningham Hall, and it was frequently prophesied that the two families would become united. Miss Jowett, however, rich as she was, did not contract any matrimonial alliance, but lived a quiet and dignified life, enjoying the good things which she had inherited, and doing her duty unobtrusively. She died on the 20th March, 1840, and by her will, dated the 16th December, 1833, after bequeathing certain legacies, amounting in the whole to upwards of £30,000, she "gave and devised all her manors, messuages, cottages, buildings, farms, lands, tenements, hereditaments, and real estate whatsoever and wheresoever, whereof she had power to dispose, unto her cousin, George Baron, his heirs and assigns for ever."

George Baron was the son of the George Baron who had married Sarah Jowett, the daughter of the Nathan Jowett who died in 1799. He was wealthy already, and lived in a handsome mansion at Drewton, near North Cave, in the East Riding. He was a man who was highly respected, possessed a cultivated mind, was good to the poor, and renowned for his integrity of character. From 1840 down to 1854 Mr. Baron enjoyed the Clockhouse estate, but never came to reside upon it, leaving its management in the hands of his steward, Mr. Ellison, and his local solicitors, Messrs. Bentley & Wood.

On the 29th July, 1854, Mr. Baron died, and was interred in the churchyard at North Cave, where a beautiful monument has been erected to his memory by the present owner of the Clockhouse property. Mr. Baron died a bachelor, without any near relation, and as he had derived the great bulk of his wealth from the Jowett family, he resolved that he would so devise it that it should revert to that family. Unfortunately, Mr. Baron was personally unacquainted with any of the members of the Jowett family, and was entirely ignorant as to who would succeed him in the possession of the estates. He was content to leave that to the law to find out. Many thousands of pounds subsequently spent in litigation might have been spared had Mr. Baron taken trouble to ascertain who was the rightful heir of the Jowetts of Clockhouse, and had he drawn his will accordingly. As it was, his will, which was prepared by his solicitors in the East Riding, according to his instructions, was vague and ill-defined so far as concerned the disposition of his real estates, and was well calculated to afford employment for the lawyers.

Mr. Baron devised his real estates to his trustees "upon trust *for such person as at the time of the testator's decease should answer to the description of heir male of the body of Nathan Atkinson, formerly of Bolton, near Bradford, whose mother was a Jowett, of Clockhouse, near Bradford, under an estate tail supposed to have been limited to him, the said Nathan Atkinson, to hold the same real estates unto and to the use of the person answering to the description last aforesaid, his heirs and assigns for ever."* And in case there should be no person who should answer to such description, then the estates were to go "unto such person as should answer to the description of heir male of the body of Samuel Atkinson, formerly of Shipley, in the county of York, who was a brother of the said Nathan Atkinson, under an estate tail supposed to have been limited to him the said Samuel Atkinson, to hold the same real estates unto and to the use of the person answering to the description last aforesaid, his heirs and assigns for ever." And in the event of there being no person answering to either of the foregoing descriptions the estates were to go "unto such person as at the time of the testator's decease should answer to the description of heir-general of the testator's deceased uncle, Nathan Jowett, late of Clockhouse aforesaid, under an estate in fee simple supposed to have been limited to him the said Nathan Jowett, to hold the same real estates unto and to the use of the person so answering to the description last aforesaid, and his heirs and assigns for ever."

No wonder that when these vague provisions became known there was much speculation as to who would come in for this splendid property. Mr. Baron's Bradford solicitors, Messrs. Bentley and Wood, were summoned to Drewton by telegram, as soon as Mr. Baron died, and the will was opened in the presence of Mr. Bentley, Mr. Wood, Mr. Francis Billam, and Mr. J. B. Burland. The trustees must have been greatly surprised to find what an important responsibility rested upon them in the carrying out of the trusts of this will. The first thing that was decided upon, therefore, was that a " case " should be prepared and laid before an eminent counsel for his opinion.

At this time there was living in quiet obscurity in the village of Bolton, an old farmer named Nathan Atkinson. He was a good specimen of the Yorkshire yeoman, and used to come to Bradford every morning, winter and summer, with his milk-cart, and carried round his milk to his numerous customers in a brusque, hearty, good-humoured fashion. He would then be between sixty and seventy years of age, and was a well-known figure in Bolton and Bradford. He was reasonably content with his lot, and his mind was in nowise troubled by ambitious projects or extravagant expectations. A farmer he had been born, and a farmer he presumed he would die. He was unaware that such a person as George Baron had ever existed, and George Baron had been equally unaware of the existence of Nathan Atkinson, the Bolton farmer. Mr. Bentley, the solicitor, remembered, however, that some time previously, in dealing with some little property belonging to Mr. Nathan Atkinson, he had had to trace that gentleman's title, and the name of Jowett had cropped up in connection therewith. This was sufficient to give Mr. Bentley the idea that possibly the person who would answer to the description of "heir male of the body of Nathan Atkinson, formerly of Bolton, near Bradford, whose mother was a Jowett of Clockhouse," was none other than this same Nathan Atkinson, the farmer. After this, the farmer began to have "expectations," and began to inquire minutely into his ancestry. It took a considerable time to get together all the branches of his genealogical tree, for neither he nor his father nor his grandfather had thought it worth while to trouble themselves about anything of the kind. By the aid of solicitors and solicitors' clerks, parish clerks, and others, however, a full pedigree was eventually made out, from which it appeared that Nathan Atkinson was in direct descent from Samuel Jowett, the purchaser of the Clockhouse estate in 1743.

This Samuel Jowett, as we have before shown, was the son of Nathan Jowett and Susanna Brooksbank, who were married in 1677. Samuel had had one brother, Nathan Jowett, and three sisters, and on Samuel dying a bachelor his real estates devolved upon the family of his brother Nathan, from whom Sarah Jowett, who died in 1840, and George Baron, were in direct descent. With the death of George Baron this line became extinct. Two of the three sisters of Samuel Jowett, the Clockhouse purchaser, died without issue; one of them, indeed, died in infancy. The third sister, however, lived to marry and have a family. She was called Susanna, was married to John Atkinson in 1725, and had children. Her eldest son, Nathan Atkinson, was born in 1726. In due course he also married, taking to wife one Mary Oliver, by whom he had issue, his eldest son, born in 1766, being named James. James Atkinson espoused Mary Jobson in 1786, and the eldest son of this couple was the Nathan Atkinson whom we are now more particularly alluding to—the Bolton farmer.

We can imagine what amazement would fill the mind of this humble vendor of milk when the news was broken to him that he was probably the heir to the immense property lately possessed by a wealthy landowner whom he had never known, and who had lived and died in the remote region of Drewton, in the East Riding ! The estates comprised about 145 farms and tenements, situated in Bradford, Bolton, Idle, Eccleshill, Manningham, Horton, Bingley, Heaton, Allerton, Wilsden, Clayton, Northowram, Hipperholme, Keighley, Giggleswick, North Cave, South Cave, Faxfleet, Drewton, Leeds, and other places in the West and East Ridings. The value of these various properties was estimated at £8,000 a year.

The friendly suit of Atkinson v. Bentley was now instituted for the purpose of establishing Nathan Atkinson's right to the real estate and residuary personal property devised and bequeathed by Mr. Baron. The cause was heard before the Master of the Rolls on the 21st April, 1855, and certain inquiries were then formally directed. Upon these, a certificate was issued on the 21st June following, declaring (1) that Nathan Atkinson answered to the description of heir male of the body of Nathan Atkinson in the testator's will named, under an estate tail supposed to have been limited to him ; (2) that Samuel Atkinson (a defendant) answered the description in the second limitation of the testator's will ; and (3) that Nathan Atkinson answered the description of heir-general of the testator's deceased uncle, Nathan Jowett. On this an order of the Court of Chancery was made, in the month following, authorising Nathan Atkinson to enter into possession of the estates devised by the will of George Baron, and into receipt of the rents and profits thereof from the time of the testator's decease. Nathan Atkinson, who had taken the additional name of Jowett, in obedience to the directions contained in the will, now formally assumed the ownership of the estates.

While these proceedings were going on, an agitation was got up on behalf of a New Leeds blacking-hawker, named Joseph Jowett, who claimed to be the rightful owner of the estates in question. He contended that he was the heir-at law of Nathan Jowett, the testator's deceased uncle, and as such he alleged he was entitled to the estates and property given by the will of George Baron, the families of both Nathan Atkinson and Samuel Atkinson having, he maintained, become extinct. Joseph Jowett was too poor, however, to enter into Chancery litigation unaided. But he found many friends and sympathisers willing to assist him. A large sum of money was subscribed for him on the understanding that if he made good his claim the subscribers would be repaid with something fabulous in the way of interest, while if he lost his case they would also lose their money. The subscribers, as well as a large portion of the public, had a firm belief in the strength of Joseph Jowett's claim, and the result of the proceedings was awaited with much interest.

Motion after motion, and appeal after appeal, were prosecuted, and on the 16th December, 1857, judgment was given by the Lord Chancellor (Lord Cranworth) and the Lords Justices. The Lord Chancellor characterised the will as most inartificially framed in the sense that it was made obscure by the multitude of words and provisions. "To imagine a testator," he said, "beginning to say that in the first instance he gives his large property to such a person answering a particular description, or answering a particular other description, as he shall by any codicil direct, is perfectly nonsensical. If he directed it by a codicil it would have gone so whether he had said that or not." Then his Lordship went on to recapitulate the limitations the testator gave in default of any such direction, the intent and meaning of which then occupied their attention, and ultimately the original construction of the will was upheld, Lord Justice

Knight-Bruce and Lord Justice Turner concurring. Joseph Jowett's contention was thus concisely put by the Lord Chancellor :—"The question which he (Joseph Jowett) had to raise involved three propositions—1, that there was nobody to take under the limitation in favour of the descendants of Nathan Atkinson ; 2, that there was nobody to take under the limitation to the descendants of Samuel Atkinson ; and 3, that there was a person to take—namely, himself—under the limitation to the heirs general of Nathan Jowett."

Joseph Jowett held that there never had been a "Nathan Atkinson, of Bolton, near Bradford, whose mother was a Jowett of Clockhouse," and the question was whether Nathan Atkinson Jowett's grandmother was or was not a Jowett of *Clockhouse*.

A number of very eminent counsel were engaged on both sides during these protracted and expensive proceedings. Mr. Bacon, Q.C. (afterwards Vice-Chancellor Bacon), Mr. Roundell Palmer, Q.C. (now Lord Selborne), and Mr. Pearson were engaged for Mr. Nathan Atkinson Jowett ; Mr. Malins, Q.C. (afterwards Vice-Chancellor Malins), Mr. Lush, Q.C. (afterwards Mr. Justice Lush), and Mr. Bilton for Mr. Joseph Jowett ; Mr. Jones for Mr. Samuel Atkinson ; Mr. Cole for the trustees ; and Mr. Craig, Q.C., and Mr. Forster for Mr. John B. Billam.

The various points were eloquently and elaborately argued by the respective counsel, Mr. Malins making a most gallant fight on behalf of Joseph Jowett ; but Joseph Jowett's claim was never entertained as tangible by the Court at all, and the objection he raised against Nathan Atkinson Jowett was looked upon as altogether untenable. Still he persevered, and still he found supporters who provided him with the funds necessary for carrying on the litigation. It might be clear enough that Joseph Jowett was the heir-at-law of Nathan Jowett, the uncle of the testator, but this was not the person, his opponents contended, that was wanted, unless, indeed, the Atkinsons of Bolton and the Atkinsons of Shipley had become extinct.

In delivering judgment on the occasion of the appeal to the Lord Chancellor and the Lords Justices, in December, 1857, the Lord Chancellor thus referred to the objection that Nathan Atkinson Jowett's grandmother was not a Jowett of Clockhouse :—" Is the circumstance of the mother of the Nathan Atkinson being a Jowett of Clockhouse a condition or not ? Are we to read it—I give upon trust, that the survivor shall convey to such person, being a male and a lawful descendant of Nathan Atkinson, deceased, whose mother was a Jowett of Clockhouse, as if he had said Nathan Atkinson, deceased, provided he was a descendant of Jowett of Clockhouse ? That is the way that it is contended on the part of the present Mr. Jowett. Now, I think that the argument would have been absolutely untenable if there had been no power of appointment reserved ; but I think that the argument must go to this, that if this testator, instead of dying without exercising the power of appointment, had, in exercise of the power, appointed to these persons, his appointment would not have taken effect, because he had previously made a condition that the person should be a descendant of Mrs. Jowett of Clockhouse. It seems to me to be a proposition absolutely preposterous ; in truth, I have rarely seen a description in a will of persons that makes it so perfectly plain who were intended to be designated. It is to be given to the 'heir male of the body of Nathan Atkinson, formerly of Bolton, near Bradford aforesaid, deceased.' There is the description ; you have the name and you have the place in which he formerly lived. If he had no male descendant, it was to be given to the descendants of Samuel Atkinson ; therefore it was a Nathan Atkinson, of Bolton, near Bradford, who had a brother Samuel. That comes pretty close. It is always

E

possible, if you exhaust every description you can think of, that there may be two persons to answer that description; but we are only obliged to act upon what after all is an immense probability in this case; and here you have a Nathan Atkinson, living at a particular place and having a brother of the name of Samuel; and that is not all, because this Samuel is described as formerly of Shipley, in the county of York, gentleman, deceased. This very Nathan Atkinson did live at Bolton, near Bradford, he had a brother Samuel, and that Samuel did live at Shipley, in the county of York. Is it possible for ingenuity to suggest a doubt that the person who answers such a description must have been the person intended? and the doubt attempted to be raised is this, that he adds 'whose mother was a Jowett of Clockhouse.' The mother of these two gentlemen was a Jowett; she died in 1772. She was a Jowett, and her brother was at Clockhouse. It is true, in one sense, she is not properly of Clockhouse, because it was the brother who purchased the estate, and not the father; but can anybody doubt what he meant when he described the right name— the mother's right name, the brother's right name, both the places of residence right, and the only error being—if it is an error—that she is described as of Clockhouse, when in truth she never was of Clockhouse, though her brother was. But I think, as was suggested by Lord Justice Turner in the course of the argument, there is no inaccuracy at all. There may be several families of Jowett for aught I know, and all he means to say by saying 'who was a Jowett of Clockhouse,' is that the Jowett of Clockhouse is to be read under a vinculum the family of Jowett, and she was of that family."

But this judgment did not put a stop to the Clockhouse litigation. Mr. Joseph Jowett now presented his appeals to the House of Lords, and the litigation continued until the 1st of March, 1860, nearly six years from the date of Mr. Baron's death.

On the hearing of this final appeal in the House of Lords, Lord Campbell being Lord Chancellor, Mr. Malins exerted himself to the utmost on behalf of his client. A portion of his speech puts the contention of Mr. Joseph Jowett so strongly that it may be well to quote it. He said :—"The appellant claims the estate on the assumption that the first and second limitations in the will have failed, and that the limitation which has taken effect is the third limitation, which, as I read to your Lordships, is that failing the limitation to the heir of the body of Nathan Atkinson, whose mother was a Jowett of Clockhouse, which is the first limitation ; secondly, to the heir of the body of Samuel Atkinson, the brother of Nathan, that also has failed ; then the third limitation is, to the heir general of the testator's uncle, Nathan Jowett, upon the assumption that the fee simple had been limited to him. The appellant claims on the ground that he is the heir general of Nathan Jowett, the testator's uncle, and that, the two preceding limitations having failed, that has taken effect, and that, under that limitation, he is entitled to the possession of the estates." Referring to the particular construction that was to be placed upon the words "whose mother was a Jowett of Clockhouse," Mr. Malins said :—"Now, your Lordships observe, the words are, 'To the heir of the body of Nathan Atkinson, of Bolton, near Bradford ;' and it is admitted that he is the heir of the body of Nathan Atkinson, of Bolton, near Bradford ; but the Nathan Atkinson to whom he must make himself out to be heir of the body is Nathan Atkinson, of Bolton, near Bradford, whose mother was a Jowett of Clockhouse. The words are—'The heir of the body in any degree either of Nathan Atkinson, formerly of Bolton, near Bradford aforesaid, deceased, whose mother was a Jowett of Clockhouse, near Bradford aforesaid.' Now, the object of the testator, no doubt, is clear in the circumstance which I have stated to your Lordships. He had derived the property from the Jowett family. I have pointed out to your Lordships that he had derived it by the devise of his cousin, Sarah Jowett. She had acquired it under the will of her grandfather. He having derived the property under her will, his object was to carry it back to the Jowett family —the Jowetts of Clockhouse—that family who had been residents of Clockhouse, who had long been owners of the estate ; and, therefore, the motive in his mind was that the property should go into the family—the Jowetts—who had been resident at Clockhouse. That, we say, is a family which has become extinct."

The following conversation then ensued between Mr. Malins and their Lordships :—

"The Lord Chancellor : When do you say that the Jowett family became extinct ?

"Mr. Malins : We say it became extinct, my Lord, on the death of Sarah Jowett, in 1840. I believe there is no dispute about that. She was the last descendant of the Jowett family. Now the object of the testator must be supposed to have been to carry back his estate to the nearest line he could find. Knowing, as he did, when he made his will in 1854, that that family had become extinct, he gave it to the descendant of Nathan Atkinson, but still the claim of Nathan Atkinson was to be that he was descended from the Jowetts.

"The Lord Chancellor : The Jowett blood.

"Mr. Malins : Not the Jowett blood only, my Lord, because Jowett of Middlesex would not have done.

"The Lord Chancellor : No, Jowett of Clockhouse.

"Mr. Malins : It must be a Jowett of Clockhouse.

"Lord Wensleydale : In some sense.

"Mr. Malins : No doubt, my Lord, in some sense ; the question is, in what sense ? We say it must be a Jowett of Clockhouse in this sense—that he must have descended from a person who had been properly of Clockhouse. Now this lady, the great-grandmother of the respondent, had never been a Jowett of Clockhouse.

"The Lord Chancellor: Does the word 'of' necessarily mean domiciled at that place?

"Mr. Malins: That is the question for decision, my Lord."

After considerable further argument, the Lord Chancellor intimated that they should dismiss the appeal; whereupon Mr. Malins expressed himself as not in the least surprised at the decision. "I am sorry to say," he said, "that it is the opinion I myself have entertained in the case from the beginning; but the stake was so great—and, considering the humble condition of life of the appellant—that I found that nothing but having the opinion of the ultimate tribunal could ever settle the question, and I felt it my duty, therefore, to acquiesce in his taking your Lordships' opinion. I can only add this—he is a man in a humble station in life. This gentleman, the defendant, will now, by your Lordships' decision, be placed in the possession of a large estate. I trust that your Lordships will not think it a case in which the appeal should be dismissed with costs. Beyond that I can add nothing.

"Lord Cranworth: What do they say to that? Perhaps they will not press for costs.

"The Lord Chancellor: Perhaps on the part of the respondents they will not press for costs.

"Mr. Bacon: My Lords, there is a very obvious reason why we should not trouble your Lordships with any word on the subject of costs.

"Mr. Malins: Then, my Lords, I must consider the case decided."

Costs were allowed, however, to Mr. J. B. Billam, the heir-at-law of Mr. Baron, the testator.

Thus ended this long legal contention, Mr. Nathan Atkinson Jowett and his eldest son, Mr. James Atkinson

Jowett, being confirmed in the title to the estates, the former as tenant for life, the latter as entitled in tail in remainder. The "law's delays" have seldom been more forcibly illustrated than in this case. The whole business ought to have been decided, had there been reasonable legal facilities at command, in as many months as it took years to do it. Those who were called upon to declare the law on the question were, in every instance and at every stage, of opinion that Mr. Nathan Atkinson Jowett was the rightful claimant of the estates. Judging from the strange mural writings one has seen in and around Bradford for these many years back, it is evident that some "artist in chalk" has got the notion that he ought to be in possession of the Clockhouse estates, but no person who will calmly weigh the matter can do other than agree in the finding of the House of Lords.

Mr. Nathan Atkinson Jowett lived several years in the quiet ownership of the wealth which came to him in his old age, and on his death his son, Mr. James Atkinson Jowett, came into possession of the property, and now enjoys it.

THE STORY OF THE LUDDITE RIOTS.

TIMES were bad — even desperate. Trade was paralysed by the long and costly war which we had waged, and were still waging, with Napoleon. Ground down by taxation, reduced to the verge of starvation by the dearness of provisions and the scarcity of employment, the poorer classes of the community were discontented and unhappy, and complained bitterly of their lot. News came now and then of a fresh victory gained by Wellington in the Peninsula, and inspired a temporary hope that the war would be brought to a close and commerce would once more resume its sway, but the weary days went by and the working-men of England were still compelled to suffer from want and privation. Wheat was sold at £9 a quarter about this time in Leeds market, and the populace, headed by a woman whom they styled Lady Lud, assailed the dealers in the market, seized the corn and threw it about the streets. At Sheffield the mob broke into the local Militia store-room and destroyed 800 guns and bayonets. Riots, indeed, were of constant occurrence, and the country was in a highly agitated and troubled condition.

During all this time the work of mechanical invention was in full progress. Inventors were busily employed in bringing out improvement upon improvement, and spinners and manufacturers in all parts of the country were adopting labour-saving machinery in their factories. It was not surprising, perhaps, in this state of things, that the un-reasoning multitude should conceive the idea that the introduction of machinery was detrimental to their interests—that it was in a great measure answerable for their being thrown out of employment. A movement was therefore started, the object of which was to put a stop by forcible means to the further use of machinery, and also to destroy such machinery as already existed.

Nottingham was the place where this unhappy feeling was first strongly manifested. The introduction of the then newly-invented stocking-loom was the means of exciting the determined opposition of the Nottingham stocking weavers, and ungovernable mobs assembled and made ferocious attacks upon the places where the stocking-frames were in use. A thousand frames were destroyed in Nottingham alone, and the rioters, who were headed by a mysterious personage, whom they denominated General Ned Lud—hence the name Luddites,—spread themselves over the whole country between Nottingham and Mansfield, and carried destruction with them wherever they went.

It was not long before the Luddite agitation reached the West Riding, which was now more largely engaged in the textile manufactures probably than any other part of the country. One of their first attempts at destruction in this district was made on the 24th of March, 1812, when they attacked the mill of Messrs. J. J. & R. Thompson, at Rawdon. The mob were armed with guns, bludgeons, and primitive weapons of various descriptions, and in the early morning they proceeded stealthily towards the mill in question. They first seized the watchman and made him prisoner; then they placed guards in possession of the cottages near the mill, and the main body of rioters entered the factory and completely wrecked the whole of the machinery that they found there. Other places in the neighbourhood suffered in the same way, and not only was the machinery destroyed but the insatiate mob cut to pieces all the manufactured goods that they could lay their hands upon.

On the 9th of April following, about 300 Luddites made their appearance near Wakefield. They marched along the highway in regular sections, preceded by a mounted party with drawn swords and followed by a similar body acting as rear guard. The peaceful inhabitants were greatly dismayed at the sight of the rioters, and were too much alarmed to make any effort to thwart them in their work of destruction. The mob attacked mills and destroyed much valuable property in the neighbourhood of Wakefield, and many other parts of the West Riding were put into terror by the visitations of these lawless people. The burning of the " gig-mill " at Oaklands, near Leeds, and of the Hawksworth corn mills, was attributed to the Luddites; and in and around Huddersfield, Holmfirth, Dewsbury, Cleckheaton, and Liversedge much damage was done by the rioters. About £500 worth of cloth was torn and cut into shreds by them in the finishing shops of Messrs. Dickenson, Carr & Shann, in Water Lane, Leeds, whose machinery they destroyed also. In addition to this, the Luddites frequently attacked the houses of the manufacturers and broke the windows, plundered the rooms, and smashed their furniture.

The movement soon began to assume alarming proportions. At first the Luddites had been content to destroy the machinery only, but as time wore on they grew more bold and more desperate in their dread work, and gradually arrived at the determination to take the lives of the obnoxious masters. The rioters used to hold their meetings in the dead of the night on the moors and commons in the district, and then and there decide what mills or masters were to be the next objects of attack. The Luddites acted with great caution. A general secret committee had the

control of all the societies, each of which had its own secret
committee for conducting the correspondence and organising
measures in concert with societies in other districts. They
were bound to each other by a fearful oath, which was
administered to each new member with awful solemnity at
their midnight meetings. The oath was in the following
terms :—

" I, ——— ——, of my own voluntary free will, do declare
and solemnly swear that I never will reveal to any person or
persons under the canopy of heaven the names of the
persons who compose this secret committee, their proceedings, meetings, places of abode, dress, features, connections,
or anything else that might lead to a discovery of the same,
either by word or deed or sign, under the penalty of being
sent out of the world by the first brother who shall meet
me, and my name and character blotted out of existence,
and never to be remembered but with contempt and
abhorrence ; and I further now do swear that I will use my
best endeavours to punish by death any traitor or traitors,
should any rise up amongst us, wherever I can find him or
them ; and, though he should fly to the verge of nature,
I will pursue him with unceasing vengeance. So help me
God, and bless me to keep this my oath inviolable."

Funds were subscribed in all parts of the country in
support of the Luddite agitation, and the movement
assumed a most threatening aspect—almost swelling to the
proportions of a rebellion. Vigorous measures were adopted
by the local magistracy for opposing the malcontents, but so
secret and determined were the Luddites in their move-
ments that it was found exceedingly difficult to arrest their
progress. Mr. Joseph Radcliffe, of Milns Bridge, employed
himself with great activity in bringing the offenders to
justice, and many of the clergymen in the district, notably
the Rev. Hammond Robertson, of Hartshead (the
Mr. Helstone of Charlotte Brontë's " Shirley "), rendered
valuable assistance. For the part he took in organising a
police system for the surprise and detection of the ring-

leaders, Mr. Radcliffe was honoured with a baronetcy. Meanwhile, in Lancashire, Cheshire, and Nottingham the police authorities, aided by the military, had been successful in apprehending a number of rioters in their own districts, and although the judges were inclined to deal leniently with them at first, they afterwards found it necessary to adopt more severe measures, and the offenders were sternly punished.

In the month of April, 1812, the Luddites, rendered desperate by the resistance which was now offered to them by the authorities, pushed matters forward to a crisis, and crime after crime followed in quick succession during this and the few following months.

On the night of Saturday, the 11th April, the Luddites, acting on a preconcerted plan, proceeded to make their well-organised attack on the mill of Mr. William Cartwright, at Rawfolds, near Liversedge. Mr. Cartwright was held in great hatred by the Luddites in consequence of his having, despite their threats, persisted in working his new machinery. Mr. Cartwright was a courageous man, and not to be deterred from carrying out his purpose. He had heard that the Luddites had denounced him, and were bent upon destroying his machinery, but feeling that he had right on his side, he was firmly resolved to stand out against the rioters to the last. For upwards of six weeks before the night of the attack, he had slept in his mill, and four of his own workmen and five soldiers were also lodged in the place. On the night referred to, this party of defenders retired to rest shortly after twelve o'clock, Mr. Cartwright having previously ascertained that his watchmen were at their posts outside. About twenty-five minutes before one, a large dog, which was kept on chain on the ground-floor, was heard to bark furiously. Mr. Cartwright immediately jumped out of bed, and on opening the door of the room where he slept he heard the violent breaking of the windows on the ground-floor, followed by a discharge of fire-arms. He also heard a furious hammering at the doors of the mill, and the sound of many voices. Mr. Cartwright and his men had piled their arms the night before, and on rushing towards them Mr. Cartwright met his four workmen and the soldiers, like himself, with nothing on but their shirts. They all seized their guns, and at once set about defending themselves in the best way they could. Mr. Cartwright had placed an alarm bell in readiness on the top of the building, and this was rung with great vigour by two men who were told off for that purpose, and who occupied themselves by turns in firing upon the mob and ringing. "Damn it, silence that bell!" cried the crowd, but the ringing was kept up until the bell-rope broke. In the meantime Mr. Cartwright and his little band maintained a continuous fire through the loop-holes of the mill, and the people without redoubled their efforts, discharging their guns and pistols with great rapidity, and uttering the most dreadful imprecations. "Bang away, my lads!" "In with you!" "Keep close!" "Damn them, kill every one!" were the cries that were heard from the outside. It is calculated that there were from 130 to 150 persons engaged in this attack, but so brave and active were Mr. Cartwright and his gallant little force that the rioters were unable to effect an entrance into the mill, and after a conflict of about twenty minutes, the Luddites slackened fire, their ammunition being probably spent, and with many curses upon the occupants of the mill, they dispersed in the direction of Huddersfield. Shortly afterwards Mr. Cartwright and his men opened the doors and went out, and found two men lying there who had been wounded.. They took the men to the nearest public-house to be attended to, and then returned to the mill, and when daylight came they proceeded to examine the condition of the building. Its appearance was very different from that which it had presented on the previous night; all the frames and glass of the windows on the ground-floor, except about nine panes of glass out of three hundred, were broken to pieces, and the door of the mill was chopped and hacked to a great extent. The two wounded men who had been left behind subsequently died, and a coroner's jury returned a verdict of justifiable homicide. The rioters had met about eleven o'clock on the night of the 11th of April in a field belonging to Sir George Armytage, near what was called the dumb steeple, an obelisk in Sir George's grounds. George Mellor, the General Ludd of the district, who was subsequently executed for the murder of Mr. Horsfall, appears to have acted as commander-in-chief, and the attacking party before proceeding to Rawfolds Mill had been formed into companies and marched off in due military form. The men with muskets went first, then the pistol-men, then the hatchet-men, then the club-men and staff-men, and lastly those who were without weapons of any kind. Mellor commanded the musket-company, and a man named Thorpe had the control of the pistol-men. In this way they marched to Mr. Cartwright's mill and made the attack in which they were so bravely repulsed.

Charlotte Brontë has used up these materials with great power in " Shirley," only, for the sake of more picturesque effect, she described the little mill in the hollow at Haworth and not the mill at Rawfolds as the scene of the midnight attack. Mrs. Gaskell, in her " Life of Charlotte Brontë," says that Mr. Cartwright's dwelling was near the factory, and some of the rioters vowed that if he did not give in they would go to his house and murder his wife and children. " This was a terrible threat," she says, " for he had been obliged to leave his family with only one or two soldiers to defend them. Mrs. Cartwright knew what he had threatened; and on that dreadful night, hearing, as she thought, steps approaching, she snatched up her two infant

children and put them in a basket, up the great chimney
common in old-fashioned Yorkshire houses."

Mr. Cartwright was twice shot at on the high-road within
a week of the attack on his mill, but nothing could make
him swerve from what he considered to be his duty.   On
the trial of the ringleaders in this affair at the York Assizes
the following January, Mr. Justice Le Blanc, in summing
up, paid a high compliment to Mr. Cartwright for his
courageous conduct ; and Mr. Cartwright received an
additional tribute of admiration from the neighbouring mill-
owners, who subscribed upwards of £3,000 for the benefit
of himself and family.

Shortly after the attack on Rawfolds Mill, the Luddites
resolved upon the assassination of Mr. William Horsfall, a
manufacturer in a considerable way of business at Marsden,
near Huddersfield.   Mr. Horsfall not only employed a large
quantity of the hated machinery, but had been heard to
express himself with much warmth against the delusions
under which the misguided workmen laboured.   He was in
the habit of attending the Huddersfield market, and on
Tuesday, the 28th of April, 1812, had gone there as usual,
and between five and six in the afternoon of that day he
started out on horseback from Huddersfield on his return to
Marsden, a distance of seven miles.   Mr. Horsfall proceeded
as far as a public-house called the Warrener House, kept by
Joseph Armitage, and stopped there for refreshment, but
without alighting from his horse.   He had a glass of
rum and water, and ordered some gin and water for
two of his workmen, who were at that time in the
public-house.   After this, he bade the landlord " good
night," and urged his horse forward towards home.
He had not got any further than the corner of a
plantation belonging to Mr. Radcliffe, about 300 yards away
from the Warrener House, when a shot was fired at him
from behind the wall and he fell forward on the neck of his

horse. Another horseman, a gentleman named Parr, was riding only a short distance behind, and heard the report of a gun or pistol and saw Mr. Horsfall fall. Mr. Horsfall raised himself up by the horse's mane and called out "Murder!" Mr. Parr saw the smoke from the gun or pistol, and observed four men in the plantation, one of whom got upon the wall as if to close with Mr. Horsfall, but Mr. Parr shouted "What, art thou not content yet?" and the men then ran off at the back of the plantation. "Good God, I am shot!" said Mr. Horsfall, as Mr. Parr seized hold of him and kept him from falling. "Good man," gasped the wounded man, from whose side the blood was gushing fast, "you are a stranger to me, and I to you; but go to Mr. Horsfall, my brother." He then fell from his horse, with his feet fast in the stirrups. Mr. Parr loosed Mr. Horsfall's feet from the stirrups, called two boys who were in the road to come and give assistance, and galloped off to Mr. Horsfall's brother's. A clothier named Bannister came up at this time, and by his aid Mr. Horsfall was conveyed to the Warrener House, where after lingering thirty-eight hours, he died.

Numerous other deeds of murder, atrocity, and outrage were committed about the same time; and the Government were at last compelled to pass a special enactment with a view to checking these crimes. The efforts of the magistracy and the police authorities were redoubled, and during the latter part of the year 1812 the arrests that were made were so numerous that special commissions for the trial of the prisoners were opened at Lancaster, Chester, and York. Rewards were offered and king's pardons to accomplices, and one way and another, a very large number of the leading Luddites were brought to justice.

The Special Commission was opened at York on the 2nd of January, 1813, and continued until the 12th of the same month. Mr. Baron Thomson and Mr. Justice Le

Blanc were the judges, and sixty-four prisoners were put upon their trial for offences connected with Luddism

On the 4th of January Mr. Baron Thomson delivered his charge to the Grand Jury, and on the following day the trials were proceeded with.

The first case was one in which four prisoners, named John Swallow, John Batley, Joseph Fisher, and John Lumb, were charged with burglariously breaking into the dwelling-house of Mr. William Moxon, at Kirkheaton, where they passed as Luddites, threatened to shoot the inmates, forced them to give them money, and then plundered the house of many things of value. A coal miner named Earl Parkin, an accomplice, turned king's evidence. According to his testimony, he and the four prisoners had met at a place called Bedford's Cabin at midnight, and after blackening their faces and putting their shirts over their clothes, had proceeded to Moxon's house, witness carrying a gun, another a pistol, and a third a sword, and by threats and otherwise had effected the robbery. Some corroborative evidence was given, and all the prisoners were found guilty, and sentenced to death. Lumb, however, was recommended to mercy, it having been stated by Parkin, the accomplice, that he and Lumb had remained about the door, and had not actually entered the house.

On the 6th of January George Mellor, William Thorpe, and Thomas Smith were indicted for the murder of Mr. Horsfall. In this case, as in the last, it was the evidence of an accomplice that procured the conviction of the prisoners. Benjamin Walker was the name of the accomplice in question, and he confessed himself one of the four men who had laid in wait behind the plantation wall for Mr. Horsfall. According to him, Mellor and Thorpe both fired at Mr. Horsfall, but the witness and Smith did not discharge their pistols. Alluding to the evidence of this wretch, Mr. Justice Le Blanc said, " That is the account given by this witness, who certainly by that account makes himself out to be one of the persons, who (if his account is true, and he had been standing at the bar) must have shared the fate which the others will, accordingly as your verdict is for or against them." All the three prisoners were sentenced to death. In the interval between the trial and the execution they refused to make any confession. Thorpe, on being asked if he did not acknowledge the justice of his sentence, said, " Do not ask me any questions." Mellor declared he would rather be in the situation in which he was then placed, dreadful as it was, than have to answer for the crime of their accuser, and that he would not exchange situations with him even for his liberty and two thousand pounds, the amount of the reward. They were executed on Friday morning, the 8th January, before a vast assembly. Every precaution had been taken to render any idea of a rescue impracticable, two troops of cavalry being drawn up in front of the drop, and the avenues to the castle being guarded by bodies of infantry. All the three prisoners had been deeply implicated also in the attack on Cartwright's mill ; Mellor, indeed, was the leader of the Luddites in his district. The eldest of the three was not more than three and twenty years of age. Numerous other capital felonies besides that for which they suffered the extreme penalty, were charged against them.

On the 7th of January John Schofield was tried for " maliciously shooting at John Hinchliffe." Hinchliffe lived at Holmfirth ; besides being the parish clerk, he was a professional singer, teaching that art to the country people, and among the rest, having the prisoner for his scholar. On the night of the 22nd of July the prosecutor, being in bed, was called to by a voice without his house, and desired to come out. Mr. Hinchliffe then recognised the voice as that of Schofield, and he got up and came to the door. As soon as he opened the door, he was seized by two men armed

F

with pistols, and dragged some considerable distance from his house. At this juncture a horse without any rider trotted up and alarmed the two men. They presumed that some one was riding up to them, and they let the prosecutor go, who escaped towards the house of a neighbour. When the men saw that the horse was riderless, however, they pursued Hinchliffe, and one of them (not the prisoner) presented his piece and fired it. The prosecutor was shot in the eye, which he entirely lost. He screamed out for help, and a neighbour coming to his aid, his two assailants fled. The following day it was discovered that Schofield had absconded, and he was subsequently arrested in London on board a ship bound for America. He did not deny his name, but denied knowing John Hinchliffe. On being brought to Yorkshire, however, he acknowledged that he was well acquainted with the prosecutor, and furthermore stated that it was because it had been hinted to him that he would be charged with shooting Hinchliffe that he absconded, though he protested he was not guilty of the crime imputed to him. At the trial at York he relied on an *alibi*, and after a long and careful investigation the jury returned a verdict of " Not Guilty," and he was released. Lord Brougham (then Mr. Brougham) was one of the counsel engaged for the prisoner.

On the 8th of January the time of the Court was occupied in trying a number of cases in which prisoners were charged with having administered the Luddite oath. Those who were found guilty of the offence were sentenced to be transported for seven years.

On Saturday, the 9th January, eight prisoners were charged with having (along with George Mellor, William Thorpe, and Thomas Smith, who had been executed on the previous day for the murder of Mr. Horsfall) been concerned in the attack on Mr. Cartwright's mill at Rawfolds. The names of the prisoners were James Haigh, Jonathan Dean,

John Ogden, James Brook, John Brook, Thomas Brook, John Walker, and John Hirst. The counsel for the Crown were Mr. Park, Mr. Topping, Mr. Holroyd, and Mr. Richardson; and Mr. Brougham, Mr. Hullock, and Mr. Williams were engaged for the prisoners. Two of the chief witnesses for the prosecution were Benjamin Walker, the accomplice and informer in the murder of Mr. Horsfall, and Joseph Sowden. The latter gave evidence strongly implicating the three Brooks, Dean, and Walker, whom he said he had often heard talk of their frame-breaking exploits. Witness said he always detested the proceedings of the Luddites. "Detesting, as you did, these proceedings," said Mr. Hullock, "why did you not instantly give information of them?" "Because I did not conceive they would ever come to the pass they did," was the answer.

"But when you found they had come to that pass, why did you not then inform? Why should you conceal these enormities so long in your own breast?"

"I acted as every other person in the same circumstances, and with my spirit, would have acted."

"Pray, sir, what kind of a spirit have you?"

"A timid spirit."

"But it seems your timidity at last gave way. How was it that at length you summoned up courage to make a disclosure?"

"When I was questioned upon oath I was then obliged to speak the truth, and leave the consequences."

Mr. Cartwright in his evidence related the details of the attack and the defence, so far as his own observation and action went, but he was not able to speak to the person of any individual concerned in the attack.

Five of the prisoners—James Haigh, Jonathan Dean, John Ogden, Thomas Brook, and John Walker—were found guilty; the other three—James Brook, John Brook, and John Hirst—were acquitted.

On Monday, the 11th January, Joseph Brook was tried for burglary at the house of Benjamin Strickland, at Kirkheaton, but was acquitted. On the same day Job Hey, John Hill, and William Hartley were found guilty of having broken into the house of George Haigh, at Skircoat, and demanded fire-arms in the name of General Ludd.

On the following day James Hey, Joseph Crowther, and Nathan Hoyle were found guilty of a similar offence on the premises of James Brook, at Huddersfield. Seventeen prisoners were liberated upon entering into the usual recognisances to appear when called upon.

Mr. Baron Thomson then proceeded to pass sentence upon the prisoners convicted, beginning with the minor offences. John Eaden, John Baines the elder, Charles Milner, John Baines the younger, William Blakeborough, and George Duckworth were severally " transported beyond the seas for the term of seven years." The unhappy persons capitally convicted, fifteen in number, were then brought up for judgment. The bar, though a large one, was insufficient to contain them all, and a seat in front was cleared for the prisoners to stand together in view of the judges. They were all comparatively young men, some of them having scarcely attained to the age of manhood. The men were placed in the following order :—John Swallow, John Batley, Joseph Fisher, John Lumb, Job Hey, John Hill, William Hartley, James Hey, Joseph Crowther, Nathan Hoyle, James Haigh, Jonathan Dean, John Ogden, Thomas Brook, and John Walker. The Clerk of the Arraigns inquired of the several prisoners, in the solemn language of the law, why judgment of death should not be awarded against them, and each unhappy man entreated that his life might be spared. The judges then assumed their black caps, and Baron Thomson proceeded to deliver the awful sentence.

One of the prisoners swooned while the judge was addressing them, and groans of anguish burst from several of the men as his Lordship spoke of the certainty and near approach of their execution.

During the short time that intervened between sentence and execution the prisoners conducted themselves in a very penitent manner, but no particular disclosures were made by any of them. Most of the men were married and had families. At eleven o'clock on Saturday morning, the 16th January, the Under-Sheriff went to demand the bodies of John Ogden, Nathan Hoyle, Joseph Crowther, John Hill, John Walker, Jonathan Dean, and Thomas Brook. They were all engaged in singing a hymn, which one of them dictated in a firm voice. Whey they arrived at the scaffold they joined in the prayers with great fervency. Joseph Crowther, addressing himself to the spectators, said, " Farewell, lads." Another said, " I am prepared for the Lord ;" and John Hill said, " Friends, all take warning by my fate. For three years I followed the Lord, but about half-a-year since I began to fall away, and fell by little and little, and at last I am come to this ; persevere in the ways of godliness, and oh, take warning by my fate." The executioner then proceeded to the discharge of his duty, and as the drop fell an involuntary shriek arose from the vast concourse of spectators.

The remaining seven prisoners were then led to the place of execution, and a similar heartrending scene occurred. All the men prayed earnestly before the fatal noose was adjusted. Large bodies of soldiers, horse and foot, guarded the place, and the spectators were very numerous.

John Lumb was respited, his sentence being commuted to transportation for life.

Thus ended one of the saddest chapters in the criminal history of this country.

THE STORY OF MARY BATEMAN, THE YORKSHIRE WITCH.

ON the evening of the 22nd October, 1808, there were a number of persons chatting and drinking together in an old-fashioned, homely Bradford hostelry. In those days people used to meet in the public-house to talk over the news of the day and discuss the prospects of trade; the era of dram-shops and rapid drinking had not then set in. There was a cheerful fire burning in the bar-parlour, and one of the company produced the *Leeds Mercury* from his pocket and began to read the news aloud, much to the enjoyment of the assembly, who smoked their pipes and drank their glasses with all the greater relish because of this intellectual accompaniment. The first thing that they would read of, probably, would be of the brave doings of Sir Arthur Wellesley and his army in the Peninsula; and after that subject had been duly debated, they would get at the smaller items of local intelligence. As luck would have it, however, there was this time a very important item of local news for them. The newspaper related that a certain Mary Bateman had been apprehended in the neighbourhood of Leeds on a charge of wilful murder. Everybody was interested in a moment, but one person amongst that bar-parlour company evinced more than interest—he uttered a cry of alarm, and immediately he heard the name and the charge jumped from his chair and left the room. This man was a Leeds clothier, named James Snowdon, and the reason he showed so much concern was that he and his wife had been the dupes—as he now suspected—of the woman who had just been taken into custody.

Mary Bateman was the daughter of a farmer named Harker, and was born at Aisenby, near Thirsk, in the year 1768. She seems to have been early schooled in vice, and adopted a career of crime almost from her cradle. When five years of age, it is said, she stole a pair of morocco shoes, and concealed them for several months in her father's barn. Numberless instances of falsehood and deception crowded upon her child life, and her father appears to have found it difficult to control her at all. In the year 1780, at the age of twelve, she left home and engaged herself as servant to a family at Thirsk. For seven years she continued to live at Thirsk, but seldom occupied a situation more than a few months at a time, something suspicious occurring generally to cause her dismissal from her engagements. In 1787 she found it necessary to quit Thirsk altogether, so she took up her abode in the ancient city of York, where she lived for nearly a year as a domestic servant. Being detected in stealing something belonging to her mistress, she suddenly departed, neither stopping for her wages or her clothes, and went to Leeds. She was now twenty years of age, and had had a varied experience. One of the situations she had held had been with a mantua-maker, and being sharp and clever she had contrived to pick up such a knowledge of the mantua-maker's art as enabled her to set up in that business on her own account as soon as she took up her residence in Leeds. But Mary was not likely to be satisfied to settle down to a quiet, respectable occupation of any kind ; she had a restlessly active mind, and but little appreciation of or regard for moral principles ; moreover, she had perceived that the public were very gullible and easily duped, and she resolved to assume the attributes of a witch and set her snares to entrap the good people of Leeds.

In 1792, while combining these two occupations, she made the acquaintance of John Bateman, a simple-minded young fellow without means or ability, and after a brief courtship of three weeks, they were married, and went to live in furnished lodgings in High Court Lane, Leeds. The couple had not been married two months when Mary broke open the box of a fellow-lodger and stole therefrom a watch, some silver spoons, and two guineas. About the same time another fellow-lodger, a young man named Dixon, missed several sums of money from his box, and it was discovered that Mary Bateman was the thief. It would have been a fortunate thing for society if she had been brought within the operation of the severe criminal law of the country at this period, but she got out of the difficulty in both cases by giving up the stolen property, or its equivalent in value.

When Mary Bateman and her husband had been married about a year they took a house in Wells Yard, Leeds, and contrived to get it pretty comfortably furnished. But Mary soon conceived a new plan of raising money, and made her own husband the victim. While John Bateman was at work one day, she went to him with a letter which she said had just come for him from Thirsk, where his father lived and acted as sexton and town crier. The letter entreated John to repair with all speed to Thirsk if he meant to see his father alive, and Mary presented it to him with many tears and protestations of sorrow. John, in sore distress at the news, borrowed a sum of money from his master to defray the expenses of his journey, and hastened off to Thirsk. To his surprise, he no sooner entered the town than he saw his " dying father " in the streets with his bell " crying " a sale by auction. " I am glad to see you so much better,"

said the astonished son. " Better ! What do you mean ? "
said the father, " There's been nothing the matter with me."
A light broke in upon John's dull intellect, and he returned
to Leeds without loss of time, and found that his heartless
wife had taken advantage of his absence to sell every article
of furniture they had. On being upbraided for her conduct,
she pleaded that she had been obliged to resort to this
stratagem in order to raise money to hush up one of her
robberies.

On a subsequent occasion she sold her husband's
clothes, and in the end so disgusted and disgraced poor
John that in a moment of fury he enlisted into the supple-
mentary militia.

In 1796 a large factory was burned down in Leeds, and
many persons lost their lives. Mary Bateman made use of
this calamity for her own purposes. She waited upon a
charitable lady named Miss Maude, and told her a harrowing story about a child having fallen a victim amongst the
rest. She said the mother had no linen to lay the child out
in, and implored Miss Maude to lend her a pair of sheets.
Miss Maude consented, and Mary walked straight to the
nearest pawnbroker's with the borrowed goods. Mary
obtained several lots of sheets under the same pretence,
and with the same result. She also went about the town
representing herself as a nurse at the Infirmary, and
collected all the linen she could with the avowed object of
using it for the wounds of the patients, but in reality to sell
for her own benefit.

When she found that her husband had joined the army
she went to him and lived with him, carrying on her base
practices in a new field. In 1799, however, John Bateman
quitted the army, and this curious couple again set up house
in Leeds, this time in Marsh Lane, near Timble Bridge.
Mary now felt herself fully primed for the nefarious work on
which she had so long set her mind—fortune-telling and

witchcraft—and she began to give it forth that she was invested with the divine gift of reading the future and effecting charms. In order, probably, to shield herself from the law, she conjured up a fictitious personage—a fortune-telling Mrs. Harris—and when servant girls and love-sick swains called upon her in order to have their horoscopes cast, she would inform them that she herself had no power to perform the mysterious rites, but that a friend of hers, a Mrs. Moore, possessed the Sibylline gift, and she would retire from the room for the supposed purpose of sending in the veritable prophetess, when shortly she herself would re-appear so cleverly disguised as to be not capable of identification. She then, in the character of Mrs. Moore, would proceed to instruct them in the way to ávoid evil and procure the desires of their hearts.

There was a certain Mrs. Greenwood whom she persuaded that only Mrs. Moore's skill could prevent her (Mrs. Greenwood) from committing suicide. Mrs. Greenwood's husband, who was in embarrassed circumstances, went from home, and "Mrs. Moore" told the simple wife that he was in danger of being arrested and placed in confinement, and that four men had been set to watch over him. "Mrs. Moore" said that unless four pieces of gold, four pieces of leather, four pieces of blotting paper, and four brass screws were produced that night and given into the hands of "Mrs. Moore" to "screw down the guards," Mr. Greenwood would be a dead man before the morning. Whether Mrs. Greenwood procured these various "pieces" or not is not stated. It is more likely that Mary Bateman defeated her own designs by the excess of her demands.

The family of one Barzillai Stead next engaged Mrs. Bateman's attentions. Barzillai was in needy circumstances, he had over-speculated in business, and was for ever haunted by the fear of the bailiffs. Mary Bateman practised upon this fear to such an extent that he took refuge from his imaginary pursuers by enlisting, but she contrived so to work upon him that he gave her, half his bounty money for the inexorable " Mrs. Moore." Having got the husband out of the way, she began to practise her artifices upon the wife, by arousing the latter's jealousy. She told Mrs. Stead that her newly enlisted spouse was about to take a young woman from Vicar Lane, Leeds, with him as his wife when he joined his regiment, and Mary requested Mrs. Stead to provide her with three half-crowns and two pieces of coal, the coals to be placed at the woman's door in Vicar Lane and afterwards laid on the fire, when the fire would throw the woman into a sleep and consume her clothes, and thus prevent her eloping. Great was Mrs. Stead's joy to find that her husband departed for his regiment the next day without taking with him the rival who had never had any existence except in the brain of Mary Bateman. Having got Mrs. Stead thus thoroughly impressed by her magic, Mary carried her imposition further and further, obliging her by degrees to sell or pawn every article in her house to avert some supposed calamity. Mrs. Stead was so reduced that she attempted to commit suicide, and on being confined subsequently, the Leeds Benevolent Society contributed a guinea from their funds to her relief. The sum was given to her by three instalments of 7s. each, out of which Mary Bateman inhumanly extorted no less than 18s., on the pretence that she might " screw down " the society so that they could not refuse Mrs. Stead relief whenever she liked to apply. She also persuaded Mrs. Stead that it was the intention of her husband's father to murder her, and that " Mrs. Moore " alone could prevent the deed being perpetrated ; and other guineas were in course of time extracted from Mrs. Stead on this excuse. At length Mrs. Stead had neither furniture nor clothes left her, and in her destitution began to suspect Mary Bateman of imposition, and some of her neighbours hardened her to threaten Mary with punishment for fraud. Upon this, the "witch" raised four guineas for Mrs. Stead, and promised to redeem the rest of her property.

Mary Bateman now thought it advisable to change her quarters, so she removed to the Black Dog Yard, Leeds, and it was while living here that she gave it out that one of her hens had laid an egg bearing upon it the inscription, "CHRIST IS COMING." Persons flocked from all quarters to see this marvellous egg, and Mary made money by the trick, a penny being charged for every person who saw it.

In 1808 she took up her residence in Camp Field, Water Lane, and here got into the good graces of the wife of James Snowdon, the man whom we have before mentioned as having been in a Bradford public-house when the news of Mary Bateman's arrest reached him. Mrs. Snowdon, it appears, had a presentiment that one of her children would be drowned, a presentiment that probably emanated, in the first instance, from Mary Bateman. Mary told Mrs. Snowdon that the intervention of "Miss Blythe" —the new name for "Mrs. Moore"—would save the child. "Miss Blythe" was represented as living at Thirsk, and a letter purporting to come from her was received, directing that James Snowdon's silver watch should be sewed up in the bed by Mary Bateman. This was speedily done. Further letters from "Miss Blythe" directed that money to the amount of twelve guineas should also be stitched up in the bed, and then the charm would take proper effect. Before long, Mary found it necessary to terrify the Snowdons still more, and foretold that the son would die and their daughter fall into disgrace, unless the family at once left Leeds and removed to Bowling. The bed, containing the charms, they were permitted to take with them, but a considerable portion of their property was to be left in the house at Leeds and the key delivered over to Mrs. Bateman.

Presently, they desired to rip open the bed and get the watch and money, but before that could be done Mary informed them they would require to drink a magic potion which she had then in preparation. This potion was to have been administered at the end of October, but before then Mary had been arrested, and the Snowdons were thereby probably saved from death. When Snowdon reached home on the day previously mentioned, he proceeded to rip open the bed, when in place of the watch and the guineas he found nothing more valuable than a piece of coal! He then went to Leeds and found his house stripped of everything. A search warrant was obtained, and most of the property was found in Mary Bateman's house.

The circumstances which led to the arrest of Mary Bateman must now be detailed.

At Bramley there lived a clothier, forty-eight years of age, named William Perigo. His wife, Rebecca, was a hale, hearty woman of about the same age, and had never had a day's illness during all the twenty years that she had been married, until she made the acquaintance of Mary Bateman. When Rebecca Perigo fell ill recourse was had to Mary Bateman's friend "Miss Blythe," Perigo himself going, on Mrs. Stead's recommendation, to consult the "witch." The first thing that "Miss Blythe" required was Mrs. Perigo's flannel petticoat, which the simple-minded husband took to Mrs. Bateman, the latter promising to send the garment by that night's post to "Miss Blythe" at Scarborough. Perigo was to call again at Mrs. Bateman's in a few days, and he did so, and a letter was shown to him from "Miss Blythe," directing what was to be done. Mary Bateman was to go to Perigo's house at Bramley, and take with her four guinea notes, which she, "Miss Blythe," had sent to her, and put them in the bed in which Perigo and his wife slept, one note in each corner. The notes were to remain there eighteen months, and Perigo was to give Mary Bateman four other guinea notes in exchange, to be forwarded to "Miss Blythe." Mrs. Bateman agreed to meet Mrs. Perigo on Kirkstall Bridge on the 4th of August, and Mrs. Perigo went there at the time appointed, but did not see Mary. Mrs. Perigo then went away, and shortly afterwards Mary Bateman arrived at the house, and William Perigo went out in search of his wife, leaving Mary alone in the house. On the return of Perigo and his wife, Mary brought out the four guinea notes purporting to be from "Miss Blythe," obtained four notes of the same value from Perigo in exchange, and then proceeded to sew the notes which were supposed to come from "Miss Blythe" in four small silk bags. Mrs. Perigo opened the bed-tick and put two of the bags inside, one in one corner and one in another, and Mr. Perigo took the two remaining bags and put them in the other corners. About a fortnight afterwards another letter came from "Miss Blythe" informing Perigo that Mary Bateman would come in a few days to his house, and that he was to get two small pieces of iron made in the shape of a horse-shoe, but they were not to be made at Bramley, and these pieces of metal were to be nailed on the door threshold by Mary Bateman, not with a hammer, but with the back part of a pair of pincers, which pincers were to be sent to "Miss Blythe" at Scarborough. Mary Bateman came to execute these instructions a few days later, and as Perigo had not got the iron prepared he went to Stanningley and got it done while Mrs. Bateman waited. On his return, Mary nailed the pieces of iron in the manner directed, and took the pincers away with her. A week or two afterwards a letter from "Miss Blythe" directed Perigo to go to Mary Bateman's with two guinea notes to exchange for two sent by her, and he was to buy a small cheese and send it to her for a particular purpose through Mrs. Bateman. Other demands for exchanges of guinea notes followed in quick succession, until poor Perigo had parted with about £70.

When guineas were not forthcoming, articles of furniture were asked for, and from December, 1806, to April, 1807, Perigo had handed to Mary Bateman, "One goose, 2 pairs of men's shoes, a goose pie, a tea caddy, several shirts, a counterpane, a piece of woollen cloth, a silk handkerchief, a silk shawl, a light-coloured gown-skirt, a light-coloured cotton gown, two pillow-slips, a new waistcoat, 60lbs. of butter, 7 strikes of meal, 6 strikes of malt, a quantity of tea and sugar, 200 or 300 eggs, a pair of worsted stockings, a pair of new shoes, a pair of black silk stockings, 3 yards of Knaresborough linen cloth, 10 stones of malt, a piece of beef, 3 bottles of spirits, 2 tablecloths, 2 barrels, 2 napkins."

About the middle of April, 1807, a letter was received from "Miss Blythe" informing the Perigoes that they would take an illness in May, and that the wife must take half-a-pound of honey to Mary Bateman, and she would put in such "stuff" as "Miss Blythe" had sent her. They were then to eat pudding for six days, and to put into it the powder which Mary Bateman would supply. On the 11th of May the Perigoes began to eat of the pudding, a powder being put in each day as directed. They became suddenly ill, and the wife died on the 24th. A doctor discovered that the pudding had contained poison, a cat and a fowl, to whom some of the paste was given, dying immediately. Perigo now ripped open the bed-tick and found that the bags contained nothing but waste paper and farthings. He went down to Mary Bateman's and charged her with deceiving him. "Ah, you have opened the bags too soon," she said. "No, I think it is too late," he answered. The next day Mary Bateman was arrested.

Her trial took place before Sir Simon Le Blane, at York, on the 17th March, 1809. The prisoner was found guilty, and sentenced to death without hope of mercy. But even at this point the woman's impudence and false-hood did not desert her; she pleaded that she was pregnant,

in order to gain time. A jury of twelve married females
were empanelled on the spot, and they declared that there
was no truth in her statement. She was executed at York
on the appointed day before an immense number of spectators, and her body was given over to the Leeds Infirmary
for dissection, and in compliance with a custom which then
prevailed, her skin was tanned and distributed in small
pieces to different applicants.

THE STORY OF THE HERMIT OF ROMBALDS MOOR.

THIRTY years ago or more the villages of Airedale and Wharfedale were occasionally visited by a strange, uncouth, weird object, that seemed to possess little kinship to the things around him. This extraordinary specimen of humanity was known as the Hermit of Rombalds Moor, and many wonderful stories were told regarding him. His appearance was anything but prepossessing, his wild eyes, and long, unkempt locks suggesting quite as much of the beast as of the man. To make matters worse, he attired himself in the veriest rags, which were fastened to his body by pieces of twine. He was evidently his own tailor, and so primitive was he in his workmanship that a skewer served him as a needle and odds and ends of string constituted his thread. In the cold weather his rude habillements were supplemented by bands of straw which he tied round his legs. In this unearthly guise, bent almost doublefold, and with a strong stick in each hand, he used to hobble through Bingley, Shipley, Burley, Otley, and other places in the neighbourhood, singing songs without tune, and accepting as a recompense the coppers which the villagers were not backward in bestowing upon the decrepit old creature. Old Job Senior, as the hermit was called, was as great a treat to

G

them as the fat woman, the learned pig, or the six-legged sheep in the caravans at the tides, and they gathered round him and listened to his singing with much enjoyment.

A more ungainly specimen of the wandering minstrel than Job was probably never seen. It was difficult to invest him with the halo of romance, for he looked as impervious to love, or poetry, or feeling as the knotted sticks which assisted him to walk. But, in spite of appearances being so much against him, a number of romantic stories were conjured up concerning him, and the damsels of the district very generally believed that a love-disappointment had been the cause of Job's falling away to the solitude and loneliness of a hermit's life. It was whispered that in the days when he was a good-looking and spruce young man he had fallen in love with a young woman who lived at Whitkirk, and that after keeping company with her for a year or two she heartlessly jilted him, causing him to renounce the world and isolate himself altogether from mankind. It is to be feared, however, that there was not much ground for this story, the truth being that Job had never been over fond of work, and on discovering that by taking up the *rôle* of the hermit he could obtain the wherewithal to live in idleness, he had made up his mind that a hermit he would be for the rest of his days.

Job Senior was a man of a low order of intelligence, and in his best days could never have shown much aptitude for getting on in the world. He was born at Middleton, near Ilkley, above a hundred years ago, and lived to be well advanced in years before he began to attract any particular notice beyond the village where he lived. He did odd jobs for farmers and others in the neighbourhood, walling fences, digging potatoes, and the like, but spent a good proportion of his time in the alehouse amongst idle and dissolute companions, and never fairly got into a settled occupation.

It was when he was about sixty years of age that he "fell in love" with an old widow named Mary Barrett, who lived alone in a cottage near Coldstone Beck, Burley Wood Head, on the borders of Rombalds Moor. Mary was then in her eightieth year, and the cottage in which she lived, as well as a potato garden and field adjoining, was her own property. It was surmised, and probably with some degree of correctness, that Job was really more in love with this little property than with the ancient dame herself. Be that as it may, Mary believed in Job's protestations of love, and in due course they were married at Otley Church in 1830 or 1831. Job's wife lived for six years after their marriage, and on her death a nephew of hers claimed the cottage, and there was a great deal of unpleasantness for Job. Originally, the property had been taken in from the moor by some of Mary's relatives.

A communication from the Rev. Robert Collyer regarding old Job will be read with much interest.

"I knew Job as far back as 1838," says Mr. Collyer. "He was then in the habit of dropping into Birch's smithy, in Ilkley, very often, especially in winter, to warm his frosty nose at the fire, gossip with the farmers' men who came in on their errands, and get his chance at any stray 'sup o' drink' which happened to be in the great brown jug. He was rather a simple old fellow at that time, not at all fond of work, but very fond of beer and tobacco, of which one of the towngate roughs told him one day he had chewed as much in his life-time as would 'theik a lathe,' and to see him at the loathsome work would compel you to think there was more truth than poetry in the remark. He used to mix hemp with his tobacco, to make it go farther, as he said, but I have wondered since then whether this might not be one of the last remnants of a habit reaching back to a period long anterior to the introduction of tobacco into England. Dr. Whittaker says that, when that half of the great tower of Kirkstall Abbey fell, in 1779, which was built before tobacco was heard of in England, remnants of short pipes were found in the wall, where they had been tucked away by the builders, from which we have to infer that some substitute for tobacco was then in use. At that time Job did a stroke of work at the coarser kinds of wool-combing now and then, and at building the old-fashioned stone drains; and Widow Barrett was getting on to eighty and to her dotage. She had a small thatched cottage, a bit of land, and as rumour went, about twenty pounds in money. All this Job, who was then under sixty, secured by marrying the widow; and while the money lasted he lived in clover. But the old woman lasted longer than the money, while Job lost what little taste he ever had for work, and so they fell on evil days, and were very poor indeed— so poor that when the silly old woman was on her death-bed they had to depend for help upon the neighbours, who were kind and generous, as the Yorkshire folks always are in such a case. Job was her nurse, and was feeding her, as he told us afterwards, 'with soft haver-breead an' baacon when shoo deed.' There was a rumour that this hastened her end; perhaps it did, but we never thought it was Job's intention to get his wife in that way out of the world; he always believed that if she could have eaten the food she might have lived. After her death, her people wanted the house and land, but Job had no idea of giving it up. They pulled the place down in his absence, but this did not answer, for he then built a sort of flue, into which he could worm himself head first, and there he slept when the weather would permit, with a dim idea that by this means he would hold on to the estate. The flue 'drew,' as managers would say. Visitors to Ilkley, with nothing in the world to do, would ride over on donkeys to see Job come out of his hole feet first. He always had a turn for singing when he was in his cups; this he turned to account by-and-by in a marvellous composition he called 't' Weddin' Anthem, i' two voices;' one was a groan, the other a yell. This he would give you leaning on his staff, and then you gave him pennies, and in the course of time the two voices grew to four. In a year or two after his wife died he was out of linen, and made up his mind to make his own to suit him. So he procured some material somehow, lay down on the floor of a barn, chalked his outline, allowing a margin, cut his cloth to the line, sewed the pieces together with twine, and got his shirts. He also made his own shoes in some such fashion; tagged his old rags together 'wi' leather wangs,' put a belt round his waist to keep all snug, mounted a hat over the whole, equally comical, and there he was, as picturesque and as dirty a hermit as ever was seen between the four seas. And Job had just sense enough to see that this was the way to such a living as he wanted. Indeed, he added little touches now and then in a way that was almost clever. He had settled down to the cell business before I left England; but he only attended to this business when visitors were in Ilkley; the rest of the year he wandered round singing his 'Weddin' Anthem,' and picking up pence and sups o' drink wherever he could find them. He often came to cook his supper in those latter days at our smithy-fire. The way he did this was to warm some water, mix oatmeal with it into heavy balls, and bolt them. The last picture of Job I have in my mind is seeing him stand eating those oatmeal balls. The simple truth is, that the man drifted gradually from the condition of a human being of a poor type, to that of a beast. There was no romance about him at all. No echo or intimation of a gift of song like that which would touch you now and then to tears, in Billy Matthews, of Addingham. No stumbling into the heart of things like that famous Pudsey Joe had, forty years ago and more, as when once he met one of the Lords Harewood in his park, and getting sixpence from him, said in great glee, 'Thank tha, lad.' Whereat a footman coming behind him was greatly scandalised, and whispered, 'Joe, don't you know that's the Lord?' 'Is that the Lord?' 'Aye, Joe.' 'Can he mak yan o' them?' pulling a blue-bell from the sward. 'No, Joe, he can't make a blue-bell.' 'Then he isn't the Lord, thah fooil.' Job had no gift of broken melody or human wit or wisdom, only that faculty of getting pennies and pints of ale, and living like beasts that perish."

Job's hermitage was but a sorry place. His plot of land measured about half an acre, and his hut was composed of coarse stones walled together without mortar, and had neither doors nor windows. He was unable to stand erect in this den, and there was not a single article of furniture to be seen. He made his bed upon a little straw, and as he laid in his narrow cell his feet would reach to the entrance.

He cultivated his little plot of ground with some success, potatoes being the only article which he cared to bother with. His system of cultivation was somewhat original. He made his ridges fully three feet broad at the base, and had a walk between each ridge. He selected the largest and best potatoes, and planted them whole in the centre of the ridge, raised about six inches above the walk, at the distance of half a yard from each other. Having thus planted them, he would place a shovelful of ashes upon each potato, then heap them up with earth to a height of half a yard. The full height of the ridges was thus about twenty-four inches above the level of the walk. The peculiar mode of cultivation adopted by the hermit was said to produce some astonishingly rich and abundant crops.

It was a very humdrum life that Job led, after all, and if it had not been for the fact that visitors from Ben Rhydding and other places in the neighbourhood came occasionally, and not only relieved the monotony of his existence but gave him money, he would in all probability have been compelled to adopt a more civilized style of living. He used to like to gossip with his visitors, however, and would talk with them or sing to them as long as they would deign to listen.

In his winter tramps through the villages of the West Riding he sometimes used to meet with rather superior entertainment to that which he was accustomed to in his Rombalds Moor dwelling. Recognised as one of the " characters " of the district, the people would often treat him to a substantial meal, and of an evening he would sometimes be drawn into the village tap-room, where he would recount his history and sing his songs for the amusement of the company. He would, in the end, perhaps be accommodated with a night's lodging in an outhouse or barn ; and early in the morning, with his straw-bands adjusted and his strings tightened up, the wretched wanderer would start out upon another day's quest. Year after year he spent in this way ; remaining at home for the reception of visitors and for the cultivation of his patch of land during the summer, and straying from village to village when the cold weather set in. It was during one of these winter tours that he at last succumbed to fate, and retired from a world which cannot be said to have been benefited by his existence. He found himself at Silsden one night, and was induced to enter a public-house, where he sat drinking and singing in his usual way for a considerable time, apparently in his customary condition of health. Suddenly, however, he was taken ill, and it was suggested that some of his alehouse companions had drugged his liquor. At all events, he deemed it expedient to make the best of his way homewards, and little by little he dragged himself back to Ilkley. It was soon seen that he was in a failing state, and he was removed to the Carlton workhouse, and there he died, and was buried in Burley churchyard. His age was 77.

There was nothing in the career of Job Senior to

encourage anyone to follow his example. He was a coarse burlesque upon the hermit of poetry and romance. There was not a single gleam of brightness in his entire life history. His hermit period was a steady, undeviating course of unmanly grovelling; and he died unpitied and unmourned —as friendless a creature as ever drew breath.

THE STORY OF JONATHAN MARTIN.

ONE of the most eccentric persons that ever set the people of Yorkshire wondering, was JONATHAN MARTIN, the brother of the artist whose great Scriptural pictures, "The Great Day of His Wrath," "The Last Judgment," and "The Plains of Heaven," have in their time attracted much notice. Jonathan claimed, however, to be a more specially gifted man than his brother John, the painter. In his "Life," published in 1828, some time before the commission of the act of incendiarism which ultimately gained him notoriety, Jonathan says: "Mark! my kind readers, the hand of God in a poor, humble cot. God has raised of us four brothers. My oldest brother He has made a Natural Philosopher; my youngest an Historical Painter, his drawings and engravings have made Kings and Emperors to wonder: the Emperor of Russia at this time has made him a present of a diamond ring: but I, the unworthiest, God has given me the gift of prophecy, which is the best of all, for I feel that God is with me."

Jonathan Martin was, indeed, a very singular being, a strange mixture of fanaticism, madness, and hypocrisy. The "Life" that he wrote was no doubt "founded on fact," but he probably was induced to infuse into it a certain leaven of fiction for sensational effect. He tells us that he was born at Hexham, in Northumberland, in 1782, "of poor but honest parents." He was apprenticed to the "tanning business," and served his time without anything particular occurring to him. In his twenty-second year, however, he wandered up to London, his "mind being intent on travelling to foreign countries." He had his desire granted in a manner that he had not thought of. One day he was standing looking at the Monument when a man accosted him, and asked him if he wanted a situation. Martin answered that he desired to go abroad, upon which the man said he could suit him exactly, as a gentleman of his acquaintance had a son on board a frigate on the Indian station, who wanted such a person as Martin, and he could give him 32s. per month, besides his chance of prize money. Martin accepted the offer, but he soon found that he had got into the hands of the press-gang. He was sent, with a number of other pressed men, down to the Nore, and drafted on board the Hercules, seventy-four guns, which formed a part of the expedition sent out to Copenhagen in 1804 under Lord Nelson. They had the Danish fleet surrendered to them, and returned home "with such a prize as England never saw before." Martin was then drafted out of the Hercules into one of the prizes, an 84-gun ship, which with seven others set sail for Lisbon, to blockade eight Russian ships that had taken refuge in the Tagus. The Russian vessels were captured and brought to England.

After that, Martin's ship sailed with others for Corunna, to cover the embarkation of our troops. "We could plainly see the French and English camps from our ships," he says, "each occupying a hill very near the other. We made every exertion to get close in. . . Our ships replied to the French as well as the heavy sea then setting would allow. By great exertion the whole embarkation was completed. They then directed their batteries against our transports, who had to slip their cables and stand out of the reach of their guns. During this scene of confusion and terror several boats were sunk by the fire from the enemy, and some by the violence of the sea. Our vessels presented an awful spectacle from the number and condition of the wounded, who occupied our cockpit, cable tier, and every spare place on board, and whose misery was rendered greater by the tempest which arose, and prevented that attention being paid to them which their situation required. A great number perished solely on this account. During the gale five transports were lost, from which only few lives could be saved, owing to the state of the weather and the rocky nature of the coast."

They landed their wounded men at Plymouth, and then sailed again for Lisbon. By this time Martin had "begun to learn what it was to be a sailor." He had served " successively on the foretop, forecastle, gunner's crew, and after-guard, and was captain of the foretop in a prize taken by Lord Nelson from the Spaniards ; and also employed as a signalman in a gunboat, and captain of a main-deck gun, a boarder, a fireman, and a mortar-boat man." On their voyage to Cadiz, he says, " the gunner's yeoman, who had charge of the stores and all the powder, shot himself through the head in the storeroom, where there were upwards of 500 barrels of gunpowder, and joining the place where all our oakum and old ropes lay. When the report of the pistol was heard in that place, the consternation became general throughout the ship's company, as an explosion was to be dreaded. Some were for making to the boats, others more desperate were for leaping overboard, expecting the ship would blow up every moment. In the midst of the panic produced, I and four of my shipmates ran below, rushed into the storeroom amidst the smoke, and soon extinguished the little fire produced by the wadding of the pistol, and then we discovered the body of the unfortunate man lying bleeding, his brains literally strewed over the floor. Thus did God put in our hearts to risk our lives, and by that means save our ship's company, 600 in number, from an awful death."

It was about this time, Martin tells us, that he began to see his "lost and ruined state as a sinner, and to cry to God for mercy and salvation." He got tired of the naval service, and anxiously looked forward for the opportunity of escape. His ultimate "deliverance," as he calls it, "was extraordinary." "But," he says, "the Lord having given me favour in sight of the whole crew, when all hands were piped to breakfast, a boat appointed for the purpose was brought under our bows, and the soldiers formed a circle on the forecastle of the ship to prevent the sentry seeing what was going forward. I dropped into the boat and got ashore, and remained in safety at the waterman's house until our ship sailed. I entered on board a transport going to Egypt for corn for our troops then lying at Messina. When I arrived in Egypt I was filled with delight on beholding the place where our blessed Lord took refuge from the rage of Herod, and where the wisdom of Joseph (directed by Almighty God) saved the land of Egypt and his own father's house from the effects of the seven years' famine, of which I had so often read. A wide range of buildings was pointed out to me by the Turks, and which they said formerly held the corn preserved by Joseph. Reflecting on these things led me to review my misspent life, and to see how often God had preserved me in many dangers, and how ill I had requited Him ; so that my thoughts troubled me sore, and I resolved anew to amend my life. I began to be comforted by reflecting that He preserved me for wise purposes, and that I should live to praise Him. Blessed be the name of the Lord, I was not disappointed."

Martin then relates "a few of those occasions on which the Lord, in an especial manner, showed him that he was under His protecting care." Once, when in Egypt, he says, he got into a scuffle with some Turks, and a dagger was raised to kill him. One of the party, however, was "moved on his behalf," and his life was spared. At another time he fell from the main-yard, but he caught at the loose end of the tracing-line, about an inch thick, and held by it until his shipmates came to his assistance. Again he fell by accident out of a gun port, but was rescued by his shipmates once more. Afterwards he was on the topgallant-yard, when the topping-lift broke, and the end he was on "went down like the end of a beam." In his fall he grappled with the back-stay and brought himself up and landed on the cross-trees. On another occasion he and a shipmate took it into their heads to desert while forming a party that had been sent on shore to procure brushwood to scour the decks. After having travelled a few miles, however, Martin says, "The Lord saw fit to disappoint us." They came to a river and found a ferry-boat, and the boatman seeing that they were English sailors refused to convey them across until com-pelled by threats. They then went to a wine-house and got drunk; and subsequently, "after travelling on some miles through a wood," Martin recovered his senses and found he had lost his trousers, but whether they had been exchanged for wine or not he did not remember. Ultimately, to their amazement, they found themselves back again at the spot where their ship lay at anchor, so Martin "saw the hand of Providence in all this," and they rejoined the vessel and received the captain's pardon.

He relates many other marvellous escapes and exciting occurrences, and in one part of his book has a full-page engraving "showing the providential escape from shipwreck and sudden death, of Jonathan Martin, four different times," which is about the rudest specimen of wood-engraving ever put before an indulgent public. Where the ship ends, or where the sea begins, it is impossible to make out; one Jonathan Martin is seen struggling in the rigging, and another Jonathan Martin is hanging suspended over the side of the ship, but the two remaining Jonathans are not discoverable even by the aid of a microscope. It would not appear that Jonathan possessed his brother's genius in the remotest degree, judging from this unique specimen.

"The last of those remarkable deliverances," he says, "occurred in our voyage from Sicily, with a cargo of sulphur. Passing through the Bay of Biscay, our men were so weak, that only four could be mustered to a watch, and during the night-watch I was stationed on the weather-quarter to keep a look-out. Casting my eyes to windward, I observed a tremendous wave coming towards the ship, and had only time to call to a man at the helm to ease off and get the ship before the sea, and as is customary, to seize the taffrail to protect me from the fury of the sea. Instead of my usual hold, I seized the iron stancheon that supported the rail, and Providence seemed to direct my grasp, as, in less time than I have been in writing this, an immense sea struck the ship full on her quarter, carried away the taffrail, bulwarks, and every moveable thing on deck. Even the bolts which secured the arm-chest were torn out of the deck. Our cargo shifted with the labour of the sea, and we started a plank under our very main chains, at which the water poured in quickly. The violence of the fall I had received completely stunned me, but still retaining my hold with the firmness of despair, and when a little recovered and looking round, I could not help shedding tears of joy to see how I had been preserved amidst the destruction of all around me : thus showing in a most particular manner God's care for me. I was constrained to cry aloud in the midst of my amazed and horror-struck companions, "Glory be to God that my soul is not in hell, and that 1 am spared to thank God for this deliverance." They next endeavoured to get the ship righted, and Martin fell on his knees and prayed for a fair wind. "While I was praying," he says, "a voice was heard crying, 'Cheer up, my lads, the ship has answered her helm, and the wind has become fair for us ;' which made every man give a shout for joy, so we set to work like true English sailors, and in twelve hours' time we had her upright, and by the help of God got safe to Portsmouth in a few days."

From that time his career was that of a religious fanatic. Having been paid off from his ship, he took coach from London to Newcastle, and went to see his parents. Shortly afterwards he obtained employment in the tannery of a Mr. Page, at Norton, in the county of Durham. While here he got married, "and in process of time the Lord blessed his wife with a son, for which he had often prayed." He had the child baptized in the name of Richard, after a brother. About this time his parents both died, and strange dreams and visions began to trouble him. He dreamed that the spirits of his mother and sister came to him, and after telling him that he would have to be hanged, instantly vanished from sight. Other warnings followed, and "forced him to the house of God, to read his Bible as well as he could." One time, he says, "the Lord was pleased to reveal himself to me as He doth not to the world. I dreamed that whilst walking in a shrubbery, I saw my Lord and Saviour approach me with a sprig of laurel in His hand, and bid me advance and look at it, and He would show me a miracle. I looked, and beheld two blossoms of different colours on the branch. Whilst I viewed them He changed the colours into one. Bidding me look again, and behold, I saw that instead of blossoms appeared fruit, one green, the other ripe. A third time He bid me look, and the fruit was all ripe. Then He said, 'If thou canst believe, all this and more thou shalt be able to do.' Seizing my hand, He bore me through the forest, and I alighted on an old altar; then He breathed upon me, bidding me have faith, and then prepared to depart. I beheld a ladder reaching to the sky, by which He ascended, and on reaching the seventh step He fell backwards. Observing His wounds bleed, I ran with pity and took Him in my arms, and placing Him on the altar,

I breathed on Him as He had done on me, and the blood disappeared. When I awoke I wondered what this could mean, as I considered it impossible that an unlearned person like me could be made the instrument of good to others, especially as I had an impediment in my speech. Yet was it not the Lord that made me? and does He not give wisdom · to all that ask it of Him? I was alternately clouded with unbelief and filled with hope for three days." Then he goes on to relate dreams and experiences. His wife, he says, endeavoured to comfort him, "as she feared for his head." He began "to run to church and chapel by turns," and after a time he joined the Methodists.

"At the end of five months," he explains, "I took the sacrament in the church at Stockton, and leaving it at half-past one o'clock, I hastened to Yarm, where the lovefeast was to commence at two o'clock. I had only half an hour to go four miles, but I was running for a prize, and was determined not to be too late. The people were astonished at my haste as I passed along, and some questioned me, thinking something extraordinary had happened. When I gave my answer, I only said I was running for a prize. I arrived before the first prayer was finished, and was not five minutes on my knees till the Lord set me at full liberty, and here, too, He showed me that I had indeed met with the people among whom I must find my way to glory."

Martin now became so enthusiastic in his profession of faith, that he gave many people the impression that he had lost his reason. He conceived a strong dislike to the Church of England, and frequently interrupted the public ministrations of the clergy. "The lukewarm state of · the Established Church," he said, "is a great grief to me." One Sunday morning he went to the church, and finding the doors shut, he was "musing how to get admittance, when a voice spoke inwardly, and said, 'Go round the church seven times and thou shalt find entrance.'" He obeyed, and "on coming the seventh time the clerk arrived," and after expressing surprise at seeing him there so early, invited him in. Then the clerk went to ring the bell, and Martin crept up into the pulpit, "shut the door and lay down." Having folded down that part of the Gospel of St. Mark, chapter 4 and verses 21, 22, and 23, he waited anxiously the arrival of the people. "And now," he says, "the time being come that I was about to speak from the pulpit, the trembling clerk had to act as constable, and when he was pulling me out by the leg, I said, ' Let me go, poor trembling soul, for I am better able to walk than you are to carry me.' . . When the clerk had left me to myself, I sat down to hear the sermon."

After that Martin was convinced that he had received a "mission," and he travelled to various places exhorting the people to repentance. At Bishop Auckland they got a constable and dragged him through the congregation, but he avenged himself by "writing papers" and posting them on the church-doors. He was also expelled from the church at Norton because of his interruptions. At the South Church, Bishop Auckland, he got up while the minister was preaching and cried out, "Thou hast no business in that pulpit; thou whitened sepulchre, thou deceiver of the people, how canst thou escape the damnation of hell?" Martin then complains that "like poor John Bunyan" he was pulled out of the place.

About this time the Bishop (of Lincoln, Martin thinks) was to hold a Confirmation at Stockton. Martin had heard that he was a good man, and "resolved to try his faith by pretending to shoot him." Martin's wife saw the pistol, and asked him what he was going to do with it. "Shoot the Bishop!" he replied. From this the authorities got to know of the business, and Martin was arrested. On being interrogated as to whether he would really have shot the Bishop, Martin said, "It depended upon circumstances.

H

I would ask him some questions out of the Creed, and if he did not answer me satisfactorily as to his conversion and the evidence of the Spirit, he must be branded as a deceiver of the people."

Martin was at this juncture confined in a lunatic asylum at West Auckland, and appears to have suffered a good deal of ill-usage. On the 17th June, 1820, he got away from the asylum, but was captured at Norton and brought back. On the 1st of July, however, he made his escape again by rubbing the rivets of his irons with freestone, which he had contrived to secrete in his room. He broke through the ceiling, got into a garret, and escaped to the roof, from whence he descended to the ground. He bursts into song in regard to what he calls his "miraculous escape" :—

> Through the lofty garret I thrust and tore my way,
> Through dust and laths and tiles, into the open day.

He made his way to the house of Mr. Kell, a distant relative, who sheltered him for a fortnight; after that he was told that the constable was in search of him, so he made his way to Glasgow, and from thence to Edinburgh. Subsequently he returned to Norton to see his wife, who was very ill; and later on he started for London, but got no further than Boroughbridge, news of his wife's death reaching him at that place. Soon afterwards he is at Hull, working in a tannery, and preaching to his workmates. "I was moved to speak to them of their drunken lives," he writes, "and what would be the consequence if they did not repent. One or two of them, more wicked than the rest, got above me with a bucket of bullock's blood, which they heaved over me; but that did not move me from my stand; and then they tried water. Then the devil put it into their minds to heave wet skins in my face, and that did not make me quit my stand until the hour was up." He claims to have converted 200 persons at Hull, but he was finally driven away, and returned to Norton to his old master,

Mr. Page, the magistrates having consented that he should not be committed to the asylum. In 1822 he was at Darlington, and worked, and prayed, and preached there until 1827. He wore a coat and boots of sealskin, with the hairy side outwards, and used to ride upon an ass, "to be more like Christ." In 1827 he removed to Lincoln, where he wrote and published his "Life," two editions being quickly disposed of, and a third of 5,000 copies issued. He now went about the country hawking his book, upon the cover of which was the following note:—"N.B.—Gentlemen and Ladies, think it not strange that I charge you one shilling for my book and the price on the title only sixpence, for the Lord says 'remember the poor.' You will find my book give you satisfaction." In concluding his biography, he expresses a hope that his wanderings and sorrows are ended, and he gives "glory to God for having at last given rest to his feet."

Jonathan Martin, however, had by no means completed his eventful career as yet.

In 1828, at Boston, (his first wife being dead) he married a young woman, twenty years his junior, named Maria Hodson, and shortly after their marriage they removed to York, and obtained lodgings with a shoemaker, named William Lawn, in Aldwark. He would go to the Minster on Sunday afternoons, and frequently left letters about. On the 6th January, 1829, the following wild epistle was found tied to one of the iron gates of the Minster choir, but at the time it was deemed too absurd to claim serious notice :—

"York, Janrey the 5, 1829.

"Hear the word of Lord, Oh you Dark and Lost Clergymen. Repent and cry For mercy for know is the day of vangens and your Cumplet Destruction is at Hand for the Lord will not sufer you and the Deveal and your blind Hellish Doctren to dseve the works of His Hands no longer. Oh, you Desevears will not milleons of the mightty and Rich men of the Earth have to Curs the Day that ever they got under your blind Docktren know to be ashamed of yourselves and wepe for your Bottls of Wine and your downey Beds will be taken away from you I warn you to repent in the name of Jesuse and believe he is able on Earth to forgeve sines, for their is no repenting in the greave. Oh you blind Gydes are you not like the man that bilt his House upon the Sands when the Thunder starmes of Gods Heavey vangens lites upon your guilty Heads a way gos your sandey Foundaytons and you to the deepest pet of Hell re Seve the Curses of millions that your blind Docktrens has Decevd and to reseve Gods Heve Curs and the Ward pronounst Depart you Carsit blind Gides into the Hotist plase of Hell to be tormented with the Deveal and all his Eanguls for Ever and Ever. Jona. Martin, a frind of the Sun of Boneypart Must Conclude By warning you again. Oh Repent repent He will soon be able to act

the part of his Father

" Derect for Jonathan Martin
    Aldwark No. 6o."

Several other communications, couched in a similar strain, were discovered, but no one suspected them to be anything but the wild ravings of a fanatic.

Martin and his wife went from York to Leeds on the 27th of January, and lodged at the house of John Quin, No. 6, Brick Street. In a few days Martin returned alone to his old lodgings in York, and he then began to lay his plans for burning down the Minster. On Sunday morning, the 1st February, he went to the Minster and heard the sermon ; he went again in the afternoon, entering the south transept as soon as the doors were open. He walked about till after the service began, and then concealed himself behind a tomb. He had before coming provided himself with " a razor with a white haft, the back of which he used instead of a steel ; a flint, tinder, matches, and a penny candle or two." He supplemented the penny candles by possessing himself of one of the wax candles used in the Minster. As the organ played he muttered to himself, " Buzz, buzz—I'll teach thee to stop thy buzzing."

When the people had all left, he walked about and began to search for a suitable spot for lighting the fire. The ringers were in the belfry during the evening, and from behind a column he watched them go out. Martin then went into the belfry, struck a light, and proceeded to provide himself with a means of escape. He cut a length of about ninety feet from the prayer-bell rope, and formed it into a ladder by doubling it and tying knots at regular distances. This done, he quitted the belfry, climbed over the gates which separated the nave from the north-east aisle, and then, by the aid of the rope-ladder, got over into the choir. He now struck a light once more, and with his white-hafted razor cut three yards of gold fringe, two gold tassels, &c., from the pulpit; also the crimson velvet curtains from the Dean's and Precentor's seats at the bottom of the choir, and those from the Archbishop's throne. He then put a small Bible in his pocket, that it might be a comfort to him during the imprisonment which he expected would follow the act that he was about to perpetrate. After that, he piled the cushions and prayer-books in two heaps, and set them on fire with matches. All this time, he said, he felt "quite happy; sometimes he prayed, and sometimes he praised God, because He had strengthened him to do so good a work."

When the place was fairly fired, Martin proceeded to make his escape. He tied one end of his rope to the machine used for cleaning the Minster, dragged the machine under the window in the west aisle of the north transept, got up to the window, broke it with a pair of pincers, got through and let himself down and successfully effected his escape. This was shortly after three o'clock in the morning of the 2nd February.

It was not until several hours afterwards that the fire was discovered. Two or three persons had observed a light in the sacred edifice, but had no idea that anything was wrong. A little before seven o'clock, however, a chorister named Swinbank made his way towards the Minster for practice, as usual. Finding the doors closed, he amused himself by sliding on a piece of ice in the Minster yard, and whilst thus engaged fell on his back, and in recovering his position saw smoke issuing from the roof of the building. He alarmed the sexton, and soon a number of people were on the spot. The fire was burning with great force in the region of the choir it was found when the doors were burst open. One of the Minster engines was brought out and put into play, and great efforts were made to rescue some of the more valuable objects. The bells of St. Michael-le-Belfry sounded the alarm through the city, and soon the terror-stricken inhabitants were rushing towards the scene of the conflagration. Expresses were sent in all directions for assistance, and for several hours a fierce struggle was kept up with the flames. Fire-engines from Leeds and other places, a strong body of military, and a crowd of active men were engaged in the work of subduing the fire, but it was not until noon that the flames were got under. The roof of the central aisle, from the lantern tower to the east window, all the interior work from the organ screen to the altar screen, the organ, the stalls, galleries, and Bishop's throne, pulpit, and tabernacle work were destroyed. The damage done amounted to about £70,000.

On Monday night a committee of investigation was constituted. Their inquiries were continued on Tuesday and Wednesday. The knotted rope, the pincers, and a bunch of matches, which Martin had left behind, all pointed to the fire being the work of an incendiary, and suspicion at once fell upon Martin, and £100 reward was offered for his apprehension.

Meanwhile Martin was not allowing the grass to grow under his feet. After leaving the Minster, as he related subsequently, he proceeded to Easingwold, and got a pint of ale ; from thence to Thirsk, at which place he arrived at eleven o'clock ; from Thirsk he went to Northallerton, where he arrived about three o'clock in the afternoon in a state of fatigue. At nine that night he got the driver of a coal-cart to let him ride with him, and in this cart he travelled all night until he reached Joft-hill pit, near West Auckland. He then walked to Alensford, on the Derwent, and slept there on the Tuesday night. At eight o'clock on the Wednesday morning he started off once more, proceeding to Riding Mill, where he had a pint of ale ; then he went forward to Corbridge, arriving about noon and drinking half-a-pint of ale ; from thence he went to Cadlaw Hill, and stayed there with his friend Mr. Kell, the gentleman who had afforded him shelter when he escaped from the Gateshead asylum, until Friday morning, when the officers of the law overtook and apprehended him.

Martin readily acknowledged that he had set the Minster on fire, and was anxious to know to what extent the build- had been damaged. He was told that the damage was estimated at £100,000; upon which he said, "If it were not for the glory of God, if that could be promoted, £200,000 would not have been too much, and I think it would have been well if all the Minster had gone together, for the worship carried on in it is idolatrous and supersti- tious."

On being charged before the York magistrates, Martin said : "The reason that I set fire to the Cathedral was on account of two particular dreams. In the first dream I dreamed that a man stood by me with a bow and a sheath of arrows. He shot an arrow, and the arrow stuck in the Minster door. I then wished to shoot, and the man pre- sented me the bow, and I took an arrow from the sheath and shot, and it struck on a stone and I lost it. In the second dream I dreamed that a cloud came down on the Cathedral, and came over to the house where I slept, and it made the whole house tremble. Then I awoke, and I thought it was the Hand of God pointing out that I was to set fire to the Cathedral. And those things which were found on me I took lest any one should be blamed wrongfully. I took them to bear witness against myself. I cut the hangings from the throne, or Cathedral, or whatever you call it, and tore down the curtains."

He was committed to the Assizes, and on Monday, March 30th, 1829, before Mr. Baron Hullock, he was tried. On being asked whether he was guilty or not guilty, he said, "My God gave me that for my hire. The Lord gave the silk to mak' a robe, like David the King, and the velvet to mak' a cap, and the tassels I took from the pulpit to hang down over my right and left ear." The question was repeated, and he again answered, "I had it given me for my hire." This was construed into a plea of Not Guilty, and the trial proceeded on the following morning. After the evidence against him had been given, he was called upon for his defence, and made a long, rambling statement as to his dreams and warnings, and the manner in which he had accomplished the firing of the Minster. He was found not guilty, on the ground of insanity, and sentenced to be confined in close custody during his Majesty's pleasure. His brother, the artist, had procured evidence of Jonathan's insanity, and ever afterwards the incendiary bore him the bitterest enmity. Martin was confined in St. Luke's Hospital, London, and died there in 1838.

York Minster was re-opened for divine service on the 6th May, 1832. The expense of the restoration was nearly all borne by public subscription. The Government gave timber to the value of £5,000, and the stone was given by Sir E. M. Vavasour, Bart., of Hazlewood. The organ was presented by the Hon. and Rev. J. L. Savile, afterwards Earl of Scarborough, and the communion plate by the Archbishop.

THE STORY OF THE CALVERLEY TRAGEDY.

IT was a dull, spiritless, November day. It wasn't exactly wet, it wasn't exactly windy,—it wasn't exactly any sort of weather. All the elemental furies seemed to have met together with the intention of neutralising each other's efforts, and the result was a chaotic mixture of all descriptions of weather, fog and drizzle being perhaps the most pronounced of the elements. It was, in fact, a true November day: a cut-throat, hang-dog sort of day—a day suggestive of suicides and murders, and foul deeds generally; and as luck would have it, it was the day I had chosen for paying a visit to the scene of one of the most notorious murders in local history. If I had not appointed this day long beforehand for making the journey, the depressing atmosphere might have caused me to relinquish the idea; but bad weather or good, I was now bound to go, and as I toiled up the hill from the Calverley Railway Station, behind a drover and his herd and an extremely active and intelligent colley, I felt that the weight of centuries was upon me. Here was I, on my way to the scene of a murder which took place over 270 years ago, my intention being to track the murderer's footsteps, and to read afresh the story of his crime, by the aid of an actual inspection of the old mansion where the awful deed was perpetrated.

Once arrived at Calverley, there was not much difficulty in finding the manorial hall wherein the Calverleys had for many generations lived their indifferent lives. I had the good fortune to meet with a young antiquary, too, who kindly officiated as guide for me; and as we proceeded to the old mansion we prepared ourselves for what we were going to see by an attempt to recall something of the history of the Calverleys. It did not take us long to tell all that there was to tell about them. How the first manorial lord of Calverley came to England in the retinue of the Empress Maude, and had lands in Airedale granted to him by one of the De Lacies; how his successors lived their wild lives out in the place which still retains their name; how in 1605 the wildest and most reckless of them all, did the deed which forms the subject of this chapter. How Henry, the son of the murderer, afterwards inherited the Calverley estates, suffered great hardships for his loyalty to the Stuarts, and afterwards, on the Restoration, was created a Knight of the Royal Oak; how this same Henry, by marriage with the daughter of Henry Thompson, of Esholt, became possessed of the Esholt estate; how his son Walter succeeded him, and adopted the name of Blackett; and how the family pedigree lengthened and lengthened until at the present day the Calverleys are represented by baronets of the Blackett and Trevelyan families.

On reaching the ancient home of the Calverleys, we found the November mists hanging round an old and somewhat dilapidated building of the Tudor period, and as we surveyed it from the outside we tried to conjure up an idea of what it would look like in the days when the Calverleys resided there. At present the mansion is divided up into cottage tenements, and is hemmed in by other buildings to such an extent as to be hidden in great part. In its original form it would, no doubt, be a house of considerable architectural pretensions, and, with the extensive park by which it would be surrounded, would constitute one of the most attractive objects in the Airedale landscape. Of the antiquity of the building there are abundant evidences in its weather-beaten, time-worn stones, and its ancient windows, but the dividing up process has, in a great measure, destroyed its original aspect. Up to a recent period the upper rooms of the hall have been used as cloth-weaving chambers, but the sound of the loom is now no longer heard there, the tenements having been given up entirely to domestic uses. We first enter a cottage, formed out of a portion of the chapel in which the Romish Calverleys held family worship. An intelligent middle-aged woman furnishes us with a candle, and we ascend the heavy stone steps into what is now a chamber, where we see such architectural arrangements as clearly prove to what uses this part of the building was devoted. From this place we proceed to the next tenement, which takes in the portion of the hall wherein the murder was done. Here we come upon strange, heavy stone staircases, with the oddest turns, and most unaccountable recesses and doors, and we advance into the living-room of the occupants, and find indications of a grand old kitchen fire-place of the period of the middle ages, and an oppressive amount of heavy oak wainscoting, and great frowning walls several feet in thickness. A damsel precedes us with a candle, and leads us upstairs into the very room where the murder was committed. It is now occupied as a bed-room, and, it is to be hoped, for the sake of the comfort of those who sleep there, that the ghost of " owd Cawverley" has by this time ceased to haunt the room. Some rudely-executed paintings are to be seen on the wainscoting, and the whole appearance of the room is, on this November day, gloomy in the extreme. Here are the very boards which were stained with the blood of the murdered children ; here it was that the affrighted wife entreated her lord to have mercy ; it was from here that the murderer rushed down those very stone stairs with the further intent of murdering his surviving child, who was out at nurse at Norton. There is something very weird about the scene as we pass to and fro, peering through the mysterious corridors, looking up at the sombre walls, and treading the creaking boards, with the damsel with the lighted candle showing us the way, as with stooping forms we proceed from room to room. We take our leave of the place with a shiver, and are glad to get out again into the daylight, even though it is but the November daylight.

Thus fortified with some amount of personal experience, I turn with greater sympathy to the story of the murder, and as I walk in the semi-darkness to the station at Apperley, the history of the crime comes back to me all the more intensely because of my having made this curious pilgrimage.

The most complete account of the tragedy that we possess was written by an anonymous author, and published in the year when the sad event occurred. This narrative was given along with the story of another contemporary crime, and the tract in which the two stories appeared, and which is now extremely scarce, bore the following title :—

"TWO MOST VNNATURAL AND BLOODIE MURTHERS: THE ONE BY MAISTER CAUERLEY, A YORKSHIRE GENTLE-MAN, VPON HIS WIFE AND TWO CHILDREN, 1605; THE OTHER BY MISTRESS BROWNE AND HER SERVANT PETER, VPON HER HUSBAND, 1605. London, by V.S., 1605."

This tract was reprinted in *fac-simile* in 1863, but only about fifty copies were struck off. One of these found its way into the hands of Mr. Abraham Holroyd, and it is from this that I am now enabled to make the extract relating to the Calverley Tragedy. The story is given in such a quaint style, and garnished so plentifully with figurative conceits and ponderous moralisings, that it would be a pity to do other than transcribe it word for word. It brings the period before us much more vividly than could be done by a simple adaptation of it to modern phraseology. It is as follows :—

"MAISTER CAUERLEY'S VNNATURAL AND BLOODIE MURTHER PRACTISED VPON HIS WIFE, AND COMMITTED VPON HIS CHILDREN.

"There hath happened of late within the countie of Yorke, not farre from Wakefield, a murther so detestable, that were it not it desires record for example sake, humanitie would wish it vtterly forgot, than any Christian heart should tremble with the remembrance of it.

" Within this county was bred a gentleman, one Maister *Cauerley* of *Cauerley*, a man whose parents were such as left him seuen or eight hundred pounds a yeare, to enrich his hopes, cherish his content, and make him fortunate. His father dying before he had reacht the years of priunege, during his nonage he was warde to a most worthy and noble gentleman in this land ; in all which time his course of life did promise so much good, that there was a commendable grauity appeared euen in his youth. He being of this hope, vertuous in his life, and worthy by his birth, was sought vnto by many gallant gentlemen, and desired that he would vnite his fortune unto their families, by matching himself, to one and the chiefe of their daughters.

"Among which number it happened, being once invited for such a purpose (a welcome guest), to an antient gentleman of cheefe note in the country (hee came), where in a short time was such an interchange of affection shot in by one paire of eies to one paire of heartes, that this gentleman's best beloved daughter was by private made Maister *Cauerley's* best beloved wife : nor could it bee kept so close betweene the paire of lovers (for love will discover itself in loving lookes), but it came to the father's knowledge, who with a natural ioy was contented with the contract ; yet in regard Maister *Cauerley* yeares could not discharge his honourable gardian had ouer him, the father thought it meete (though the lovers could have wished it otherwais) to lengthen their desired haste, till time should finish a fit houre to solemnize their happy wedlock. Maister *Cauerley* hauing spent some time there in decent recreation, much abroad, and more at home with his new mistresse, at last he bethought himself that his long stay made him looked for at London. And hauing published his intended departure, the father thought it convenient, though the vertuous gentlewoman danced a loth to depart upon his contracted lips. Maister *Cauerley* came to London, and whether concealing his late contract from his honorable gardian, or forgetting his priuate and publike vowes, or both, I know not, but Time, mother of alterations, had not fanned ouer many daies, but he had made a new bargaine, knit a new marriage knot, and was husband by all matrimonial rites to a courteous gentlewoman, and neere by marriage to that honorable personage to whom he was ward.

"Rumour, with his thousand tongues and ten thousand feete, was not long in travel before he had delivered this distasteful message to his first mistresse eares, who, looking for a more lovely commendations, and hauing hearde but part of that, such as truly it was, the wind of her sighs had so raised vp the tide of her teares, that she clipped the report, ere it could be tolde out, into many pieces. And as she would faine haue asked this question (as it is indeede)? she was faine to make vp her distracted sillables with the letters of her eyes. This gentlewoman, Maister *Cauerley's* (if vowes may make a wife) took, with an inward consideration, so to heart this vniust of wrong, that exercising her houres only in continual sorrow, she brought herself to consumption; who so plaide the insulting tyrant over her unblemished beautie, that the cruel contention dwelt in her face of white and redde was turned to a death-like paleness; and all her artires wherein the spirite of life mixed with blood doth runne, like giddie subjectes in the empire of her bodie, greedie of innovation, took such vngentle parte with this forraigne vsurper, that where health before was her peaceable soueraigne, now distracted sickness and feeble weakness were her untimely conquerors ; yet under this yoke of griefe shee so paciently indured that, though she had great reason, a foundation whereon shee might haue baild arguments to have curst his proceedings, and where others would haue contrasted sillibles both of reproache and reproofe agaynst him, shee only married these letters together : I entreat of God to grant both prosperous health and fruitful wealth to him and his, though I am sick for his sake.

"But to Maister *Cauerley*, who hauing finished this wrong to this gentlewoman, and begun too much distresse to her that he married (as too soon appeared) ; for though the former, conquered by the gentlenesse of her nature, forgave his fault, yet revenge being alwaies in God's hand, thus it fell.

"This gentleman had not lieud many months with his wife, but he was so altered in disposition from that which he was, and so short from the perception which he had, as a body dying is of a life flourishing : and where before his thoughts onely studied the relish of vertue and her effects, his actions did now altogether practice the vnprofitable taste of vice, and her fruites.

"For though he was a man of so good reuenew as before, he continued his expence in such exceeding riot that hee was forced to mortgage his lands, run in great debts, entangle his friends by being bound for him, and in short time so weakened his estate, that, hauing not wherewithall to carry that port which before he did, he grew into a discontent, which so swaid in him, he would sit sullenly, walke melancholy, be thinking continually, and with steady lookes naild to the ground, seeme astonisht that when his wife would come to desire the cause of his sadnesse, and intreate to be a willing partner in his sorrow ; for,

Consortium rerum omnium inter nos
Facit amicitia,

hee would eyther sitte still without giuing her an answer, or rising vppe, depart from her with these words :—A plague on thee ! thou art the cause of my sadnesse. The gentle-woman, which without question this report is true of, neuer so much as in thought offended him, and hauing been sundry times curst without cause, once came to him, and making her teares parlee with her words, she thus intreated him : Sir, Maister *Cauerley*, I beseech you by the mutuall league of love which should be betwixt vs, by the vowes we made together, both before and after our marriage, and by that God that registers our thoughts, tell me what I haue done, the remembrance of which should afflict you, or what I may do that I might content you : as you desire the three lovely boyes you haue been father vnto should grow vp and make your name liue in your country, acquaint me with your griefes ; and what a wife can shew to manifest her love to her husband shall be perfected in me. Maister *Cauerley*, fixing himselfe with a stedy eie vpon her, at last delivered this : I now want money and thou must help me.

"O ! Maister *Cauerley* (quoth shee), though God selfe know I am no cause of your want, yet what haue I to supply you, either in iewels or rings, pray you take : and I beseech you, as you are a gentleman, and by the love you bear to your children, although you cannot for me, looke back into your estate, and restrain this great feond of your expense before your house be utterly ouerthrowne. You know, sir (quoth shee), your land is morgaged already, yourselfe other-wise greatly in debt, some friends of yours that are bound for you like to be vndone. But as shee would have gone forward, he cut her off with these words : Base strumpet ! (whom though I married I never loued), shal my pleasure be con-fined by your wil? If you and your bastards be in want, either beg or retire to your friends. My humour shal have the antient scope. Thy rings and iewels will I sel, and as voluntarie spend them, as when I was in the best of my estate. The good gentlewoman's eyes being drawne full of water with these words, made him no other replie but this: Sir, your will be done. But he fled on in this vehemencie of bloud: I protest, by Heauen, I will ever hereafter lothe thee, till thou gie thy consent thy dowrie shall be solde to maintaine my pleasure, and leave thyselfe and children destitute of maintenance. Sir (answered she), in all this I will be a wife: what in all this the law will allow me to doe, you shall commaund. See thou doost it (quoth he), for no longer then I am full of money shalt thou partake from me a taste of kindnesse.

"Mistresse *Cauerley*, going forward with this intent to sell away her dowrie, was sent for vp to London by that honorable friend whose neece she was, and whose warde she had beene; who, having heard of her husband's prodigalitie, at her coming vp began to question her about her estate, and whether he bore himselfe as a husband should do in familiar love to her? The gentlewoman, though she knew how desperate his estate was, and her tongue could too well haue tolde his vnkindnesse, she answered both thus: For my husbande's estate, I make no doubt but it is in the same height his father left it to him, but for our love one to another, I am assured, and I prayse God for it, we live like *Abraham* and *Sarah*, he loving me, I obedient to him.

"Howsoever (answered this honourable friend), your words are an ornament a good wife should haue, and you seek to shadow the blemishes his actions have cast vpon your life: let this suffice you; I know his prodigal course. I know how his land is all, or the most part of it morgaged, himself in debt to manie; yet censuring these infirmities to proceed of no other cause, but from the rash heate of youth, which will in time, no doubt, be supprest by experience; and for that I believe your words to be true, and I am glad to hear of his kindnesse toward you. I will take such order for him, as he shall continue still Maister *Cauerley*, in the

I

same degree, or better, than ere his ancestors were in Yorke-shire : and at your return to certifie him withall, that he hasten vp to Court.   Nor let the feare of his creditors abridge his comming vp to Court, for I will protect him, both from them, and also provide some place in Court for him, wherein he shall finde I am his honourable kinsman.

"The good gentlewoman was so struck with ioy at this comfortable promise, that she was scarce able to speake out her duetifull thanks.   And thinking her husband would be satisfied with this preferment, hoping that kindnes would be contracted again betwixt them, and assuring herselfe there would be now no need to make sale of her dowrie (for that was also a part of her busines), hauing taken leaue of her honourable kinsman, she returned towards *Cauerley.*

"During this her absence Maister *Cauerley* maintained his accustomed habite, and indeede grew from bad to worse ; for mischiefe is of that nature, that it can not stand, but by strengthening one euil with another, and so multiply in it selfe vntil it come vnto the highest, and then falls with its own weight, so Maister *Cauerley* being given to excesse, rioting, as dicing, drinking, reuling, and it is thought, etc., fed one euel with another, and in such continual vse, that his body was not in temper without the exercise of sinne : for who knowes not, *sine Cerere et Bacco friget* Venus ?   So, without money pleasure will hardly be maintained.

· "And this gentleman, hauing now made wracke of his estate, and finding himselfe not able to maintaine his plea-sure, when his desire was as great as before (for pleasure being once delightfull vnto the memorie, is as hard to be resisted as madnesse) first he fel vnto a hatred with his wife, and in this her absence to such a loathing of his children, that in what company soeuer hee had happened, hee could not containe his rage, but would openly proclaime his wife was a strumpet, his children were bastardes.   And although theyr marriage was made by honourable personages, her selfe nobly descended, from the first houre he embraced her to that very minute hee did loathe her. Some would mildly perswade him from phrensie, others would courteously reproove him, saying, It was not fitte. And all, whose modestie thought it vnmeet to meddle betwixt man and wife, knowing her vertuous life, didde vtterly condemne him.

"But he continued this publication in all places where he came; and at one, among the number there happened a gentleman to be, who having knowne the discreetnesse of his wife from her very cradle, and hearing him so wilde in his abuses, prepared himselfe confidently to correct him: and hauing beganne his speech of chasticement, the other not enduring to be detected, both being soone inflamed, fel to quarrelsome tearms, and in such heate, that Maister *Cauerley* did not spare to say, That he might wel be his wife's friend, for ought he knew; nay, there was great presumption for it, since he should bee so easily stirred vp in his wife's excuse. The gentleman, not enduring to heare her reputation, but especially his owne, to be touched, so answered Maister *Cauerley*, and agayne Maister *Cauerley* him, that they both agreed to purge themselves in the field. Both mette, and after some thrustes chaunged between them, Maister *Cauerley* was hurt, yet he would not giue ouer; so that after he became at the gentleman's mercie; but hee of that humane condicion did to desire his life, nor so much blood as was, had he not been vrged, bade him rise, and left him with these words: Maister *Cauerley*, you are a gentleman of an antient house; there hath been much good expected from you; deceyue not men's hopes: you haue a vertuous wife, be kinde vnto her. I forget my wrong, and continue to be your friend.

"But Maister *Cauerley*, vnsatisfied with this, his hart flew to his mouth as it would have leapt out after him for reunge: yet knowing he could get little by following him, but hurts such as he had already, prepared to turn his wrath another way. Then looking upon his wounds, and seeing them bleede, said to himselfe, Strumpet! thou are the cause that I bleede now, but I will be the cause that thou shalt bleede hereafter. So, taking his horse, rode presently home, where, before his wounds were thoroughly healed, his wife came from London, and the first greeting given to her by her husband was, What! hast thou brought the money? Is the land sold? She answered: Sir, I hope I have made a iourney shall redound both to your comfort and mine: so accquainting him with the precedencie, which was his promised preferment by her kinsman, and expecting a louing acceptance, the first thanks he gaue her was a spurn. And looking vpon her as if his eies would have shot fire into her face, Haue you bin at London to make your complaint of me, you damnable strumpet (quoth hee), that the greatness of your friends might ouersway the weaknesse of my estate? and I, that haue liued in that rank of will which I haue doone, that freedom of pleasure, should forsake it now? Shall I, being a *Cauerley* of *Cauerley*, stoope my thoughts so low to attend on the countenance of your alliance, to order my life by their direction, and neither doe nor vndoe anything but what they list? which if I refuse to doe, your complaints haue so wrought with them, and haue so possessed them of my estate, they will enforce mee forsoothe for your good and the good of my children. Was this your tricke to save your dowrie, the which I swore you should sell? Was this your going to London?

"The good gentlewoman being almost blown to death with this vehemencie of his wrath, fell at his feete, and desired him to heare her, when (poor soule) she was as full of griefe, she had not the power to speak; yet having eased the way with a few sorows drops, she beganne to pleade this true excuse to him, that (like one had lost all his senses) had scarce patience to heare. Sir (said she), God knowes the words I speake haue no fashion of vntruth: my friends are fully possesst your lands are morgaged; they know to whom, and for what; but not by me, I beseech you believe; and for any difference betwixt yourself and me, which I doubt would offend more than the morgaging of your land, I protest yet there is no occasion of suspect. If you think I have published anything to him with desire to keep the sale of my dowrie from you, either for mine owne good or my childrens, though it fits I should have a motherly care of them (you being my husband) passe it away how you please, spend it how you will, so I may enjoy but welcome lookes, and kind wordes from you : and when all which you call yours is gone, ere you or yours shall want, I will work for your maintenance ; neither of which extreamities, sir, neede, if you please, if you will but accept preferment in Englands Court, being offred you *gratis*, which many men would purchase with cost, and cannot compass it.

"At which words, though thus mildly vttered, and on her humble knees, he was so without cause enraged, that had not one of his own men come up in the instant, and told him there was a gentleman from one of the Universities staid to speak with him, he had offered her present violence.

"Maister *Cauerley* went down to speak with this gentleman, leauing his wife stuffed with griefe vp to the eyelids; and shee, good soule, hauing eased her heart with a long fetcht sigh or two, laid her downe vpon her bed, where in carefull slumbers we will leau her, and attend the conference between Maister *Cauerley* and this gentleman. Maister *Cauerley* had at this present a second brother who was o good standing in the University, who vpon some extremitie Maister *Cauerley* was in, for so he would plead himself to be his friend, when he would haue them bound for him, had passed his bond for a thousand pounds; this bond was forfeited, suied, and this young gentleman being reputed of staied government, the execution was served vpon him, and he at this instant prisoner for his brothers debt. About this business came this gentleman to Maister *Cauerley*, who being master of the college where his brother had his instruction, and having ever noted his forward will in the exercise of vertue, in pity vnto his estate, being moved thereunto by the young student, came purposely thither, who without long circumstance told Maister *Cauerley* the cause of his coming was toe stirre vp his conscience to haue regard to his brother, for hee heard hee was carelesse, and indeed dwelt so sharply, and forcibly, in laieing open to him that scandal the world woulde throwe vpon him, that judgement from God should fall vpon him for suffering his brother to spend the glory of his youth, which is the time young men of hope seeke preferment, in prison by his means, did soe harrowe vp his sole by his invincible arguments that in that minute he made him looke back into the errore of his life, which scarce in his life he had done till this instant.

"This gentleman hauing spoke his minde asked him what he meant toe doe with his brother, for he now waited his answer. Maister *Cauerley* made him this milde reply: Sir, I thanke you bothe for your paines and good instruction to me in my brothers behalfe, and I must confesse I haue done him wronge. Soe calling for a cup of beere he dranke toe him and bade him welcome. Now, sir, quote Maister *Cauerley*, if you please to walke downe and see the grounds aboute my house one of mye men shall goe along with you, at your returne I will giue sufficient answere that my brother bye you shall be satisfied, and be a prisoner but a few houres.

"This gentleman thanked him, and told him that in performing that naturall office, he shoulde bothe gratifie God, satisfie the worlde, and he himselfe shoulde account his paines profitable.

"This stranger is gone to walke with one of Maister *Cauerleys* men to oueruiew his ground, and Maister *Cauerley* retires himselfe into a gallery, where being alone he felle into a deep consideration of his state, how his prodegall course of life had wronged his brother, abused his wife, and vndone his children, and the misery he should leave his children in. Then he saw what an vnnatural part it was his brother should lie in prison for his debt, and he not able to deliver him. Then he saw that his wife being nobly descended, vnless her owne friends tooke pitty vpon her, should with his children be driven to beg remorce of the world, which is composed of flint. Then he saw the exterpation of his family, the ruin of his house, which hundreds of yeares had been gentlemen of the best reputation in Yorkeshire, and every one of these out their severall objects did create distraction in him. Some time he would teare his hair, and bye and bye teares would rush into his euies, strait breake out into the exclamation, O I am the most wretched that ever was borne of woman! O that I had been slayne in my mothers wombe, and my mother had beene my sepulchre! I have begotten my children to be nothing but wretchednesse, made a wife to eat her bread in bitternesse, and a brother to be full of care.

"As he was thusse tormented by the remembrances of his owne folly, his eldest sonne, being a childe of aboute foure yeares old, came into the gallery to scourge his toppe, and seeing his father stand in a study, came prettily vp to him, saying, How do you do, father? which lovely looke and gentle question of the childe, raised againe the remembrance of the distresse he should leaue him in. And as the sea being hurled into furious billows by the rageing of the windes, hides bothe heaven and earth from the sight of men, so hee, being ouerwhelmed by the violence of his passion, all naturall loue was forgotten in his remembrance, caught his childe vp by his necke, and striking at him with his dagger, the childe lente him such a looke that would haue driven a hand, seuen yeares prentice to murder, to an ague; (yet hee) would it had neuer beene donne, it might neuer haue beene told ; though his armes seemed twice to remember him of the monstrousenesse of the fact, he strooke the louely infant into the head, and holding the bleeding childe at armes lengthe, that it might not sprinkle his cloaths, which had stained his hart and honour, he soe carried it into a meare chamber, where his wife laye asleepe vpon a bed, and the maide was dressing another childe bye the fire (here is to be noted his other childe was at nurse) ; but the woman seeing him come in that cruell sort—his childe in one hand —his reeking dagger in the other—the childe bleeding—he staring—started from the fire, and, with the childe in her armes, cried out, but he, letting goe the boy he had wounded, caught the other violently out of her armes, and this chamber doore being at the toppe of a very high paire of staires, carried her forthe by maine strength, and threwe the poore woman downe to the very bottome, who in tender pity, by precedent of the one, woulde haue preserued the other.

"The childe that was wounded was all this while crying in the chamber, and with his woefull noyse wakened his more woefull mother, who seeing one childe bleeding, the other lying on the grounde (while he stroue to throwe the maide downe staires), shee caught vp the youngest, and going to take the elder, which was going towards the doore, her husbande coming backe met her, and came to struggle with her for the childe, which shee sought toe preserve with wordes, teares, and whatever a mother could doe, from soe tragicall an end.   And when hee saw hee could not get it from her, hee most remorcelessly stabbed it three or foure times, all which shee saued the childe from by taking it toe herselfe ; and hauing a paire of whalebone boddice on, it pleased God his dagger soe glaunced on them that shee had but one wounde on her shoulder.   But hee, more crewell by this resistance, caught holde of the childe in his mother's armes, and stabs it toe the heart, and after giuing his wife two or three mortall woundes she fell backwarde, and the childe dead at 'her feete. The maide that was throwne downe staires, with the greatness of the fall, the staires being high, laye in a swoand at the bottome ; the noyse of this brought the servants toe helpe the maide, thinking that she had felle by mischance (not knowing that which was most tyranous), did their best toe to comforte her beneath while the father and mother were striuing, one to preserue the infant, the other to kill it.

"The childe that was first wounded sought toe get toe the doore, and hauing recouered the toppe of the staires, by expence of bloud and the greatness of the wounde, hauing nobody to comforte it, fell alsoe downe the staires ; and the armes of the servants helping the maide at the staires foote were faine to let her goe to receiue him. Some caught at the dead infant, some helped the maide ; all amazed at this tragick alteration, knewe not what to think ; yet one of the men, more hardy than the rest, came vp staires and met his maister in the chamber, where he saw his mistress lye on the ground, and her dead infant at her feete, and said to him : 'O sir, what haue you done ?' 'That which I repent not of, knaiue,' answered he ; and hauing his dagger still in his hand, came toe stab at him, but the fellow seeking toe defend himselfe, as also to attack his maister, they both fell a struggling. Maister *Cauerley*, which was knowne before, was a man of weak constitution, was in the strife toe hard for the fellow, who was reputed of a uery able body, and in the wrestling together did soe teare him with the roweles of his spurs, both in the face and legs, that there he left him, not being able to follow him.

"Maister *Cauerley* went downe staires, and presently towards the stables ; by the way he met the gentleman who had told him aboute his brother being in prison who before was walking in his groundes, who, wondering to see him in such a heate, asked : 'What aill you, sir ?' He answered, 'No greate matter ; but, sir, I will resolue you within, where I have taken orders for my brother's businesse.' Soe the gentleman walked in, and Maister *Cauerley* hasted to the stable, where finding a gelding readdy saddled, backed him, and fled away presently. The gentleman coming in was entertained with outcries and shriekes, the mother for the children (for by this time shee was almost recouered), the men-servants at their sad mischaunce, and all dolefully lamenting that a father should be soe vnnaturall. The gentleman, doubting that which was of Maister *Cauerley's* escape, left all the house making elegies of sorrow, and betooke himselfe to his pursuit, and hauing forthwith raised the towne and heard which way hee went, followed him with the quickest haste. Maister *Cauerley* being well horst, spurred on as fast as they, not earnest to escape, but thirsty for more blood; for hauing an infant, half-a-year old, at nurse some twelve miles off, hee, pricked by his preposterous fate, had a desire to roote oute all, his generation, and onely intent to murther it, was carelesse what became of himselfe. Hee rode hard for an act of sin, and they for an act of iuestice. But God that ordereth the losse of a realme, hath then a care for His reasonable creatures, and though Caine was suffered to kille his brother Abel, God bound him not to destroye him. Soe far Maister *Cauerley*, as God permitted the sin to blush at his vnnaturall acts, yet He suffered him not escape without his revenge, for when hee was at the towne's end, within a bowshot where the childe sucked that hee came to murther, and his hart had made sharp his knife to cut his owne infant's throat (Oh, God, how iuest Thou art!), his horse that flew with him from his former tragedie, as appointed by God, to tie him from any more guilt and to presurve his infant's life, in a plaine ground where there was scarce a pebble to resist his haste, his horse fell downe and Maister *Cauerley* vnder him. The horse got vp, and breaking from the hold his maister had to staye him, came violently toward the towne, leauing Maister

Cauerley not able to stirre from thence, where hee was soon ouertaken by the pursuit, and indeed, seized on by those who did both lament his fate and pitty his folly. From thence hee was carried to a worshipful gentleman's, one Sir John *Sauile*, who hauing heard the tempest of this euil, and knowing from what ancestors hee had sprung, did bewaile his fate, yet being in the office of iustice, he was forced to ask him the cause that made him soa monstrousse. Hee, being like a strumpet, made impudent by his continuence in sinne, made this answer : ' I haue done that, sir, I reioice at, and repent this, that I killed not the other. I had brought them to beggary, and I am resolued I could not please God better than by freeing them from it.' ' Oh, sir,' answered that Worshipful Knight, ' you haue donne soe much that when you yourselfe thinke vpon the terrours of death, the remembrance of this will make you wish you had neuer beene borne.' But his hart being hardened, hee was from thence committed to Maister Keys house, a gaile but lately built vp in Wakefield—for at this time the infection of the plague was uery uiolent in Yorke.

" The way to Wakefield from Sir John *Sauile's* lay direct by Maister *Cauerley's* house, agaynst which when hee came he intreated of the multitude that were his conduct, he mighte speake with his wife before he came to prison, who he heard was aliue, though in great daunger ; that libertie was granted him. The distressed gentlewoman when shee saw him, forgot her owne wounds and the death of her two children, and did as louingly kisse him and tenderly imbrace him as hee had neuer donne her wrong ; which straunge kindness soa strook to his hart, remembering the misery he had heaped on her, that imbracing one another, there was so pittifull lamentation betweene them, that had flint had eares it would have melted into water. And could either wordes or teares haue perswaded his keepers to hauue left him in her armes, shee, Mistress *Cauerley*, before the bloode was washed off from her cloathes (which hee pierced out of her and her infants bodyes) gaue occasion, would have altered them.   But here they were divurced, shee vnable to rise to follow him, and hee inforced to leaue her; and bye the waye hee should passe from his house, the graue chamber of his ancestors, which hee neuer should see agayne.   Euen on the threshold lay his two children to take their farewell with bleeding tongues, which when hee beheld, his euies were scarce able to bear vp the couers, nor was hee distracted with the sight, but all like a pillar of salt; and the remembrance of their liuely shape reflected such a naturall heate upon him, that hee was melted into water, and had not power to take any farewell of them, but onely in teares.

"It was not long before he came to Keys House; he was not long there, but the memorie of his children sate in his euies, so that for the one he repented all the day, and for the other lamented all the night; nor can the pen of the diuinest poet express half the griefe in words that he conceived in hart.   For whereas before he told Sir John *Sauile* he was glad he had rid the world of beggars, he now employed his howres in these wordes : ' I would I had these beggars, either I to beg with them, or they to ask Heaven's almes for me.' "

The crime seems to have made a deep impression throughout the country at the time of its commission, for not only was it, as we have seen, made the subject of a popular pamphlet, which was sold, it may be presumed, in all parts of the kingdom, but it was dramatised, much after the fashion adopted in more modern times, when it has been the custom in minor theatres to represent on the stage the most notorious crimes of the period.   The murderous deeds of Patrick Reid at Mirfield, the murder of Maria Martin in the Red Barn, and other acts of sanguinary criminality have been amongst the subjects which have been seized upon even in our own time for dramatic delineation, although better judgment has condemned these things as morbid and unhealthy. In Shakspeare's time, grand as it was in its dramatic realisations, the people drank more deeply of horrors even than we do to-day, so that such a tragedy as the fearful one that was enacted at Calverley could not escape the notice of the dramatists of the time. The high .position of the parties, as well as the romantic nature of their surroundings, made the subject all the more attractive, so that it is not surprising that very soon after the event took place a play, dealing with the horrible incidents of the Calverley tragedy, was brought out at no less a place than the Globe Theatre, while that temple of the drama was in the full tide of prosperity, and partly under the management of Shakspeare. Shakspeare himself had probably by this time ceased to act at the Globe, and had given himself up entirely to the writing of plays. It is not improbable that Shakspeare had something to do with the writing of *The Yorkshire Tragedy*. The play was published in 1608, and had our immortal bard's name on its title-page; but Shakspeare's part in it can hardly have amounted to more than a slight "touching up" here and there, as there are few passages which have the Shakspearian ring about them, and the construction is not at all Shakspearian.

The registers of Calverley Church contain the following entry :—

"1605. April. William and Walter, sonnes of Walter Calverley, Esqr., buried ye xxiiii day."

The murderer was brought to trial four months after the commission of the crime. He saved his estates from confiscation by refusing to plead, and was sentenced to be pressed until he either pleaded or died. Heavy stones were placed upon his chest, and he resisted to the last, when, in answer to his piteous cries, it is said his own servant pressed the last breath out of him, for which kindly office he was himself executed. The local saying, "A pund o' more weight; lig on!" is supposed to have had its origin in this incident. An affecting interview took place between the wife and husband before the latter was submitted to the final ordeal, and she forgave him for what he had done. Tradition says, that the body of Walter Calverley was stolen by his servants, and afterwards secretly buried in Calverley Church, and the fact that, at the restoration of the church a few years ago, a man's skeleton was found imbedded in plaster and buried without coffin, is considered to give some confirmation to this story.

The widow of the murderer married a second time, and became the wife of Sir Thomas Burton, a Leicestershire gentleman. She was a daughter of Sir John Brooke, son of Lord Cobham. The surviving son, Henry Calverley, lived in the old hall, until his death, fifty-six years after the murder. Henry's son, Sir Walter Calverley, married Frances, daughter and heiress of Henry Thompson, of Esholt, and built the hall at Esholt, where he died on the 22nd October, 1749. Sir Walter, his son, who soon afterwards assumed the name of Blackett, sold the manor of Calverley to Mr. Thomas Thornhill, of Fixby, in 1755.

THE STORY OF A YORKSHIRE STABLE-BOY.

IN the year 1809 there was born at York, into the humble family of a groom, named Ward, a boy who was destined to take a prominent part in the world when he came to grow up to manhood's estate. The father of this boy was in the service of Mr. Ridsdale, a trainer of horses, and it was with difficulty that he managed to provide for the wants of his family. It was, therefore, with no very favourable surroundings that the lad, who was named Thomas, after his grandfather, passed the early days of his childhood. To make matters still more unpleasant for young Tom, he had the misfortune to lose his mother when he was in his infancy. His father did not long remain a widower, but married again, with a result that does not seem to have been conducive to his boy's comfort, for when only seven years of age Tom ran away from home and took refuge under the roof of his grandfather, a labouring man, who lived in a small cottage at Howden. The grandfather seems to have been deeply attached to the boy, and as far as his means would allow, had him carefully trained and instructed. Tom went to the Church school of the village from the time of taking up his abode with his grandfather until he was twelve years of age. He was an apt and attentive pupil, and considering the condition of educational training at that period in a remote country school, made good progress.

When he reached the age of twelve it was considered desirable that he should return to York, and with feelings of deep regret, he left the village in which he had spent five happy years, and again took up his residence with his father and stepmother. He was sent to a national school at York, and it was remarked that he there showed himself to be a boy of parts, and was uncommonly well informed in regard to religious matters. What particular direction his talents would have taken had he been in a position to advance to higher grades of study, it is impossible to say ; but unfortunately—or, perhaps, fortunately—he was set to earn his own living soon after his return to his native city, and his schooling (in the ordinary sense of the term) was brought to an end.

His father obtained him, in the first place, some menial occupation in the stables of Mr. Ridsdale, and he discharged his duties with so much satisfaction to his employer that it was not long before he received promotion. Whatsoever he was desired to do he did to the best of his ability, and was conscientious and honest in all things. Such sterling qualities as these could not fail to command attention even in an atmosphere of grooms, and jockeys, and trainers, and it is therefore not surprising to find him steadily advancing to higher duties. At the age of fourteen he quitted the employment of Mr. Ridsdale, and entered upon an engagement of a more responsible character. He is described as being at that time an active, smart, clever little fellow, and possessed of a shrewdness beyond his years. He was "Yorkshire" in everything.

In the month of October, 1823, one of those lucky opportunities in which there would almost seem to be the directing-finger of fate occurred to him. A York trainer entrusted him with the duty of taking a horse to a noble customer residing at Vienna, and young Tom, although entirely ignorant of the country and its language, made his way safely to the Austrian capital with his charge, and acquitted himself in the most satisfactory manner of the important trust which had been reposed in him.

Vienna must have appeared to the Yorkshire stable-boy a gay and bustling place in comparison with the dull Cathedral city which he had left. Indeed, so much was Tom impressed by the new life that was revealed to him in the metropolis of the Hapsburgs, that he made up his mind to remain there for a while, and acting on that resolve, began to cast about for employment. His good fortune did not desert him even at this trying juncture; he secured an engagement in the service of Prince Aloys von Lichtenstein "in the department of the stables." While fulfilling the duties of this post he was, of course, thrown much into the company of great personages, his success as a jockey and as a trainer gaining him the favour of many of his master's intimate associates. He was a fearless rider, and being compactly built and of light weight, was often selected to ride in the principal races. He continued in the service of Prince Lichtenstein for some time, and by his good moral conduct and close attention to the interests of his employer, was gradually advanced to higher posts in the Lichtenstein stables.

In course of time, Tom Ward was induced to enter the service of the Duke of Lucca, who had a strong liking for English horses and English grooms, and being in want of an under-groom, and having the Yorkshire lad recommended to him, took him into his establishment, and for many years Ward had full charge of the Duke's stables, and conducted himself in such a faithful and exemplary manner as to inspire his master with a true feeling of friendship for him.

The Duke of Lucca resided chiefly at Vienna. "Although a Bourbon and a son of France," says Sir Bernard Burke, "he never cultivated any very intimate connection with Louis XVIII. or Charles X.; while he

K

regarded the Emperor Francis as a father. Himself a great grandson of Maria Theresa, he was still more closely connected with the Imperial family through his beautiful Duchess, who was twin sister to the wife of the son and heir of the Emperor. He thus was adopted as a son of the house of Austria, and regarded Vienna as his capital, while in common with his neighbours of Florence, Parma, and Modena, he looked up to the Austrian Emperor as the supporter of his sovereign authority, and respected him as his political chief."

Tom Ward applied himself with so much devotion to the care of his master's stables that, as time wore on, the Duke conceived the idea that he would like to attach his Yorkshire groom more closely to his personal service, and with that view invited Ward to become his under *valet de chambre*. Ward accepted the offer, and thenceforward became a member of the Duke's domestic establishment. If the saying that no man is a hero to his valet be true, how much more true it must be that no valet is a hero to his master. But the Duke of Lucca discovered—not with the startling suddenness with which Royal favourites are usually discovered, but by a gradual process of observation and experience—that he had got a hero in his Yorkshire stable-boy.

It could not have been because of a distinguished personal appearance that Ward gained the confidence of the Duke, for he was a plain, simple, under-sized man, with nothing whatever striking about his features, unless it was his quick, penetrating, grey eyes. He was scrupulously neat in his attire, and of the most regular habits.

The next advancement that Ward received at the hands of the Duke of Lucca, was the granting to him of the highest post in his master's dressing-room. This situation was filled by him until the year 1836, when he was created the Duke's confidential attendant, in which capacity he continued for six or seven years.

In the summer of 1838 the Duke was seized with a strong desire to enlarge the sphere of his experiences, and he set out upon a round of travels, taking Ward with him. After attending the coronation of his brother-in-law, the Emperor of Austria, at Milan, as King of Lombardy, he proceeded to England, where he was well received at Court, and mixed freely with the notables of the time, staying for a short time as a guest of Her Majesty at Windsor Castle, and subsequently visiting certain members of the aristocracy at their country seats. Ward was always in attendance upon him, and during that round of visits, the *valet de chambre* must have been privileged to see many important political and diplomatic personages, though at a most respectful distance.

The Duke grew more and more attached to his confidential valet as the length of his service increased. Never had the Duke met with such integrity of character, such fidelity to duty, as were displayed by this once stable-boy. And further than this, he had rarely met, even in the highest circles, with a greater amount of good sense and shrewdness than was embodied in this faithful servant. The Duke at length began to place so much trust in Ward that he confided to him his most intimate concerns, and was glad to seek his advice and counsel in times of perplexity. The influence that Ward thus came to acquire over the Duke was very great, but he had the good sense never to abuse his power. In all that he did he showed himself actuated by an earnest desire to promote the best interests of his master, and never allowed himself to be governed by selfish motives.

It was not to be expected that all this could take place without its being known outside the palace walls; but the people of Lucca, like their Sovereign, believed in the Yorkshireman's sincerity, and he became quite a popular personage. His modesty, no less than his fidelity, secured him the attachment of the people. Years before, he had married a young woman of Vienna, in his own station in life, and a quiet little house near the palace served them for their abode at a time when he might well have afforded to keep a large establishment.

In the year 1843 another of Ward's grand opportunities for advancing his fortunes occurred. The Duchy of Lucca had by bad management been plunged into a condition of financial crisis. The revenue had been misappropriated, and even the Duke's private funds had been embezzled. Under the distress of mind caused by the discovery of the disordered state of his finances, the Duke of Lucca fell ill; his Duchess, however, bore up with much fortitude, and determined that she herself would make a desperate attempt to save her husband from ruin. Knowing in what high esteem the Duke had always held his servant Ward, and herself highly appreciating the Yorkshireman's intelligence and devotion, the Duchess applied to Ward for advice, and he plainly told her that the only way of averting ruin from the ducal house of Lucca was to immediately dismiss the minister who had been the chief means of bringing this trouble upon them. It was no easy task to induce the Duke to act with the necessary firmness at this critical moment; and it is probable that the proper action would not have been taken had not the Duchess decided to call in the aid, as adviser and arbitrator, of her uncle, the Archduke Ferdinand, cousin to the Emperor, and Governor of Galicia. She confided her idea to Ward, who at once fell in with it, and he was selected by her as ambassador to the Archduke. It was a highly difficult task that was thus entrusted to him, but he nerved himself for the duty, and quietly prepared to make the journey to Galicia. He was not furnished with the customary written instructions, lest he should be robbed by the way, or should be examined at the frontiers which he had to pass. The only written communication that Ward had given to him was a single line from the Duchess to the Archduke, testifying to Ward's identity, and assuring his Imperial Highness that in everything Ward said he was to be implicitly trusted.

This journey had to be kept a secret from the Duke, and it was with considerable difficulty that he could be got to grant Ward the three weeks' leave of absence that would be necessary for the fulfilment of his mission. Ward gave out that he was going to Dresden; and in order to keep up the deception, he sent several letters addressed to his wife at Lucca, under cover to a confidential friend at Dresden, to be posted from that city from time to time during his absence, so that they might reach Lucca with the Dresden postmark upon them.

This done, Ward at once set out for Galicia, and after he had crossed the Hungarian frontier and was no longer in fear of having his papers seized, he spent one or two nights in compiling a succinct statement of the Duke's affairs, instead of sleeping, composing the statement in German, which he spoke and wrote fluently.

Arriving at Lemberg, the capital of Galicia, he lost no time in presenting his credentials to the Archduke, who received him in a very friendly manner. On being desired to explain the nature of his errand, Ward produced his written statement, and was about to quote facts and figures from it, when the Archduke requested him to leave the paper with him, and call the next day to discuss the matter. Ward obeyed, and on the following morning he repaired once more, full of anxiety, to the Archduke's presence. His Imperial Highness complimented him on the distinctness of his statement, and then wanted to know how he could be instrumental in improving the condition of the Duke of Lucca's affairs? It was now that Ward had to explain verbally and at length what it was that the Duchess had thought of, and so well did Ward plead his master's cause, that the Archduke expressed himself willing to assume the trust which the Duchess wished him to undertake, provided that the Duke himself requested him to do so.

Ward now returned home with all speed, acquainted the Duchess with the success of her scheme, and then, with great tact and delicacy, broke the news of what he had done to the Duke. Not long afterwards, the Archduke Ferdinand came upon the scene, as had been arranged, and the unfaithful minister was dismissed and the Duchy saved from ruin.

The Duke now looked with greater favour than ever upon his quondam stable-boy, and had no hesitation in urging him to accept the portfolio of the dismissed minister. But Ward's good sense did not leave him even then. Hitherto he had been simply a private servant of the Duke's, and to jump all at once from that humble post into the position of a first Minister of State, and to assume before the public the duties and responsibilities of such a dignified office, was more than he could bring himself to think of for a moment. He represented to the Duke that his proposition was an untenable one altogether; that it would expose them both to ridicule, and that all he wished was to remain the Duke's private servant as of old. "I am but an uneducated English groom," said Ward, "and quite unfit in every way to be elevated in the manner proposed by your Royal Highness." The Duke, however, was not to be turned from his purpose so easily; he still insisted upon Ward taking the office, and in the end, with much reluctance, the Yorkshireman consented, and on receiving the portfolio of Minister of Finance, was created Baron Ward.

In commenting upon Ward's position at this period, Sir Bernard Burke says: "He must have been a consummately clever fellow who could apply all his native Yorkshire shrewdness to a new sphere, and turn to his sharp intelligence for guidance in novel and difficult circumstances. A certain freedom of speech, with a bold hardihood of character, based entirely on a conscious sense of honour, attracted at first the notice of his master, who felt such pleasure in the open frankness of the man that he frequently took opportunities of conversing with him and asking his advice. Ward always spoke out his mind, and by the force of strong native sense and unswerving determination, he impressed his master with the fact that his best counsels were to be derived from the truthfulness of his Yorkshire groom, and not from the flattery of the titled and decorated crowds that thronged his chambers of audience."

Ward soon became virtually Prime Minister, and it was through him that all the arrangements between the Duchy of Lucca and the other Italian States were made. In 1845 he settled, greatly to the advantage of the Duke of Lucca, an old standing dispute between that Prince and the Grand Duke of Tuscany; and having concluded a treaty for the acknowledgment of the Lucchese public debt, as well as the Customs Union between the two Governments, he was decorated by his master with the first-class of the Order of St. Louis, and was created a Baron of the Duchy of Lucca. The Grand Duke of Tuscany also made him a Noble of his States, and decorated him with the Order of St. Joseph.

Baron Ward himself, in his own not very polished style, thus alluded, in a letter to his father, to these events :—
" Afterwards a very serious question arose between the Duke of Lucca and the Grand Duke of Tuscany, which lasted for two years, and ended in a very disagreeable manner, by the Grand Duke protesting publicly. I at that time was confided with the Finance Department, as Minister of State and State Councillor. Our Minister of Foreign Affairs, who had treated the above affair, gave it up as impossible to make anything more out of it. My indefatigable spirit would not allow me to see a scandal of

that kind given up so cowardly, and it was, at my request, confided to me. I was laughed at when I took it in hand by all. Some said I was presumptuous, some said I was a fool, and some said I was an ignorant fellow. I let them all have their talk, and to work I went; and this was my first step as a diplomatist. I was so successful that in two months' time the Grand Duke was so convinced of his wrong that he was obliged to withdraw his protest, which had been publicly placarded by his Government throughout the Duchy, and confirmed the Duke of Lucca's right to his credit against the Duchy of Lucca in two millions of livres. And in three weeks afterwards I signed another treaty for a Customs Union betwixt the two States, and was fortunate enough to succeed, as well as the raising of a public loan. All this went step after step, so quick that I had not time to look round me. . . . And all at once I found myself launched into the world, without really knowing how I got there. And for why do all make such a fuss of me? Invitations on all sides, all admiring a wonderful talent that I know nothing of."

One day, about this time, it is related, Ward entered the Duke of Lucca's room, and found him occupied with a pencil and paper. "Ward," said his Royal Highness, "I am devising a coat-of-arms for you. As a mark of the esteem in which you are held by the Duchess as well as myself, you shall have armorial bearings compounded of her arms and my own. I will give you the silver cross of Savoy, with the golden *fleur de lis* of France in dexter chief." With many expressions of gratitude, Ward desired to be allowed to add something emblematical of his native country; and as he had heard that coats-of-arms sometimes had supporters, he would like to have the cross of Savoy and the lily of Bourbon supported by the English *John Bulls!* "So be it," said the Duke; "you shall have two bulls regardant for your supporters."

It was in 1847 that the Duke of Lucca carried out his long cherished idea of abdicating his crown. He knew that ere long he must inherit the Duchy of Parma as his birthright. So it came about that Ward's diplomatic powers were employed in negotiating the cession of the Duchy of Lucca to Tuscany, and through his active agency everything connected with the business was amicably settled.

This had hardly been done when the Archduchess Maria Louisa died, and Ward's master became Duke of Parma. Parma, unfortunately, was in a very unsettled condition. The atmosphere was heavy with political troubles. Ward was hastily summoned from Florence to his master's side, but he only arrived in time to see him overthrown. The Duke was compelled to fly from the capital, over which he had reigned but a few weeks. Ward accompanied him. They traversed a portion of Italy in disguise, and gaining the coast, embarked for France, where they landed, and from thence proceeded to Weistropp, near Dresden, where the Duke owned a chateau and small estate.

"From Weistropp," says the authority previously quoted, "Baron Ward was despatched, in the summer of 1848, to fight his master's battles in the diplomatic circle of Vienna, and in the camp of Field-Marshal Radetsky. He displayed the greatest energy and the most consummate prudence in negotiating for the interests of the Duke, or rather for those of his family; for the Duke himself had decided on abdicating his sovereignty to his son, and he only waited for the downfall of Charles Albert, and the restoration of legitimate authority in Northern Italy, in order to execute his design. Ward was invested with full powers to act for the Duke both at Vienna and in Italy; and he was, in fact, nominated as his *alter ego*: a degree of confidence which was indeed fully merited by him, but which has very seldom been extended by a prince to a subject."

When the abdication had been concluded, and his

master's son had been placed on the tottering throne of Parma as Charles III., Ward assumed the position of chief adviser to him, as he had done to his father. Writing to England, describing these events, Ward says: "Though feebly placed, having no cannon and no soldiers, with God there is no need of them, as is evident in our case. I expect to be in Milan in a short time again, if the clouds clear away; if not, I have succeeded in assuring the incontestable rights of a family to whom I was, from a sense of gratitude, devoted; and I shall content myself with the day's work allotted to me being accomplished, and retire to rest. The young Duke did wonders at Parma, pleased everyone, and was found in the eyes of all sensible, active, honourable—*pieno di caraltere.* He seems born for a sovereign. The tact which he displayed was like magic. He is now at Malghera with Radetsky, displaying as much courage as any common soldier. In short, he seems determined to make up lost ground."

In July, 1849, he says: "Prince Schwarzenburg was rather hard upon me about a month ago, respecting a quarrel we have with the Duke of Modena. I was to have been silenced by force; the order was imperious. But Albion's sons do not understand any language but honour; so I made the affair short, and as a *sine qua non*, the free liberty to defend the rights of my royal master without any restraint, or else Ward retires from office. Ten days elapsed without an answer, and a hundred might have done so before I would have humbled myself. My straight-forwardness at last gained the day. The Prince sent for me, inviting me to have the kindness to come to him! And ever since, I flatter myself that there is not a man in Vienna he esteems more. Since then I have concluded a treaty with the Minister Brück, in Milan, for the free navigation of the Po, as well as a postage convention, and also a military one."

Ward continued to be Prime Minister of Parma during the reign of Charles III. He resided chiefly at the Court of Vienna, to which he was accredited as Minister Plenipotentiary, and from which he governed the Italian Principality.

In 1854 Charles III. was assassinated. One of the first acts of the Duchess, his widow, was to depose Baron Ward from his ministry, and sentence him to banishment. By this time a considerable party had sprung up with unfriendly feelings towards the Englishman who had done so much to promote the interests of the Ducal family. Ward now retired into private life, and undertook a large farming establishment in the neighbourhood of Vienna, spending the remainder of his days in the enjoyment of domestic happiness with his wife and children.

Baron Ward, it is worth recording, never forgot his relatives at York and Howden, but in the days of his fame and prosperity administered to their wants, and did his best to make them comfortable. In 1848, in addition to a handsome new year's gift, he settled a pound a week upon his father, payable every Monday morning ; and from time to time he forwarded considerable sums as presents to his grandfather and brother, settling a comfortable allowance upon both, the allowance to his brother being permitted to accumulate, he being at sea. He adopted Walter Ward, the son of his father's younger brother, educated him, and procured for him a commission in the Austrian army, which he left, and then joined the German Legion, and afterwards went to the Cape. During nearly the whole of the time he spent in the service of the Dukes of Lucca and Parma, it was Ward's custom to visit England on horse-buying or other expeditions yearly; but no matter how full he might be of business, he always made time to pay a visit to his relatives in Yorkshire, and on one occasion took a box full of orders and decorations to show his father and grandfather.

Ward died in 1858, at the early age of forty-nine. In his career we have presented a wonderful example of what can be achieved by integrity, ability, and courage. He made his way by his own efforts from the humble position of stable-boy to that of Prime Minister, and for some years exercised a really important influence over Continental affairs. Of course, the Premiership of Lucca or Parma was a very different thing from the Premiership of England or France; still, it was an undoubtedly exalted position, and it was a surprising circumstance that it should come to be filled by a man of such humble beginnings and connections as Ward. Metternich alluded to Ward as a "heaven-born Minister;" and Lord Palmerston said of him that he was "one of the most remarkable persons he ever met." The history of this stable-boy conveys a wholesome lesson, and his name is well worth being held in regard in the county where he was born.

THE STORY OF THE HEBDEN-VALLEY MURDER.

TIMES are bad as bad can be. Flour is selling at 8s. a stone, and oatmeal at 5s. It is the early part of the year 1817. Waterloo has become a thing of the past; the allied armies are on the point of being withdrawn from French territories; and peace, after long years of war, tumult, and oppression, has once more resumed its sway. Still, the country is suffering the keenest distress. Trade is completely paralysed, and the labouring classes are on the verge of starvation. The people are clamouring for reforms of various kinds, and in some parts of the kingdom open rebellion seems to be impending. On his return from opening Parliament, the Prince Regent is assailed by a riotous mob, and the Royal carriage is attacked with stones and other missiles. So alarmed do the governors of the land become, that many of them consent to forego a large portion of their emoluments. Even the Prince Regent, "sympathising with the sufferings of a generous public," as Lord Castlereagh announced in Parliament, relinquishes £50,000 per annum of his income, the whole of the members of the Ministry dispense with one-tenth of their official salaries, and altogether the work of government is an extremely difficult and perilous undertaking. Strong detachments of military are quartered in the large towns of the north, and arrests, trials, and convictions for treason are of constant occurrence.

There is plenty of news to talk over in the public places in this year of grace 1817, even though the work of news transmission is as yet a slow-paced affair, railways and electric telegraphs being still hardly foreshadowed. There is one particular inn at Hebden Bridge, called the "Hole in the Wall," which on Saturday afternoons and evenings is much frequented. In the bar-parlour of this quaint hostelry the affairs of the day are anxiously discussed. One man—a stout, well-preserved yeoman trader, commonly known as Sammy o' Kattie's, but away from the vernacular more properly called Samuel Sutcliffe— has been in the habit of dropping in at this house over the bridge every Saturday afternoon for years, on his way home from Halifax market. He is a bachelor, and has reached the ripe age of eighty. There is no one in the entire district round about Hebden better known than Sammy o' Kattie's. He lives in a solitary house at Hebden Hay, near the bottom of the slope descending from Whitehall Nook to the brawling Hebden, one of the chief tributaries of the Calder. A funereal yew tree spreads its umbrageous shade in front of the whitewashed dwelling, and close by is the road leading to Upper Hepton. At this place Sammy o' Kattie's carries on the manufacture of worsted pieces in a small way, and for a considerable time he has also farmed the land attached to the house. He is, indeed, a man of some substance, having by industry and thrift been able to save a tidy sum of money. He has living with him a nephew, William Sutcliffe, who does something in the fustian trade on his own account, and like his uncle, does a little farming. These two men live all alone in this secluded spot, their only neighbour being a weaver, named William Greenwood, who lives in a cottage which joins up to the residence of the Sutcliffes. Old Sammy, despite his eighty years, regularly attends the market at Halifax, about eight miles distant, making the journey always on foot.

On Saturday, the 1st of February, 1817, Sammy performs his usual business pilgrimage to Halifax market, and on his way home drops in for his customary glass of ale at the " Hole in the Wall," at Hebden Bridge. There he meets with a number of friends, and chats with them on the grave position of public affairs, lamenting with them over the dearness of provisions and the lack of trade, discussing the need for Parliamentary reforms, and divining much danger in the alarming attitude of the crushed and starving population. Personally, Sammy has little to fear ; his means are all-sufficient for his modest wants, and he possesses the respect and esteem of his neighbours. This Saturday night he is probably accompanied home by his nephew William. The latter is about to leave home on Monday for a short business tour through Lancashire, Craven, and Westmoreland, and to-day he has had to visit Halifax to make certain arrangements in connection with his proposed journey. He takes these trips three times a year, starting on the Monday and getting back home some time towards the end of the week. As the two walk forward from Hebden Bridge to the whitewashed farmhouse at Hebden Hay, this February Saturday night, they dwell much in their converse upon the prospects of William's proposed business trip to the north.

The next morning William is up betimes to milk his cows, and while it is yet early, customers begin to arrive with their cans for their morning's supply of milk. One of these customers is a man named Michael Pickles, otherwise " Old Mike," who has for a long time been filling two distinct characters. He lives in a low, one-storeyed cottage at Northwell, on the road leading from Heptonstall by

New Bridge to Haworth. For fifteen years he has lived in this little two-roomed cottage, and in the small garden attached to the house he keeps a number of bee-hives, and in one corner, years ago, he planted a Scotch pine. Mike is a member of Birchcliffe Baptist Chapel, both he and his wife having long passed the ordeal of public immersion. As an expounder of the Scriptures, Mike is considered rather able, and never loses an opportunity of " holding forth " to his friends and neighbours on the beauty and happiness of a Christian life. It is by his aptitude for religious discourse, and his seeming goodness and serenity of heart, that he has been able to gain the friendship of old Sammy. Mike is accustomed to sit with the old bachelor during the long winter evenings, and is never tired of reading the Scriptures to him, talking with him upon the events of the day, or directing his thoughts to heavenly things. In this way Mike and old Sammy have been friends for several years.

When Mike comes for his milk this Sunday morning, he doubtless goes forward into the house to see the old man, and pleases him by saying he'll come up and sit with him during the lonely evenings of the coming week, while William is away in the north. Sammy is grateful for the attention given him by Mike, for, hale and fearless as the old man feels, he finds his evening hours made brighter by the companionship of so good and worthy a person as Mike.

But there are those who suspect that old Mike is not all that he seems to be to the world at large, and to Sammy o' Kattie's in particular, and he is suspected of doing many things under the cover of the darkness that he would scarcely like to have brought before the light of day. His age at this time is forty-one ; he is a strong, broad-set, powerful man, with cadaverous face and "large rolling eyes." Moreover, he is left-handed, and is renowned for his strength of grasp, the story being that he is what is called double-jointed. He is also considerably " knock-knee'd," and altogether not over human in his outward aspect. He has no particular occupation, but does " odd jobs " for anybody about. Sometimes he digs up a garden for a neighbour, sometimes he weaves a bit, and sometimes he is engaged upon such labour as drywalling. It is whispered of him that he walks abroad much o' nights, that he has been seen at untimely hours conveying plunder to his cottage, and that he has dug out underneath his bed a cave or secret hiding place for stolen property, the hole being covered by a moveable flagstone. Above all, he is suspected of being a great stealer of bee-hives. Horsemen have been startled in the dead of the night by the sight of his ungainly figure moving heavily along with a hive of bees on his head, and half a score people can be got to testify against. him in a similar way. But of all this Sammy o' Kattie's remains in ignorance ; or if he hears anything of it, he at once dismisses the idea as preposterous ; and thus it comes about that during the absence of the old man's nephew, Mike comes up to the farm as usual, and is received with every trust and confidence.

During these visits to the house at Howden Hole, as the place is called, Mike naturally becomes acquainted with old Sammy's most intimate concerns, gets to know what money he has in the house, and is thoroughly familiar with all the ins and outs of the place. Many a time, no doubt, it occurs to him, as he is sitting with the old man, that he would like to be possessed of a portion of Sammy's hoardings, and he thinks that the opportunity of helping himself thereto can never be better than now that the nephew is away. Such thoughts trouble Mike no little at this juncture of affairs, and his will stands poised in the balance, hesitating between cupidity and honesty.

On Thursday, the 6th of February, however, there comes

L

to Mike's cottage a visitor known in the district as " Joan o'
t' Bog-eggs," who suffices to turn Mike's wavering mind in
the wrong direction. Joan o' t' Bog-eggs is a weaver about
twenty-nine years of age, with light hair, and undecided
features. He and Mike are married to sisters. Joan lives
in a cottage attached to a farm in Wadsworth, called Bog-
eggs, above Old Town, and a little below the moorland
prominence called Tomtitiman. Joan is out of work,
without money, and his family have no bread in the house.
In these desperate circumstances he walks across to his
brother-in-law's cottage.

"Lend me some brass, Mike," says Joan, "we're pinin'.'

"I havvant a penny i' t' world, lad," replies Mike ; then
dropping his voice to a whisper, he adds meaningly, "but I
know where there is some."

"Where ?" asks Joan, impatiently.

Mike then proceeds to inform Joan that old Sammy o'
Kattie's has got lots of money stowed away in a small oak
box which he has lately bought, and which he keeps in his
bed-room, and that nothing can be easier, now that the
nephew William is from home, than to enter the house
secretly in the night-time and rifle the box of its contents.
With poverty and hunger pressing him so strongly, Joan
o' t' Bog-eggs is not long in being won over to Mike's
villainous scheme, especially as Mike assures him that the
robbery can be effected without the least danger. Joan
goes back home, carrying with him something to eat, which
Mike has given him for his little household, the arrangement being that the two shall meet again at Mike's cottage
in the evening.

After nightfall Joan makes his way back to Mike's house,
and Mike despatches his wife and children to bed. Mike
then lights his pipe and the two men sit before the fire for
a long time in silence. Mike feels that the whole responsibility of the scheme rests with him, and as his tobacco

smoke ascends in curling whiffs up the cottage chimney, his thoughts pass out into the night with it, and in his mind he goes over, again and again, the plan of operations which he has for the last day or two been slowly maturing. Meanwhile, Joan, comfortably relying on his brother-in-law's knowledge and ability to pull him safely through, has fallen asleep, and sleeps on placidly until the little clock in the corner strikes the hour of midnight, when Mike rouses him from his slumber, and says, "Come, Joan, lad; it's time to be going."

"All right," says Joan, yawning himself awake.

Mike knocks the ashes out of his pipe, takes down his gun from its resting-place, puts in a fresh charge, and then the two men, with as little noise as possible sally forth on their midnight errand, Mike locking the cottage door as he passes out.

The two walk along a field called Adcock, to the left of and above the public road leading to Whitehall Nook. Thence they proceed through the steep, rough wood to Hawden Hole. There is no moon as yet. Half-past twelve is the time for it to rise, and as the robbers make their way amongst the crackling brushwood a sense of terror steals over the heart of the younger of the two, and three separate times he halts with fear, and tells Mike he dare not go through with the business. Each time, however, Mike overcomes Joan's scruples, partly by persuasion, and partly by threats, and at last they find themselves in front of the solitary farm-house where old Sammy is peacefully reposing.

Darkness rests over the scene, and not a sound is to be heard except the murmuring of the stream below. Mike stations Joan before the door of the house, with the gun in his hand, and directs him to shoot any person who should interrupt them. Joan tremblingly obeys, and then Mike stealthily proceeds to take out one of the windows at the west end of the house. This done, he enters the house and unfastens the door near which Joan stands sentry. The door is not only locked, but has a stout wooden bar placed across it, with the ends inserted in holes in the masonry. Mike now passes out of the front door, and goes and secures the door of Wm. Greenwood, the neighbouring cottager, so as to prevent any interruption from that quarter. He places the wooden bar across the doorway, and fastens the "sneck" to the bar with a piece of string.

The way has now been made clear, and Mike and Joan enter the farm-house together, Joan remaining downstairs while his more venturesome companion stealthily ascends the stone stairs into the room where the old man is sleeping. Mike loses no time in securing the oak box in which Sammy keeps his money. He also plunders the bed-room of three cotton pieces and four warps, a piece of woollen coating, a pair of shoes, and a new shirt.

Unfortunately for everybody concerned in this dark night's work, old Sammy awakes just as Mike is on the point of leaving the room with all his booty. Starting up in bed, the old man calls out, "William! William! William!" thinking thereby to bring his neighbour, William Greenwood, to his assistance, perhaps. Alarmed at this outcry, Mike rushes to the bedside, and with that terrible left hand of his grips his old friend by the throat, nor does he relax his hold until the last spark of life has been extinguished.

William Greenwood, in the little cottage adjoining, is himself disturbed by the noise in Sammy's house, and asks what is the matter. No reply comes, however, so he concludes the old man has been merely talking in his sleep, and troubles no more about the matter. Moreover, the wind has become very boisterous by this time, and whistles round the buildings and through the solemn yew tree in a furious manner, so that the old man's voice seems but a part of the ordinary noises of the night.

When Mike descends the stairs he horrifies Joan by

telling him he is afraid he has killed old Sammy. They now lose no time in making off with their plunder, and plunge into the wood again on their way to Mike's cottage. The wind tears madly through the leafless branches, which crack and snap around them, and great angry clouds drive gloomily overhead, as if trying to shut out the light of the moon from the scene. Whether the voice of the wind is to the murderers as a voice crying for revenge, or whether the dark, frowning clouds are to them like pursuing demons, as ought to be, there is no possibility of knowing. They are silent, and afraid—that is all we can say. The guilt of murder weighs heavy on their souls as they hurry back to Mike's cottage at Northwell. Arrived there, the flag-stone under the bed is removed, and the cotton pieces, the warps, and the shoes are deposited in the cavity, which has so often been used for the hiding away of stolen goods. Mike's wife, who has evidently been in the secret of the intended robbery, wakes up when the men are about the division of the plunder, and is anxious to know how they have fared. Her husband at once expresses his fear that he has killed old Sammy, and the wife is much alarmed and distressed, and begins to cry. Indeed, this horrible deed is not to be crushed out of their thoughts; it haunts Mike with such force, that the simple-minded Joan is able to gain an advantage over him in the sharing of the spoil, and secretes a one-pound note unknown to Mike. In dividing what remains after the pocketing of this note, they have one pound ten shillings and sixpence each. That is all! For this poor, paltry sum, a human life has been sacrificed.

When Joan gets up to depart, Mike impresses upon him the importance of his keeping the night's work a secret from his wife, telling him that it is a hanging matter for both of them, if it should become known. Joan does not go straight home, but in pursuance of a plan agreed upon, instead of crossing the valley at Foster Mill goes down towards Mytholmroyd, and crossing the Calder at Carr Bridge, throws the papers and documents obtained from Sammy's box upon the ground, the idea being that suspicion will thereby be diverted from Mike and Joan to someone living in the Cragg valley, where, it is well known, there are to be found a number of desperate and notorious characters. When Joan has done this, he makes his way home to Bog-eggs: the thought that he had contrived to cheat the crafty Mike out of a pound-note diverting his mind somewhat from the harrowing thoughts of murder.

All this time poor old Sammy o' Kattie's is lying dead—murdered—in the lonely farm-house. Before daylight, a man named James Greenwood, of Lobb Mill, calls at the house to ask Sammy for a balance of four shillings due to him for some work he has been doing for the manufacturer. To his astonishment, he finds the door wide open. Fearing that something may have gone wrong, he goes to William Greenwood's cottage, and calls to him to come out. Greenwood at once comes to the door, but finds it fast, and James Greenwood discovers that a wooden bar has been placed on the outside so as to prevent the door being opened from the inside. He removes the bar, out hurries William Greenwood, a word or two of explanation is given, a lighted candle is procured, and together the two Greenwoods enter the farm-house. They soon see that the place has been entered by robbers, and, worse than all, that Sammy has been foully murdered. The old man's mouth s full of blood, and some has run out upon the bed-clothes. William Greenwood sees that the cotton pieces are gone, and finds outside the door a bucket in which the oak money-box has been kept. He also discovers the mark of a bare foot near the window which has been taken out. The weaver is much shocked at the sight that is thus revealed to him in the early morning, for he was sitting up with Sammy until half-past ten the previous night.

The news that Sammy o' Kattie's has been murdered soon spreads all over the district, and the neighbourhood is greatly excited. Mr. Thomas Dinely, surgeon, of Hebden Bridge, is summoned to the spot, and pronounces the opinion that Sammy has been strangled.

Then comes the grave question—Who is the murderer? At present there is no clue, but the local authorities are actively engaged in investigating the matter. The papers and documents which Joan o' t' Bog-eggs dropped at Carr Green are picked up by Olive Heyhirst as she is going to fetch milk on the morning of the murder, but this fact is not of much assistance to the authorities in their search after the criminal. A messenger is sent to hasten the return home of William Sutcliffe, but he does not arrive until the Saturday afternoon. He is unable to do anything except to testify as to what money his uncle had in his possession. One important fact he is able to state, however, and that is, that one of the notes which have been stolen was issued by the Mytholm Bank, and does not contain the usual signature, "Turner, Bent & Co." He also knows that the number of the note is "63." This note is the identical note which Joan o' t' Bog-eggs pocketed unknown to Mike. In due course an inquest is held on Sammy's remains, a verdict of "wilful murder against some person or persons unknown" is returned, and the body is interred in Heptonstall churchyard in the presence of a vast concourse of people. Upon his tombstone this simple record is placed: "In memory of Samuel Sutcliffe, of Hebden Hay, in Heptonstall, who died February 7, 1817, aged eighty-one years."

During all this time, the two criminals walk about as usual, but it can hardly be said that they are unsuspected. Mike is ill at ease, as he afterwards confesses. The day after the murder he can neither eat, drink, nor sleep; he is in constant fear of having the murder brought home to him.

On the morning of the murder he meets a woman in North-well Lane, and says, "Have you heard that old Sammy's murdered?" With astounding outspokenness, the woman replies, "If he is, it's thee 'at's done it." On the Friday night he goes into a barber's shop in Heptonstall to be shaved, but he is so restless and agitated that the barber finds a difficulty in fulfilling his office; and after Mike has gone he turns round to some customers who are in the shop and says, "Yond's t'man 'at's murdered Sammy." A worse trial still awaits Mike when he attends the service in Birchcliffe Chapel—the place he has attended so regularly for years, where he was baptised and admitted a joined member. The minister, Mr. Hollinrake, preaches a sermon on the text, Matthew xxiv. 43,—"But know this, that if the goodman of the house had known in what watch the thief would come, he would have watched, and would not have suffered his house to be broken up." Mr. Hollinrake alludes to the circumstances of the murder in the most touching manner, and denounces the perpetrator of the deed in the strongest terms. The sufferings which Mike endures during the time he is listening to this discourse must have been intense: and one can well believe, as he afterwards declared, that anyone looking him earnestly in the face might have discovered that he was the murderer.

And now the one-pound note which Joan o' t' Bog-eggs had secretly appropriated begins to play an important part in the unravelling of the mystery of the murder. Joan, in the first place, goes to see a brother, John Greenwood, who is living at Luddenden, gives the note into John's hand, then receives it back again, and all this is done as a matter of form, to enable Joan to say that he got the note from his brother. After this, Joan purchases a clock from one Thomas Greenwood, of Birchcliffe, and gives him the un-signed one-pound note and other money in payment. Then the note passes into the hands of a woman called Betty

Wadsworth, who, having had an illegitimate child, has been disowned by her relatives, and is now living "afore t' friend" at Rawholme, with another William Greenwood. Betty sells a chest of drawers to Thomas Greenwood, the furniture broker; for she, like so many of her neighbours, finds it hard to make ends meet in these bad times. She receives in payment for the chest of drawers the one-pound note which the broker had received from Joan o' t' Bog-eggs. This is on Tuesday, the 11th of February, nearly five days after the murder, and the same night she goes to the shop of John Hoyle, at Woodend, and offers the note in payment for some groceries. Hoyle notices that the note is unsigned, and refuses to receive it, and, in consequence of this, on the following morning, she sends the note back to the broker, with rather a sharp message for having paid her a note which is not genuine. Betty then gets some current coin instead of the note, and her connection with the fatal paper ceases. Thomas Greenwood, the broker, however, is somewhat puzzled as to what he shall do with the note. Mr. John Sutcliffe, of the Lee, for whom he wove, had paid him a Halifax bank-note for wages, and not being able to read, he is unable to say whether the note which he has now returned on his hands is the one that Mr. Sutcliffe paid him, or the one he received from Joan o' t' Bog-eggs. He decides to make application to Mr. Sutcliffe before trying Joan; he is a little bit doubtful whether Joan would be able to give him a good note for the bad one, even supposing that Joan is the person from whom he got it. Away the broker goes to Mr. Sutcliffe's works, and finds Mr. Richard Aked, who is learning the business with Mr. Sutcliffe. Thomas Greenwood gives the note to Mr. Aked, says that Mr. Sutcliffe must have paid it him in mistake the day before, and asks to have a good one given to him in place of it. Mr. Aked takes the note to Mr. Sutcliffe, who is just then in the house having his breakfast. Mr. Sutcliffe has heard about this unsigned note having been amongst the notes stolen from Sammy o' Kattie's, and at once feels the importance of the clue that has been placed in his hands. He calls Thomas Greenwood in, and, after questioning him a little, ascertains that the note has come from Joan o' t' Bog-eggs. Thomas Greenwood is detained, and the constables are sent for. Shortly afterwards James Wilson, the constable, sizer, of Hebden Bridge Lane, George Hargreaves, John o' Paul's (Greenwood), and John Uttley, commonly called John Clerk, being the clerk of Heptonstall Church, arrive upon the scene, and have the matter explained to them. Then the constables, accompanied by Mr. John Sutcliffe and Thomas Greenwood, proceed to Bog-eggs, and Joan is met with and taken into custody. The explanation that he has to offer is that the note has been paid to him by his brother William. On this the constables set Joan at liberty, and proceed to Luddenden, and there apprehend William Greenwood. The same day William is taken to Halifax, and brought before Mr. Thomas Horton, justice of the peace, in the justice-room in Copper Street. Feeling convinced that there is some danger surrounding his brother, William Greenwood refuses to give any account of the note. He preserves his silence until Friday—possibly hoping that Joan has made use of the time that has thus been gained and run away—and then he confesses what passed between him and his brother in reference to the note. The constables now return to Bog-eggs to re-apprehend Joan, and succeed in doing so, Joan not having made the least attempt to effect his escape. On being confronted with his brother at Halifax, Joan declares that he received the unsigned one-pound note from Old Mike. William Greenwood is now released, and the constables set off in quest of the actual murderer. But Mike is missing. On enquiring for him at his cottage, his wife informs the officers that he has gone off in search of employment.

On Sunday, the 16th February, however, Mike is discovered at his brother's house at Cowside, near Blackshaw Head. He is detained in custody that night at an inn at Heptonstall, and on being visited by the Rev. J. Charnock, declares that he is as innocent as a child unborn.

On the Monday morning Mike is taken forward to Halifax, and brought before Justice Horton. Up to this time sixteen or seventeen persons have been apprehended on suspicion of being concerned in the murder of old Sammy; but finally the prisoners detained on this charge are weeded down until only Joan o' t' Bog-eggs and Mike remain. The proceedings are conducted in a very loose manner indeed; Mr. Horton jumps at conclusions on the slightest bits of evidence. When brought face to face with Joan, Mike stoutly denies having given Joan the one-pound note; and Joan, in his statement concerning the matter, contradicts himself as to the day of the week and month when he went to Mike's to borrow money. This, Justice Horton assumes, is quite sufficient to exonerate Mike, so he is set free. Joan must be tossed by strange feelings when he sees his companion in crime—the actual murderer of Sammy o' Kattie's—go out of the justice-room a free man.

Joan is consigned to prison to await further inquiry, and there is visited by his father, who implores him, if he knows anything of the robbery, to make a clean breast of it. Thus entreated, Joan is brought into the justice-room again, and makes an unreserved confession of the whole of the circumstances connected both with the robbery and the murder. John Uttley, the constable, who is in court, now rushes off in pursuit of the liberated Mike. John mounts a horse which he has left at a neighbouring inn, and is soon galloping along the high-road towards Heptonstall. But there is no need for much haste. Mike has not been in a hurry to get out of the way; he has called at a little shop to buy a square of "parkin," and is now walking leisurely up King

Cross Lane on his road home. Uttley gallops up to the murderer and calls out, "You must come back with me." Mike's coolness and audacity desert him at this sudden command, and in his alarm he says, "What! has he been tellin' summat?" Uttley does not stop to parley with him, however, but takes Mike back to the magistrate's room.

Mike now feels that the game is up, and on being again confronted with Joan, declares the full measure of his own and Joan's guilt. Joan grows excited, and has to be removed until Mike's confession is completed. But, in the end, the prisoners are committed to take their trial at York on the charge of "wilful murder."

On Friday, the 14th of March, 1817, the trial of the two prisoners takes place at York. Mr. Hardy is the counsel for the prosecution. The indictments charge them with murdering Samuel Sutcliffe, and also with having committed burglary. Both deny the murder but admit the burglary. The judge recommends them to plead "Not guilty" to both indictments, and they do so. There are no fewer than twenty-two witnesses examined for the prosecution, and the evidence against the prisoners is of the most complete kind.

The *Leeds Mercury*, of the 22nd March, 1817, in its report, says :—" The prisoners being called upon for their defence, Michael Pickles said : John Greenwood came to my house and said he was pined, and asked me to go with him to Sammy's, of Hawden Hole, which I did, and he took the gun with him. When we got to the old man's house, we got in at the window, and we both went into the chamber where the old man was. He started up in bed when he heard us, and we both ran away, and I never touched the man.—John Greenwood said : The robbery was proposed by Michael Pickles, for I did not know there was such a house—I had never been there in my life. When we got to the house, Pickles went in at the window, but I stayed at the outside. I was never in the biggin' at all, but stood at the shop end all the time, and Pickles brought out all the goods to me that he had taken out of the biggin'. He then told me that he had taken the old man by the neck, and was afraid he had killed him; and I said, 'Surely thou hast not hurt the old man?' Michael Pickles gave me the gun to carry, but I tied my handkerchief in two knots over the lock, for fear I should do some mischief with it. When we got back to Pickles's house, he told his wife he was afraid he had killed the old man; and his wife began to cry. Pickles charged me that I should keep it a secret from everyone, even from my wife, for if I told I should be hanged.—Three witnesses were called. Two of them spoke favourably of the character of John Greenwood. The third stated that he had a wife and three children, but that he did not know much about his character."

The Judge in his charge to the jury said that if they were satisfied that both the prisoners had gone to the house of the deceased for the purpose of committing a robbery, and that one of the men, to prevent any alarm or discovery, had by violence occasioned the death of the deceased, it would be murder in them both, though one of the prisoners should not have been in the house at the time, and should have given no consent to the murderous deed, or even not have known of its being committed.

"The jury turned round in the box for a moment" (says the report referred to), "and then pronounced against both prisoners the fatal verdict of 'Guilty.' His Lordship proceeded, after a most solemn and affecting address, to pass the sentence of the law, which was, that they were both of them to be hung by the neck on Monday until they were dead, and that their bodies should be delivered to the surgeons for dissection. John Greenwood fell on his knees, begging for mercy, and protesting his innocence of the murder."

Subsequently Joan confessed to the chaplain that he was

in the house at the time of the murder, and stood at the foot of the steps with the gun. Mike also made a full confession; and on Monday morning, the 17th March, 1817, less than six weeks after the crime was committed, and only three days after the sentence of death, they were both executed in front of York Castle in the presence of a vast crowd of people. The execution took place a few minutes before eleven o'clock, and after the bodies had been suspended the usual time, they were delivered to the surgeons for dissection, Mike's body being sent to the Dispensary at Halifax.

In presenting the story of this crime, and of the bringing to justice of its perpetrators, we have been largely indebted to the Leeds papers of the period, and to Mr. Baring Gould's story of the "One Pound Note." The *Hebden Bridge Chronicle* also published in 1856 many particulars concerning the crime.

THE STORY OF THE BISHOP BLAIZE FESTIVALS.

At the Tower entrance of the Bradford Exchange stands the statue of the reputed inventor of the art of woolcombing—St. Blaize, or Blase, or Blasius. Saints have not, as a rule, been much associated with trading pursuits, and there is probably not another instance on record of one of that holy order having made himself famous as an inventor of mechanical appliances. True, we have in modern times the case of the Rev. Mr. Cartwright, who invented the power-loom; but there is an immense gap in point of sanctity between an ordinary clergyman and one who occupies the exalted position of saint, bishop, and martyr in the calendar of the Church of England. St. Blaize, however, seems to have been altogether an exceptional kind of bishop, for he was famed in other ways than as the inventor of woolcombing. He was bishop of Sebast, in Armenia, during the early part of the fourth century, and according to Butler, was receiver of the relics of Eustratius, and executor of his last will. It is further related of St. Blaize that he lived in a cave, whither wild beasts came daily to visit him, and be cured of him; "and if it happened that they came while he was at prayer, they did not interrupt him, but waited till he had ended, and never departed without his benediction." Bishop Blaize seems to have been more successful in his dealings with the animal world even than St. Francis or St. Anthony, for the patron saint of the woolcombers not only preached to and admonished the brute creation, but gave relief to their physical sufferings. Indeed, St. Blaize's power was, according to tradition, most powerfully displayed in administering to those who were afflicted by sickness or disease. Prayer was the only medicine that he considered it necessary to have recourse to, and his appeal to the Supreme power was looked upon as more efficacious than all the physic in the world. On one occasion, having been discovered in his retirement and cast into prison, he cured, by praying, a youth, who had a fish-bone stuck in his throat. It was for a long time a custom amongst the Greeks to invoke the spirit of St. Blaize in cases of affections of the throat. Ætius, an ancient Greek physician, gave, it is stated by Ribadeneira, the following recipe for a stoppage in the throat :—" Hold the diseased party by the throat, and pronounce these words—*Blase, the martyr and servant of Jesus Christ, commands thee to pass up or down.*" Bland informs us that candles offered to St. Blaize were formerly said to be good for the toothache, and for diseased cattle.

> " Then followeth good Sir Blase, who doth
>   a waxen Candell give,
> And holy water to his men,
>   whereby they safely live.
> I divers Barrels oft have seene,
>   drawn out of water cleare,
> Through one small blessed bone
>   of this same holy Martyr heare :
> And caryed thence to other townes
>   and cities farre away.
> Each superstition doth require
>   such earnest kinde of play."

The " Golden Legend " says that a wolf having run away with a woman's swine, she prayed St. Blaize that she might have her swine again, and St. Blaize promised her, with a smile, she should, and the wolf brought the swine back ; then she slew it, and offered the head and the feet, with some bread and a candle, to St. Blaize. " And he thanked God, and ete thereof ; and he sayd to her, that every yere she sholde offre in his chirche a candell. And she dyd all her lyf, and she had moche grete prosperyte. And knowe thou that to thee, and to all them that so shal do, shal well happen to them."

Howsoever it may be as regards these matters, all chroniclers are agreed upon the fact that Bishop Blaize was put to death by being tormented with iron combs, by the order of Licinius, in 316. This, some think, is the sole reason for Bishop Blaize having been adopted by the wool-combers as their patron saint. Others maintain that if he did not actually invent the art of woolcombing, he at least made considerable improvements in it. Ribadeneira gives a highly imaginative account of the martyr's death. He relates that " St. Blaize was scourged, and seven holy women anointed themselves with his blood ; whereupon their flesh was combed with iron combs, and their wounds ran nothing but milk, their flesh was whiter than snow, angels came visibly and healed their wounds as fast as they were made ; and they were put into the fire, which would not consume them ; wherefore they were ordered to be beheaded, and beheaded accordingly. Then St. Blaize was ordered to be drowned in the lake ; but he walked on the water, sat down on it in the middle, and invited the infidels to a sitting ; whereupon threescore and eight, who tried the experiment were drowned, and St. Blaize walked back to be beheaded."

From time immemorial it has been the custom to honour the memory of Bishop Blaize in this country. At one time it was usual on St. Blaize's Day to light fires on the hill tops or other conspicuous places. "So determinedly

M

anxious were the country people," says Mr. Robert Chambers, in his *Book of Days*, " for the celebration by a blaze, that they would sacrifice articles of some importance to make one. Country women went about during the day in an idle, merry humour, making good cheer ; and if they found a neighbour spinning, they thought themselves justified in making a conflagration of the distaff."

In Yorkshire, however, the Bishop Blaize celebrations have been almost wholly confined to the woolcombers' festivals, and these have taken place not only in Bradford, but in Wakefield, Leeds, Halifax, and other towns of the West Riding. Bradford has naturally claimed the right of taking the lead in these celebrations, and during the early part of the present century, when woolcombers formed a large and important portion of the Bradford population— when the woolcombing machine was not yet invented—it was the custom to hold Bishop Blaize Festivals at septennial periods. In 1811, in 1818, and in 1825 these celebrations were of a very imposing character ; especially in the last-named year, when Bradford exerted itself to such an extent that it has never been able to get up another display of the kind.

There was a Bishop Blaize Festival in London on the 3rd of March, 1730. It was the Queen's birthday, and a procession of a hundred woolcombers proceeded through the streets to St. James's Palace. The men wore woollen caps, and shirts over their clothes, and they had with them a person on horseback, representing Bishop Blaize, who carried a woolcomb in one hand and a prayer-book in the other. He addressed the King and Queen, who appeared at the window, and thanked His Majesty for the encouragement they had so far received, and entreated his further protection.

The Bishop Blaize Festival which stands out prominent from all the rest, however, is the Bradford festival of 1825, when the town gave itself up heart and soul to the celebration. The year had begun with signs of considerable prosperity, and on the 3rd of February, 1825, the commercial outlook was of a favourable and reassuring character. For three or four years there had been a good trade, and the woolcombers were a numerous and well-paid race of operatives. In the year 1825 there were, within a radius of six miles round Bradford, from 7,000 to 8,000 woolcombers employed.

Thursday, the 3rd of February, 1825, found Bradford in full holiday aspect. The factories were all standing, the shops were closed, and the inhabitants seemed to have divided themselves into two classes only—processionists and spectators. The morning dawned brightly, and by an early hour the streets were thronged with people, visitors from adjoining towns and villages having arrived in great numbers—some by coach, or other special conveyance, but most of them on foot. In those days, when railways were not, and when people were accustomed to work early and late, they made long days of pleasure as well as long days of labour, and were up and about betimes. Days of rejoicing were few and far between in those times, so when they *did* come, the people made the most of them. On this particular Thursday morning the worsted legions poured in from Bingley, Shipley, Horton, Thornton, Eccleshill—old and young, male and female—intent upon seeing the great procession, the preparations for which had occupied their thoughts for many weeks before. Very quaint and picturesque the town looked that morning, compared with its aspect in the present year of grace. There was not a single public building in the town of any architectural pretensions. The Piece Hall was the only edifice of anything like importance; the Exchange, at the bottom of Piccadilly, had yet to be built; there was no Mechanics' Institute, and stuff warehouses, as we know them now, had not come into existence. Power-looms had not yet been introduced in Bradford—it was in 1826 that the fatal riot took place at Horsfall's mill, on the attempt being made to set up power-looms there—and gas had only just superseded the old oil-lamps in the streets. There were only two churches in the town—the Parish Church and Christ Church—and the third Wesleyan Chapel in the town, that at Eastbrook, was just on the point of being opened. The beck was as yet comparatively unpolluted, and the twenty or thirty factories, which were all that then existed in the town, could not make the air noxious with their smoke to anything like the same extent that was afterwards the case when the mills were multiplied so greatly. It was the time of stage-coaches and knee-breeches. He whom flattery had designated "The First Gentleman in Europe" was on the throne of England, and Bradford had still some years to wait before it was to be permitted to send a representative to Parliament.

The public-houses were then an important feature of the daily life of Bradford. They formed the rallying ground for every description of gathering or celebration, and the leading merchants, spinners, and manufacturers did not consider it beneath their dignity to frequent them. The Talbot was the great political rendezvous for the landed gentlemen and Tories, while such old-world hostelries as the Bull's Head obtained the patronage of the commercial classes. On this February morning of 1825 the crowd was greatest in that part of Westgate where the Bull's Head stood, for it was there that the organisers of the great festival were to meet, and from which the procession was to start. Mr. Matthew Thompson, father of the present Mr. M. W. Thompson, was the chief mover in the getting up of this trade pageant, and by eight o'clock in the morning the people who were to take part in the procession had begun to assemble. The streets were by this time crowded in every direction, and almost all the vehicles for twenty miles round had been brought into requisition. Never had been seen such stir and animation in the town. Mr. Thompson, Mr. Richard Fawcett, and their fellow-organisers, employed themselves with great activity in getting the processionists into their places, but it was a work of considerable difficulty, and it was not until ten o'clock that the various sections could be arranged in their proper order. We can well imagine the fire of chaff that the processionists would have to undergo during these preparatory stages; how curious the wool wigs, the scarlet stuff coats, the red cockades, and the coloured " slivers " would look on the weavers; and how uneasily many of the woolsorters would feel on horse-back for the first and only time in their lives. Then there would be the marshalling of the bands of music, and the " ordering up " of the important personages who had to assume the characters of the Bishop, King, Queen, Jason, &c. These, with the continual moving about of flags, banners, fleeces, and so forth, would make Westgate a very busy place that morning.

The number of persons taking part in the procession was as follows :—Twenty-four woolstaplers, 38 spinners and manufacturers, 6 merchants, 56 apprentices and masters' sons, 160 woolsorters, 30 combmakers, 470 woolcombers, and 40 dyers. When the procession was ready to move off, Mr. Richard Fawcett, who was on horseback at the head of the spinners, advanced to the front, and with head uncovered, delivered the following lines, which it had long been customary to repeat on these occasions :—

> Hail to the day, whose kind auspicious rays
> Deign'd first to smile on famous Bishop Blaize !
> To the great author of our combing trade
> This day's devoted, and due honour's paid :
> To him whose fame thro' Britain's isle resounds,
> To him whose goodness to the poor abounds ;
> Long shall his name in British annals shine,

And grateful ages offer at his shrine!
By this, our trade, are thousands daily fed,
By it supplied with means to earn their bread,
In various forms our trade its work imparts
In different methods and by different arts :
Preserves from starving indigents distress'd,
As combers, spinners, weavers, and the rest.
We boast no gems, or costly garments vain,
Borrowed from India or the coast of Spain ;
Our native soil with wool our trade supplies,
While foreign countries envy us the prize.
No foreign broil our common good annoys
Our country's product all our art employs ;
Our fleecy flocks abound in every vale,
Our bleating lambs proclaim the joyful tale.
So let not Spain with us attempt to vie,
Nor India's wealth pretend to soar so high ;
Nor Jason pride him in his Colchian spoil
By hardships gain'd and enterprising toil :
Since Britons all with ease attain the prize,
And every hill resounds with golden cries.
To celebrate our founder's great renown
Our shepherd and our shepherdess we crown ;
For England's commerce, and for George's sway,
Each loyal subject give a loud " Huzza ! Huzza !"

The name of the author of these now historic lines does not appear, which is rather unfortunate, for his couplets are ensured of a fame which many poets who think they count for something in the world of letters, may sigh for in vain. How scornfully he bids Spain not with us to "attempt to vie," and with what pride he declares that Britons can "with ease attain the prize" which Jason only gained after many hardships ! It was evident, too, that the Bishop Blaize laureate did not see so far into the future as to perceive that other countries besides our own were destined to supply us with wool for our manufactures. His sense of hearing must have been somewhat acute, though, for him to hear every hill "resound with *golden cries*."

But the general tone of the composition would be so thoroughly in accord with the sentiments and feelings of the crowds who listened to its delivery, that it is hardly likely that any fault would be found with it. It was received with a ringing cheer from "each loyal subject," and then the procession moved off in the following order :—

Herald bearing a flag.

Woolstaplers on horseback, each horse caparisoned with a fleece.

Worsted Spinners and Manufacturers on horseback, in white stuff waistcoats, with each a sliver over the shoulder, and a white stuff sash ; the horses' necks covered with nets made of thick yarn.

Merchants on horseback, with coloured sashes.

Three Guards.   Masters' Colours.   Three Guards.

Apprentices and Masters' Sons on horseback, with ornamented caps, scarlet stuff coats, white stuff waistcoats, and blue pantaloons.

Bradford and Keighley Bands.

Mace bearer, on foot.

Six Guards. KING. QUEEN. Six Guards.

Guards. JASON. PRINCESS MEDEA.   Guards.

Bishop's Chaplain.

BISHOP BLAIZE.

Shepherd and Shepherdess.

Shepherd Swains.

Woolsorters on horseback, with ornamented caps, and various coloured slivers.

Comb Makers.

Charcoal Burners.

Combers' Colours.

Band.

Woolcombers, with wool wigs, &c.

Band.

Dyers, with red cockades, blue aprons, and crossed slivers of red and blue.

The appearance of these festive personages was highly imposing, and the crowds greeted them with much enthusiasm as they passed along. An old man, named William Clough, of Darlington, was the King, he having filled the regal office at four previous celebrations. Jason, the mythological hero of the Golden Fleece, was personated by an individual bearing the homely cognomen of John Smith; and another John Smith, who is described as "a personage of very becoming gravity," appeared in the important *rôle* of Bishop Blaize, he also having enjoyed his pontificate on several former occasions. What damsel personated the fair Medea, the chroniclers of the period have not deigned to leave on record. The part of the bishop's chaplain was assumed by one James Beetham. "The ornaments of the spinners and manufacturers," we are informed, " had a neat and even elegant appearance, from the delicate and glossy whiteness of the finely-combed wool which they wore. The apprentices and masters' sons, however, formed the most showy part of the procession, their caps being richly adorned with ostrich feathers, flowers, and knots of various coloured yarn, and their stuff garments being of the gayest colours; some of these dresses were very costly, from the profusion of their decorations. The shepherd, shepherdess, and swains were attired in light green. The woolsorters, from their number and the height of their plumes of feathers, which were for the most part of different colours and formed in the shape of *fleur-de-lis*, had a dashing appearance. The comb-makers carried before them the instruments here so much celebrated, raised on standards, together with golden fleeces, rams' heads with gilded horns, and other emblems. The combers looked both neat and comfortable in their flowing wigs of well-combed wool; and the garb of the dyers was quite professional. Several well-painted flags were displayed, one of which represented on one side the venerable Bishop in full robes, and on the other a shepherd and shepherdess under a tree. Another had a painting of Medea giving up the golden fleece to Jason; a third had a portrait of the King; and a fourth appeared to belong to some association in the trade."

From the Bull's Head in Westgate, the procession moved forward down Kirkgate. It was in Kirkgate, opposite the house of Miss Preston, that Mr. M. W. Thompson (then a boy of the age of five) recited—"with great distinctness and animation," it is said—the lines which had been previously spoken by Mr. Richard Fawcett. Forty-three years after the event—in February, 1868—Mr. Thompson, then M.P. for Bradford, speaking at a dinner given by the Bradford Overlookers, referred to the circumstances under which he made this his "first public appearance in Bradford." "My father thought it right," said Mr. Thompson, "that I should take part in the procession, and he had me up every morning at breakfast until he had drilled into me a certain number of verses. I was put on the top of a door, or out of a window at the bottom of Kirkgate, and spouted those verses to an immense number of people, although I daresay nobody heard me three or four yards off. I was then taken on a pony down into the Holme, and spouted the same verses to a number of workmen assembled round a table." Young Thompson, mounted on a fine Shetland pony, was, indeed, regarded as one of the most interesting features of the procession.

From Kirkgate the cavalcade passed up Darley Street, along Rawson Place, and forward to Manor Row, and down Cheapside (then known as Skinner Lane). From this point, the procession went along Well Street, ascended High Street, and pushed forward to Garnett's mill in Barkerend Road. Halting there a brief period, they then returned to the front of the vicarage, near the church, and halted again. From there they passed along Vicar Lane and up to Mr. Duffield's mansion near Wakefield Road, returned by way of Bridge Street, and then turned on

Tyrrel Street to Mannville. From Mannville they proceeded to the Holme, or Fawcett Holme, where Fawcett's, Thompson's, and one or two other mills were to be seen dotted here and there. The Holme, however, then presented a large open space, all of which has since been absorbed in the busy thoroughfare of Thornton Road, its many off-branching streets, and gloomy array of business premises.

It was one o'clock when the procession reached the Holme, and in the spacious field in front of Mr. Fawcett's factory the men were regaled with sandwiches and ale, of which they partook freely—in some instances, indeed, too freely, it was afterwards confessed.

Two hours were spent over this simple repast; the time being whiled away by the re-recital of the Bishop Blaize verses by young Thompson, the pet of the day, and by sundry speechifyings. At three o'clock the procession was re-formed, and proceeded up Little Horton Lane to Little Horton, from thence crossed to Manchester Road (then called Bowling Lane), back again to Tyrrel Street, along Market Street, up Kirkgate, and down Ivegate to the Sun Inn, where they were dismissed. The procession, which was over half-a-mile in length, had been moving about (except in the interval allowed for refreshment) from ten in the morning until five in the afternoon—until dark, in fact. At many places along the route the procession stopped until some one repeated the now familiar verses. Mr. George Thompson Lister was the reciter at one point, and Mr. John Rand at another.

After the dispersion of the procession, the streets gradually became less crowded, the country visitors hurried off to their homes, and everybody seemed well satisfied with what they had seen. A few showers of hail and snow had fallen at intervals during the day, but they were of short duration, and were succeeded by bright sunshine. No accident occurred to mar the proceedings, though there was one or two cases of robbery reported. The Rev. Mr. Bayley, of Drighlington, had his pocket cut and his pocket-book extracted, but fortunately it only contained two pound notes; and Mr. Bates, of Hartshead, had his pocket-book stolen, containing notes to the value of forty guineas.

During the evening there were further rejoicings on the part of the masters, masters' sons, apprentices, &c: The spinners, manufacturers, and merchants dined together in the large room of the then Court House, and the apprentices and masters' sons at the Sun Inn. The dinner at the Court House was a very sumptuous affair. Nearly a hundred gentlemen sat down, Mr. Matthew Thompson presiding, and Mr. G. T. Lister officiating as vice-president. After the cloth had been drawn, " Non nobis Domine " was sung, the company standing. The president then gave " The King," with " four times four," and the National Anthem was sung. " The Duke of York, and the rest of the Royal Family," was the next toast, also proposed by the president; after which there was more harmony : " Hail, Star of Brunswick !" and " The Fleece," being sung by the glee party engaged for the occasion, and afterwards the song, " The Sheep Shearing." Mr. Thompson now proposed " The Immortal Memory of Bishop Blaize," and in doing so made a brief but appropriate speech. I have been favoured with a copy of a report of the speeches delivered at this dinner. They were published by Mr. W. H. Blackburn shortly after the commemoration was held. Viewed by the light of our later experience, the speeches present many points of great interest. Mr. Thompson in proposing the toast referred to, could not, he said, forbear offering his congratulations upon the then prosperous state of the country generally, and of this neighbourhood in particular. " At our last septennial commemoration of the memory of Bishop Blaize," he said, " you did me the favour of appointing me your chairman; and then it was with sincere gratification we hailed the return of peace, and, to us connected with the manufacture of long wool, a considerable degree of prosperity. The whole of this populous neighbourhood connected with the manufacture was then fully employed, yielding to every branch of our artisans an ample remuneration for their services. I wish I had it in my power to say such was the case at present; but, unfortunately, there is one part of our manufacture languishing, and a class of workpeople, who in their situation in life, yield to none in respectability, unable to gain sufficient employment, and suffering also such a reduction in wages as to render them totally unable sufficiently to support their families. Gentlemen, seven years ago, we stood nearly alone in our prosperity. Agriculture, the great origin of national wealth, languished; the iron, cotton, and silk trades, unable to sustain the shock occasioned by so great a change, became almost extinct; indeed, in many instances the furnaces were blown out, and the wages of the workpeople reduced to so low a state, that, with the greatest economy, it was impossible for the artisan and mechanic to sustain without parochial relief his once contented family. The general inquiry was: What is to be done with the unemployed population of the country? But, gentlemen, I am happy to say no such inquiry now exists. Ingenuity and invention are now put to the rack, to know how labour can be abridged and what can be done by machinery to supply its place. Unexampled are the exertions now making by the silk and short wool manufacturers; and as to the iron, so great is the demand, that the furnaces appear to make one general illumination from Carron to the Land's End. Whilst I am attempting, around this convivial board, faintly to describe the national prosperity, the senators of the land are at this moment assembled to teach us, and I doubt not we shall be taught by His Majesty's speech delivered this day, that the country never enjoyed so great a degree of prosperity in agriculture, manufacture, and commerce. I have no doubt that our manufactures will be very greatly extended, and that the continuance of peace, which opens fresh channels to commerce, and conveys to savage nations the arts of civilised life, will in a few years cause our ships to visit every country and every port in the world, will impart renewed energies to our trade, and diffuse cheerfulness and content all around us." Mr. G. T. Lister proposed "Prosperity to the town of Bradford; and may liberal hospitality and distinguished advances in the arts and sciences accompany the increase of its wealth and commercial importance." Mr. Lister alluded to the "manufactured article" as "a faint and sickly plant, to which our climate seems no longer congenial, ready to start from our shores to other regions where it will be more favoured and cherished." He further added that, "as the raw material was exclusively our own, so were the finished productions of it, and it ought to have been the last article on which the theory of Free Trade should have been tried." Then the glee, "Life's a bumper," was sung; after which Mr. Richard Fawcett proposed "The health of Mr. Stuart Wortley, the upright and independent member of this county, the tried friend of commerce." Mr. Fawcett maintained that the permission to export wool or yarn with a low duty must eventually produce mischief to this country; that every pound of wool or yarn taken from it, either in a raw or partially manufactured state, must to that extent be injurious to the artisan and manufacturer. The song that followed this was, "When order in this land commenced." Mr. Joshua Mann then proposed "The health of the Lord-Lieutenant;" they then sang "Auld Lang Syne;" after which Mr. John Rand, jun., proposed "The Ladies." Mr. John Rand, sen., gave "The health of the Vicar of Bradford," for whom Mr. Fawcett returned thanks. "The landed and commercial interests, and may they ever be cordially united," was given by Mr. R. Thornton; "The Land we live in," by Mr. T. Marshall; "Prosperity to the Manufacturers of the West Riding of Yorkshire," by Mr. Milthorp; and a number of miscellaneous toasts followed. Altogether, the dinner seems to have been a very successful and enthusiastic affair.

On the following evening a "Stuff Ball" was given at the Court House. One hundred and forty tickets were issued, and the whole number were taken early in the day. At eight o'clock in the evening the company began to assemble, and before ten the room was crowded. The dresses of the ladies, we are told, though uniform in fabric, assumed all the forms that fashion and taste could impart. The masters' sons appeared in the scarlet stuff coats which they had worn in the procession on the previous day. The ball-room was brilliantly illuminated, and in each window there was a transparency. In the "centre front window" the device was "Commerce," and on each side "The Fleece." In the two back windows were the designs, "Plenty," and "Harvest" respectively; while over the orchestra was a transparency of "His most gracious Majesty, George the Fourth." Even the floor of the room was decorated with various tasteful devices, the centre figure being that of the Fleece. Dancing commenced at half-past eight, being led off by Mr. Matthew Thompson and Mrs. Stockdale; after which the company indulged in country dances and quadrilles alternately until eleven o'clock. At that hour a sumptuous collation was provided by Mr. Hirst, of the Sun Inn, and then dancing was resumed, and kept up with great spirit until between two and three o'clock in the morning, when the company separated, highly delighted with the entertainment of the evening, and rapturous in their praises of the festival of the Golden Fleece.

Thus ended the last great Bishop Blaize festival. Those who took part in it little imagined the disastrous cloud that was even then hovering around. Before the year advanced to summer there were 20,000 people out on strike in Bradford ; trade was really paralysed, and for many months the greatest distress prevailed in the district.

In 1833 an attempt was made to get up another festival, but without sufficient success. A bill, of which the following is a copy, was posted in the streets of Bradford at that time :—

BISHOP BLAIZE.

Whereas, a number of evil-disposed persons lately assembled, and wilfully and maliciously
Burked
The Venerable and Reverend Father
in God,

BISHOP BLAIZE.

It has been determined by a number of his Friends, out of Respect to his Memory, to give his *Remains* public and honourable *Burial*, on the *Third day of February next.* The Band and

Funeral

Procession to meet at the *Piece Hall Gates* precisely at Ten o'clock in the Forenoon, and it is requested that as many as possible who gain their *Livelihood* by the exercise of his Invention, will, out of gratitude to the Founder of the Trade of Bradford, follow his Remains to the grave.

A Committee is appointed to receive contributions to defray the expenses.

The Committee Room, Talbot Inn, January, 1832.

From this time forward things went badly with the woolcombers. Inventors were hard at work trying to supplant hand woolcombing altogether, and in course of time they succeeded, and the old hand-comber's occupation was gone completely. No wonder that the Bishop Blaize festivals were discontinued! It was the custom, however, for some time afterwards for persons engaged in the worsted trade to meet on the Bishop Blaize anniversary and dine together, but beyond this no attempt was made until 1873 to revive the old Bishop Blaize procession.

In September, 1873, however, when the boy who in 1825 had cut such a prominent figure on his Shetland pony had come to be Mayor of Bradford, and when the new Town

Hall had to be opened by him, a procession was got up which far outvied in costliness and splendour the pageants of 1825 and former years. Although the procession on this occasion, taken as a whole, was rather a procession of trades guild than a commemoration of Bishop Blaize, still the woolstaplers, woolcombers (masters), spinners, and others united in reviving on a grander scale than ever the ancient Bishop Blaize display, and this formed the principal feature of the procession of 1873. The Woolstaplers led the procession, headed by the Buttershaw Brass Band, and in front of them was borne a banner of blue and scarlet silk, upon which the motto "The Wool Trade" was inscribed. On a waggon that was suitably ornamented, there was a real woolsorter at work at a real sorting board, and in front was carried a representation of the "Golden Fleece" carved in wood, and being the same that was used in the celebration of 1825. Immediately following came Mr. Timothy Horsfall on horseback, then a number of well-filled carriages and a number of horsemen. Eight decorated wherries came next, loaded with every description of English, foreign, and colonial wools, and covered in by a neat canopy of Gothic design. Over thirty classes of wool were represented. From sixty to seventy woolsorters in check pinafores followed, and banners and flags were profusely distributed amongst them. Along with each specimen of foreign wool was the flag of the country in which it was grown. The most prominent features of the procession, however, were supplied by the combined efforts of the Combers, Spinners, and Manufacturers, and consisted of a most striking array of trophies. Foremost came the Bishop Blaize trophy drawn by six horses, each led by a gorgeously-costumed "beef-eater." The front of the waggon represented a bower of lilies, enclosing an old spinning wheel, emblematical of the origin of this branch of manufacture. Seated on a richly-draped throne above this bower was the representative of the famous old Bishop, attired in his priestly robes and holding the usual Bishop's crosier. Behind the Bishop two ancient 'pad-posts,' originally worked by hand-combers, were erected, and two men were to be seen vigorously working at them as in the old days. Then there was a man represented in the act of shearing a sheep. On this one waggon, indeed, all the stages of wool manipulation, from the time of its being taken from the back of the sheep to the time of its being ready for spinning, were shown. Over all these was spread a canopy of divers colours plentifully adorned with flags; and immediately preceding the trophy was a large orange and blue flag, bearing the inscription, "Hail! Bishop Blaize, our Patron Saint." Then there came a band, and about fifty employers on horseback and in carriages. The Wool-combers came next—a very different body from that of 1825—with a scarlet banner, bearing on its front the words, "Associated Woolcombers." Holden's Brass Band accompanied them, and on a waggonette there was conveyed a model of Noble's combing machine. The trophy which followed was mounted on a richly-draped waggon, drawn by four horses, each led by a "beef-eater." On a high dais were arranged numerous examples of wool after it had passed through the washing and combing processes. Then came the Spinners, with a trophy; then the Weavers, with a representation of the *Argo*, drawn on a car, and in the vessel stood figures personating Jason and Medea, attired in classical costumes, and over their heads was borne aloft the emblem of the "Golden Fleece." Following these were the Sizers, then the Dyers, then the Merchants, with a stupendous trophy representing Britannia, with the traditional trident, sitting on a granite rock, with the globe at her feet. The globe was supported by four human figures, representing the four quarters of the earth, and dressed in appropriate garb. Four trade trophies came next, and then a large body

N

of clerks and warehousemen. Then were to be seen three
stately heralds and a dozen men-at-arms, preceding a bril-
liantly-painted vessel—the Enterprise—conveyed on a waggon, and having Prudence for her helmsman. There were
numerous gaily-attired figures manning the ship. Then
came the representatives of the miscellaneous trades—
Drapers, Printers, Butchers, Brewers, Fishmongers, Iron-
founders, Soapmakers, Joiners, Sweeps, and what not; and
this was the last attempt that Bradford made to revive the
Bishop Blaize pageant. The town was crowded with people,
and, in spite of a steady downpour of rain, the procession
was one of the most impressive that was ever seen either in
Bradford or elsewhere.

THE STORY OF THE HALIFAX GIBBET.

EVERY one is familiar with the old saying, "From Hell, Hull, and Halifax, good Lord deliver us!" From the first-named place we even now fervently pray to be delivered, but as regards Hull and Halifax there remains no special reason why we should require to be saved from them any more than from any other Yorkshire town. The aspect of things has changed since Hull was avoided by thieves and vagabonds, because of the extraordinary vigilance of its officers of the law, and since Halifax had to be avoided by the same people in consequence of the operation of its severe gibbet laws. The decadence of the feudal system saw the disappearance from amongst us of a whole host of special laws, local customs, and absurd manorial privileges, and the right of exercising the gibbet as an instrument of execution upon offenders within the boundary of what was known as the Forest of Hardwick, and included the present townships of Halifax, Skircoat, Ovenden, Warley, Sowerby, Rishworth, Midgley, Errington, Langfield, Heptonstall, and Wadsworth, was abolished after the execution, in 1650, of John Wilkinson and Anthony Mitchell.

From that period onwards nothing remained but the site of the ancient gibbet and the records of the parish, to keep this tragic chapter of local history in memory.

In course of time even the gibbet site itself passed from view, and for more than a century the inhabitants of Halifax were unable to point to the precise spot upon which the gibbet stood. There were Gibbet Lane and Gibbet Hill, it is true, but the exact mound upon which this primitive instrument of execution—the forerunner of the guillotine—used to be erected was not discovered until the year 1840, when in excavating for some building extensions behind Gibbet Lane, the raised earthwork which formed the abiding place of the gibbet during its long reign of terror, was found.

The mound was at once laid bare, as in its original state, and steps were taken to preserve this remnant of bygone days to future generations. An enclosure was formed around it, and to-day, in a back-yard to the right of Gibbet Lane, the place upon which so many criminals were put to death, is still to be seen, much in the same condition as when the fatal axe used to be uplifted there over the necks of the condemned. The mound is about thirteen feet square and four feet in height, and is faced on each side with stone walling. On the higher side is a flight of four or five well-worn steps, which the criminal, his executioner, and attendants would have to ascend. An ancient pole axe is reared against the mound, and the iron railings which fence off the enclosure are appropriately formed in the shape of similar warlike instruments. The ground surrounding the platform is laid out as a garden, and on a stone near the entrance to the enclosure appears the following inscription :—" The Remains of the Halifax Gibbet within this enclosure were discovered in the year 1840 under a mound of earth known as Gibbet Hill, and were enclosed by the Trustees of the Town. The Public Records preserve the names of fifty-three persons Beheaded on this spot between the years 1541 and 1650. The first on the list is Richard

Bentley, of Sowerby, Executed March 20th, 1541; and the last were John Wilkinson and Anthony Mitchell, both beheaded April 30th, 1650. This fence was erected at the cost and in the Mayoralty of the Worshipful Samuel Waterhouse, A.D. 1852." The ancient, gibbet-axe itself, which weighs seven pounds twelve ounces, is preserved at the Rolls Office, Wakefield. Its length is ten inches and a half, and it measures seven inches in breadth at the top and nearly nine inches at the bottom, while in the centre its breadth is about seven inches and a half. A model of the gibbet is deposited in the Halifax Museum. This curious structure consisted of two upright pieces of timber, fifteen feet high, joined at the top by a transverse beam. Within the upright timbers a square block of wood was placed, which moved up and down in grooves, and had fastened to its under side an axe of the description mentioned. The machine thus formed was drawn up to the top of the frame by means of a cord and pulley, the cord being held by a pin until the moment of execution, when the pin was withdrawn and the fatal knife descended with great force upon the unfortunate culprit, severing his head from his body instantaneously. Holinshed, in his " Chronicle," thus describes the instrument and the *modus operandi:*—"The engine wherewith the execution is done is a square block of wood, of the length of four feet and a half, which doth ride up and down in a slot, rabet, or regall, between two pieces of timber, that are framed and set upright, of five yards in height. In the nether end of the sliding block is an axe, keyed or fastened with an iron into the wood, which being drawn up to the top of the frame, is there fastened by a wooden pin (with a notch made into the same, after the manner of a Samson's post) unto the midst of which pin also there is a long rope fastened, that cometh down among the people; so that when the offender hath made his confession, and hath laid his neck over the nethermost block, every man there doth either take hold of the rope (or putting forth his arm so near to the same as he can get, in token that he is willing to see justice executed), and pulling out the pin in this manner, the head block wherein the axe is fastened doth fall down with such violence that if the neck of the transgressor were so big as that of a bull, it should be cut in sunder at a stroke, and roll from the body a huge distance. If it be so that the offender be apprehended for an ox, sheep, kine, horse, or any such cattle, the self beast, or other of the same kind, shall have the end of the rope tied somewhere unto them, so that they being driven to draw out the pin whereby the offender is executed."

The Halifax Gibbet law is believed to have existed from a very remote period, probably having been imported by some of the Norman barons from their own country. Such a law was appurtenant to the right of outfangtheof and infangtheof possessed by the Lacies and exercised by them on their domains both in Cheshire and Lancashire. One of the enactments of Edward the Confessor, subsequently confirmed by the Conqueror, makes express mention of the right of infangtheof, thus :— "Justitia cognoscentis latronis sua est, de homine suo, si captus fuerit super terram suam." There is nothing in this enactment, however, to indicate the privilege of out-fangtheof—the power of the lord to put to death any thief taken within his manor, although the robbery might have been committed away from his proper jurisdiction. At Halifax, though, it would seem, the manorial lords enjoyed this privilege, as sufficiently appears from some of the entries in the public register, amongst which there are the following :—"Quidam extraneus capitalem subüt sententiam, the die, Jan., 1542." "Richard Sharpe and

John Learoyd, beheaded the 5th day of March, 1568, for a robbery done in Lancashire."

The Forest of Hardwick was coextensive with the parish of Halifax, and it was the custom that if a felon was taken within that liberty, "with goods stolen out or within the liberty of the said forest, either *Hand-habend, Back-berand, or Con-fessand*, of the value of thirteenpence-halfpenny, he should, after three markets or meeting-days within the town of Halifax next after such apprehension, be tried, and being condemned, to be taken to the gibbet, and have his head cut off from his body." The Lord-Bailiff of Halifax, who was called the Sheriff of Sowerbyshire, had the superintendence of all matters relating to the trial and execution of criminals. No sooner was an accused person apprehended than he was brought before the Bailiff, who, by virtue of his authority, kept a common gaol in the town. The Bailiff then proceeded to summon a jury, issuing his summons to the constables of four several towns within the forest, commanding each of them to procure four frith burghers to appear before him on a certain day, to examine into the truth of the charge laid against the prisoner. On the day of the trial, the accuser and the accused were brought face to face before the jurors, and the thing that had been stolen was produced. The evidence was then gone into, without any oath being administered, and the jury condemned or acquitted according to the best of their judgment. Bishop Hall, in his "Satires," however, insinuates that the jurors were not altogether above suspicion, his lines,

> " Or some more straight-laced juror of the rest,
> Impanelled on a Holy-fax inquest ;"

implying that integrity was a somewhat exceptional commodity amongst these people. If it happened that the accused party were acquitted, he was liberated on payment of his fees ; on the other hand, if he were condemned, no time was lost in bringing him to execution. The principal market-day, however, was always selected for the day of execution, the idea being that the lesson intended to be conveyed by these acts of justice ought to be impressed when the greatest number of people were likely to be present. The condemned criminal had to sit in the stocks from the time of sentence to the time of execution, with "the stolen goods on his back, if portable, if not, before his face." The party from whom the goods had been stolen was not permitted to compound the felony, but was bound to bring the prisoner, with what he had taken, to the bailiff at Halifax, and prosecute the thief according to the custom, otherwise the goods became forfeited to the lord of the manor.

The proof of certain facts appears to have been necessary before a felon was condemned to the gibbet. " 1st. He was to be taken within the liberty; and it appears that if he escaped out of the liberty, even after condemnation, he could not be brought back to be executed; but if ever he returned into it again, and was taken, he was sure to suffer; as was the case with one Lacy, who, after his escape, lived seven years out of the liberty, but, returning, was beheaded on his former verdict, A.D. 1623. This man was not so wise as one Dinnis, who, having been condemned to die, escaped out of the liberty on the day destined for his execution (which might be done by running about five hundred yards), and never returned again. Meeting several people, they asked him if Dinnis was not to be beheaded that day? His answer was, 'I trow not,' which, having some humour in it, became a proverbial saying amongst the inhabitants, who, to this day use the expression, 'I trow not, quoth Dinnis.' 2ndly. The fact was to be proved in the clearest manner. The offender was to be taken either handabend or backberand, having the stolen goods either in his hand or bearing them on his back, or lastly, confessand, confessing that he took them. This is what writers have called by the name of furtum manifestum, answering to the Open Dybb in the 61st chapter of the laws of the Danish King Canute, which is there said to be a crime not to be atoned for; and perhaps the bad opinion which our ancestors had of this offence might give rise to the Baron's power of punishing it, for nothing surely could more effectually deter from the practice than to take off the offender's head, without much trouble or expense to the prosecutors, in the public summary way, without a possibility of either pardon or reprieve, if they were found guilty. It is worth remarking that neither of the last executed criminals were taken either handabend or backberand, but that both were convicted on their own confession, and it seems that John Wilkinson escaped merely by not confessing: for Anthony Mitchell charged him directly with stealing a black colt, and Abraham Wilkinson with assisting him to rob the tenter of Samuel Colbeck. Does it not, therefore, follow that the two others might likewise have saved their lives had they used the same precaution? But if so, there was a great defect in this mode of proceeding, for unless a man was taken with stolen goods in his actual and immediate possession (which would very seldom be the case), his silence was sure to bring him off, and the person concerned had no further redress, for it is to be presumed that the criminal could not be again arraigned for the same offence in the King's Court. Thirdly, the value of the goods stolen must amount to thirteenpence-halfpenny, or more; and if, at the judgment of the jury, it be but at the utmost value worth thirteenpence-halfpenny, and no more, or of less value, by this custom they are to acquit the felon and he shall not die for it." Dr. Grey, in his notes on *Hudibras*, seems to think that thirteenpence-halfpenny may have been called hangman's wages, in allusion to the Halifax law.

The beheadings took place only on a Saturday, which was the great market-day, and if a felon were condemned on a

Saturday he would be led to the block there and then. This was the case with the last two malefactors who suffered; they were sentenced and executed on the same day. The members of the jury were compelled to attend the executions. As the old record tells, "the bailiffs, jurors, and the minister chosen by the prisoner, were always on the scaffold with him." According to Wright, "the fourth psalm was played round the scaffold, on the bagpipes; after which the minister prayed with him awhile, till he underwent the fatal stroke." The custom of playing the bagpipes as an accompaniment to an execution, must have been anything but soothing in its effects upon the terror-stricken criminal, one would think.

Dr. Whitaker inclines to the opinion that the Halifax Gibbet Law did not come into operation till the general introduction of the woollen manufactory rendered a special protection necessary for that species of property; but the probability is that the law dates from a much earlier period, and that the clothiers of Halifax were merely having recourse to an old enactment in appealing to it as a protection against trade depredations. It is an error to suppose, too, that punishment by decollation was practised in no other part of England but Halifax. The Harleian MSS. set forth that "anciently, the several customes of places made, in those dayes, capitall punishments severall. Apud Dover infalistatus, apud Southampton submersus, apud Winton demembratus, veldecapitatus, ul apud Northampton," &c. The Earls of Chester exercised the power of beheading, as appears from a document referred to by Watson, which says, "the serjeants or bailiffs of the earls had power to behead any malefactor or thief who was apprehended in the action, or against whom it was made apparent by sufficient witness, or confession, before four inhabitants of the place, or rather before four inhabitants of the four neighbouring towns." Then follows an account of the presenting of several heads of felons at the Castle of Chester, according to custom, by the earl's serjeants. In a Roll of the 3rd Edward II., this practice of beheading is alluded to as the custom of Cheshire. The beheading of criminals, therefore, cannot have been peculiar to Halifax, but was exercised in other parts of the kingdom. In the second volume of *Holinshead's Chronicle*, printed in 1577, there is a wood-cut representing the execution of a man who attempted to murder Henry III., and the instrument of execution corresponds in its main features with the representation of the Halifax gibbet, published in " Moll's Maps of England and Wales," issued in 1724, where the bailiff, or some other person, is shown in the act of cutting the rope. In the original edition of "Foxe's Book of Martyrs " there is also an engraving of a similar description. Evelyn, in his " Memoirs," says : " At Naples they use a frame, like the one at Halifax." The machine was well known also in several parts of Germany early in the sixteenth century. There is a print extant, by Aldergraven, repre-senting Titus Manlins standing to see the execution of his own son, for fighting contrary to his orders. The axe hangs over his neck, suspended by a cord ; there are hollows cut in the two uprights, to direct it in its descent, but being a side view, the method made use of to cause it to fall is not represented. An officer, who stands by the side of Manlins, has his left hand on the criminal's head. Earl Morton, when Regent of Scotland, introduced a similar instrument into his own country. It is said that as he was passing through Halifax on a certain occasion, about the middle of the sixteenth century, he witnessed an execution on Gibbet Hill, and being so much struck by the efficacy of the gibbet in cases of capital punish-ment, ordered a model to be made of the Halifax one ; and on his return to Scotland, had a similar instrument constructed, which, remaining long unused, was called " The Maiden ; " but on the 3rd June, 1581, he was himself executed by it. This identical instrument is now deposited in the Museum of the Society of Antiquaries at Edinburgh.

The custom of beheading criminals by means of the gibbet was kept up in Halifax as long as ever the clothiers could possibly retain it—to a later period, indeed, than elsewhere. The executions came to be so common, it is averred, that the inhabitants became indifferent to such exhibitions. It is related that on one occasion a country-woman, who was riding by the gibbet with her hampers on the way to market, just at the execution of a criminal, "when the axe chopped his neck through with such force that the head jumped into one of her hampers, or (as others say) seized her apron with the teeth, and there stuck for some time." Be that as it may, as feudalism died out, and more civilized notions came into vogue, the gibbet became distasteful to the people of Halifax generally. Between 1623 and 1650 there were no fewer than twelve executions by the Halifax gibbet, and signs of discontent began to be manifested at the cruelty of the old law. When the last double execution took place, in 1650, the mob assailed the bailiff with shouts of disapproval, and he was threatened that if the like were ever attempted again, he himself would be made an example of. It does not seem that any law was passed by Parliament abolishing the gibbet, but it fell naturally into disuse as soon as the people awoke to a sense of its unjust application and barbaric form as an instrument of death.

The following is a full list of the persons gibbeted at Halifax, since entries of such executions began to be made in the Parish Register :—

Richard Bently, de Sowerby, decollat 20 die Martii, 1541.—Quidem extranius capitalem subiit sententiam, 10 die Jan., 1542.

Joh'es Brygg, Capellanie de Hiptonetal.—Capitalem subiit sententiam, 16 Septembris, 1544.

Joh'ee Ecoppe, de Eland, capitalem subiit sententiam ultimo die Martii, 1545.

Thomas Waite, de Halifax, capitalem subiit sententiam, and fuit sepultus, 50 die Decomb, 1545.

Richard Sharpe, de Northm., John Learoyd, de Northm., beheaded the 5th day of March, 1568, for a robbing done in Lancashire.

William Cokekere, was headed the 9th day of October, 1572.

John Atkinson, Nicholson Frear, Richard Garnet, were headed at Halifax the 9th day of January, 1572.

Richard Stopforthe, was headed the 19th day of May, 1574.

James Smith, de Sowerby, was headed at Halifax, the 12th Feby., 1576.

Henry Hunt, was headed at Halifax, the 3rd of November, 1576.

Robert Baystall, *alias* Fernesyde, was headed the 6th of Feby., 1576.

John Dicconsone, de Bradford, was headed the 6th Jan., 1578.

John Watus, was headed at Halifax, March 16, 1578.

Bryan Cassone, was headed at Halifax, the 15th of October, 1580.

John Appleyard, de Halifax, was headed the 19th of February, 1581.

John Staden, was headed at Halifax, the 7th of February, 1582.

Arthur Firthe, was headed the 17th of January, 1585.

John Duckworth, was headed at Halifax, the 4th of October, 1586.

Nicholas Hewett, de Northouram, Thomas Masone, vagans, were headed the 27th of May, 1587.

Thomas Roberts, de Halifax, was beheaded the 13th day of July, 1588.

Robert Wilson, de Halifax, was beheaded the 5th of April, 1589.

Decollatus Petrus Crabtrye, Sorbvr, 21 December, 1591.

Decollatus Barnard Sutcliffe, Northowram, 6th of January, 1591.

Abraham Stancliffe, Halifax, capite, truncatus September 23, 1602.

Ux Peter Harrison, Bradford, decoll February 22, 1602.

Christopher Cosin, decollatus December 29, 1610.

Thomas Briggs, decollatus April 10, 1611.

George Fairbanke, per ditissimus nebulo vulgo vocatus Skoggin, ob nequitiam, anna ejusdem Georgii Filia spuria, ambo meritissime ob surtum manifestum dicollati December 23, 1623.

John Lacy, puditissimus nebulo and latro, dicollatus January 29, 1625.

Edmund Ogden, decollatus April 8, 1624.

Richard Midgly, of Midgly, decollatus April 13, 1624.

Ux Johan Wilson, decollata July 5, 1627.

Sara Lume, Hal., decollata Dec. 8, 1627.

John Sutcliffe, Sk., decollatus 14 May, 1629.

Richard Holle, Hept., decollatus October 20, 1629.

Henry Hudson, ux Samuel Ettal ob plurima surta decollati August 28, 1630.

Jeremy Bowcock, de Warley, decollatus April 14, 1632.

John Crabtree, de Sourby, decollatus September 22, 1632.

Abraham Cligg, Morland, decollatus May 21, 1636.

Isaac Illingworth, Ovenden, decollatus October 7, 1641.

John Wilkinson, Anthony Mitchell, Sowerby, decollati April 30, 1650.

In all 49.—

5 in the last six years of Henry VIII.
25 in the reign of Elizabeth.
7 in the reign of James I.
10 in the reign of Charles.
2 during the Interregnum.

Few particulars remain of the incidents or circumstances connected with the men who suffered by the gibbet at Halifax. The story of the escape of Dennis, or Dinnis, seems to have been the one that has fastened itself most firmly upon the popular mind. I have before me a play-bill of the Halifax Theatre, which shows that on the 27th February, 1837, "by particular desire, for this night only," there was played a drama entitled, *Dennis, or the Gibbet Law of Halifax*. It was on a Monday evening, and the occasion was the benefit of Mr. Gordon, who respectfully appealed to "the gentry and public in general of Halifax and its vicinity" to give him their liberal patronage. The characters were—Sir William Wentworth (Lord Bailiff of the Liberty of Hardwick), Master Colbeck (a wealthy merchant), Master Lacy Dennis (in love with Marian Lacy), Martin Matchlowe (Head Constable of the Liberty of Halifax), Lambert Lightheel, (Deputy Constable of the Liberty of Halifax), Master Varley (Clerk of the Court), Gibbet Jack (a reported thief and deer stealer), Jailor, Marian Lacy (betrothed to Dennis), and Prudence, (with a song, "Hints to lovers"). Mr. Gordon played the part of Sir William Wentworth, Mr. J. W. Simpson that of Dennis, and Miss Gurney Read that of Marion Lacy. The first scene was an apartment in Lacy's mansion, where the lovers met and lamented the hardness of heart of the damsel's father in time-honoured form. Sir William scorned Dennis because of his poverty, and now, cast adrift, as it were, upon the world, Dennis vowed that he would accomplish some desperate act that should gain him the approbation of the stern baronet. Master Colbeck, the villain of the piece, who is also desirous of marrying Marion, overhears Dennis's determined resolve, puts a foul construction upon his words, and makes up his mind to use them against his hated rival. News of a great robbery of cloth is presently heard, and, by the machinations of Colbeck, Dennis is accused of being the thief, and is consigned to gaol. Then comes a scene in the "Hall of Trial," where Dennis is brought face to face with his accuser, and is subjected to "the peculiar mode of trial by the Gibbet Law." He makes an eloquent defence, but all to no purpose, his doom is sealed, and the awful sentence of "Death by the Gibbet Law" is pronounced upon him. Then there is a scene in the prison, where Dennis bemoans his fate in the most pitiable style. Following that, there is a mysterious meeting between Colbeck and Gibbet Jack in "An Antique Chamber in the Mansion of Colbeck." Then there is a view of Crown Street, the "procession of Dennis to the place of execution." After this the scene changes to Gibbet Hill, as it stood in the reign of Elizabeth, in which scene was exhibited "a fac-simile of the real gibbet and axe, and mode of decapitation exercised on the criminals of Halifax." There is a great commotion, of course, and thanks to the scheming and plotting of his betrothed, Dennis is enabled to make his escape to Sanctuary Bridge, beyond which the Gibbet Law is powerless to reach him. To wind up with, there is a view of Beacon Hill and the Forest of Hardwick, and the piece terminates with "the death of the real criminal," Master Colbeck. Such were the old-fashioned lines upon which Mr. Gordon sought to obtain the sympathies of the Halifax public in the year 1837. How often the piece has been played since (if at all) I do not know, but such a bill-of-fare, with the drama of *The Wrecker's Daughter* to precede it, *The Golden Farmer* to follow, and dances, clog hornpipes, and comic songs between the pieces, ought to have been sufficient to ensure the *beneficiare* a good house.

THE STORY OF ROBIN HOOD.

AMONGST the legends and traditions which have been handed down to us from the ancient days when printing was unknown, none stands more boldly forth, or takes firmer possession of the popular mind, than the story of Robin Hood. There are those who would have us believe that no such person ever existed, but that the name of Robin Hood was merely used to symbolise that feeling of resentment to oppression and opposition to priestly tyranny, which in Plantagenet times was so strongly felt by the people. Signs, emblems, and symbols no doubt meant much in those days, but the strict narrative form adopted in the series of ballads dealing with the life and adventures of the outlaw hero, and the fact that so many of our early prose writers have so pointedly alluded to him as an actual personage, may be regarded as sufficiently evidencing his having been something more tangible than a legendary myth. Nearly all the heroes of ancient romance have had their existence undermined by those modern iconoclasts, who would fain demolish everything that is not supported by formal documentary proof. William Tell has been almost argued into nonentity in Switzerland, and Robin Hood has been in danger of meeting with the same fate in England. Fortunately, however, there still survives a deep reverence for the traditions of the past, and it is not likely that the name and fame of Robin Hood will be suffered to pass into the regions of disbelief.

In Yorkshire—indeed, in all the northern counties, from Nottingham to Cumberland—the local associations connected with the name of Robin Hood will preserve his memory from gliding into oblivion. There is a Robin Hood's Bay between Scarborough and Whitby, a Robin Hood's Cave at Halifax, a Robin Hood's Well near Nottingham, and innumerable other places bearing the ancient freebooter's name. The most interesting spot of all, however, connected with Robin Hood, and the place where his identity seems to be most clearly marked, is at Kirklees, where in the park attached to Kirklees Hall, and belonging to Sir George Armytage, is the supposed grave of the outlaw, and the cottage in which he is said to have died. Access to these relics of a bygone time is not so easy as might· be desirable, perhaps ; but the rights of property must be respected, and a landed proprietor must have wild game preserved for the special slaughter of himself and friends, whether public curiosity be satisfied or indulged or not. Robin Hood's grave is situated in the midst of the "shady sadness" of a beautiful wood, where immemorial beeches tower high above the ancient tombstone, and a more peaceful seclusion is ensured than could be obtained in any consecrated burial-ground. It is enclosed in a walled-off space, with fluted columns at each corner. Strong spiked iron rails rise from the wall on its four sides, while over the top stretches a network of iron wire. Thus, it will be seen, the owner of Kirklees takes great care of the outlaw's grave, although he may not be disposed to follow the example of the Duke of Devonshire and other noblemen and gentlemen, in admitting the public to view this and other relics of national interest which lie within his domain. There used to be a superstition in the neighbourhood that a piece of Robin Hood's tombstone would act as a certain cure for the toothache, and suffering villagers have so often stolen through the park under cover of the darkness and

o

chipped off bits of the stone, that although the stone existed entire in 1750, the toothache people have reduced it so much that not more than a quarter of it remains. The probability is that if Sir George Armytage had not taken steps to protect the stone, it would by this time have been completely gone. The piece of stone had to be placed under the pillow of the sufferer, and by acting powerfully on the imagination, or perhaps by inducing a counter irritation, the remedy must have been considered efficacious, seeing that its use was kept up for so long a period. It is said that there was originally a cross carved on the stone, of the form in use at the beginning of the 13th century, and this would seem to denote that the tombstone must be that of an ecclesiastic of that period. A very plausible suggestion has been advanced in regard to this, however. The Nunnery of Kirklees, which was not far distant from Robin Hood's grave, had many ancient tombstones in its burying-ground at the time of the dissolution of the monasteries, and it is thought probable that one of these stones was removed to the place of the outlaw's interment, and thenceforward served " to mark a place which perhaps an older memorial had ceased to record." The only record existing in connection with the spot is the well-known inscription, which now appears upon a small square stone, evidently of modern date, inserted in the wall, and may or may not be identical with the inscription on the original tombstone. It runs thus :—

> " Hear undernead dis laitl stean
> Laiz robert earl of Huntingtun
> near arcir der az hie sa geud
> an Pipl Kauld im robin heud
> sick utlawz az hi an iz men
> Vil England nivr si agen.
> Obiit 24 Kal Dekembris 1247."

Antiquaries are disposed to consider this epitaph a modern fabrication. It was found amongst the papers of Dr. Gale, Dean of York. Thoresby visited Kirklees, and his record was that "the noted Robin Hood lies buried under a grave-stone that yet remains near the park, but the inscription *scarce legible*." Dr. Whitaker, who twice visited Kirklees, said there was *no lettered gravestone* over Robin Hood.

The site of the Nunnery of Kirklees is in one of the most romantic positions in the park. Not much of the ancient edifice remains. It was a Benedictine Nunnery, founded by Regner de Fleming, in the year 1155 (2nd Henry II.), and was dedicated to the Blessed Virgin and St. James. The first Superior was Elizabeth de Staynton, who entered it at its foundation, along with her two sisters, Agnes and Mary. The tombstones of these three sisters are still visible, the inscription being still very legible. The part of the Nunnery, however, which most concerns us in our endeavour to trace the history of Robin Hood, is the old gatehouse, which still stands and is in excellent preservation, its heavily-timbered walls and quaint carvings forcibly re-calling the remote period to which it belonged. It was in this little house, it is said, that the notorious outlaw breathed his last. In an upstairs room, with narrow windows, and heavy frowning walls of great thickness, they show the place where the robber spent the last hours of his eventful life. Here, it is recorded in the Sloane MSS., "being distempered with could and age he had great payne in his lymnes, his bloud being corrupted, therefore to be eased of his payne by letting bloud, he repayred to the prioress of Kyrkesley, which some say was his aunt, a woman very skilful in physique and surgery ; who perceyving him to be Robin Hood, and waying howe fel an enimy he was to religious persons, toke revenge of him for her own howse and all others by letting him bleed to death." The cunning of the prioress is quaintly set forth in the ancient ballad :—

> "Will you please to sit down, cousin Robin," she said,
>   "And drink some beer with me ?"
> " No ; I will neither eat nor drink
>   Till I have been blooded by thee."

" Well, I have a room, cousin Robin," she said,
" Which you did never see ;
And if you please to walk therein,
You blooded by me shall be."

She took him by the lily white hand,
And led him to a private room ;
And there she blooded bold Robin Hood
Whilst one drop of blood would run.

She blooded him in the vein of the arm,
And locked him up in the room ;
Then did he bleed all the live long day,
Until the next day at noon.

The ballad goes on to describe how weak he became, and
that having "set his horn unto his mouth " and blown out
" weak blasts three,"

Then Little John, when hearing him,
As he sat under the tree,
" I fear my master is near dead,
He blows so wearily."

Then Little John to fair Kirkley is gone,
As fast as he can dree ;
But when he came to Kirkley Hall,
He broke locks two or three.

Until he came bold Robin to,
Then he fell on his knee ;
" A boon, a boon," cries Little John,
" Master, I beg of thee."

" What is that boon," quoth Robin Hood,
" Little John, thou begs of me ?"
" It is to burn fair Kirkley Hall,
And all their nunnery."

" Now nay, now nay," quoth Robin Hood,
" That boon I'll not grant thee.
I never hurt fair woman in my life,
Nor man in woman's company.

" I never hurt fair maid in all my life,
Nor at the end shall it be ;

But give me my bent bow in my hand,
And a broad arrow I'll let flee ;
And where this arrow is taken up,
There shall my grave digg'd be."

The little window through which he fired this last arrow looks straight across to the grave where the outlaw is said to have been buried. It is 575 yards distant: a fact which goes to prove that even in his dying moments the archer must have possessed a considerable amount of strength.

Having thus briefly indicated the interesting associations to be met with at Kirklees in connection with Robin, it may be as well to attempt to form some outline of his actual career, from such scattered evidences as are to be met with in our early literature.

There is little doubt that some of the ballads relating to Robin Hood were sung or recited by the minstrels who in the Middle Ages wandered from place to place recounting the heroic deeds of their contemporaries and predecessors. The whole tenour of the Robin Hood ballads shows that the people believed in his existence; indeed, it is difficult to imagine how such a mass of literature could have been inspired by a mythical personage. The earliest mention of him is in the *Vision of Piers Plowman* (1362), in which one of the allegorical characters, *Sloth*, owns that he does not know his *paternoster* perfectly, but he does know "rimes of Robin Hood." As soon as printing came to be invented, these "rimes" received the honour of being put into more enduring form. Wynkyn de Worde, one of the earliest printers, at one time assistant and afterwards successor to Caxton, issued "A Lytell Geste of Robin Hode" in or about the year 1489. After that the collection of "rimes of Robin Hood" seemed to grow rapidly, and from the fourteenth century there is direct evidence of the deeds of this famous outlaw being familiar to the peasantry of England. Not only did the people sing of Robin Hood, but they had their Robin Hood Festivals year after year, much as in more modern times we have had our Guy Fawkes celebrations and our May Day festivals. Bishop Latimer tells how he was hindered from preaching on a certain occasion by one of these popular demonstrations. "I came once myself to a place," he says, "riding on a journey homeward from London, and I sent word overnight into the town that I would preach there in the morning, because it was holyday, and methought it was holy-day's work. The church stood in my way, and I took my horse and my company, and went thither. I thought I should have found a great company in the church, and when I came there the church door was fast locked. I tarried there half-an-hour and more; at last the key was found, and one of the parish comes to me and says, 'Sir, this is a busy day with us; we cannot hear you; it is Robin Hood's day. The parish are gone abroad to gather for Robin Hood. I pray you let [hinder] them not.' I was fain then to give place to Robin Hood. I thought my rochet should have been regarded, though I were not; but it would not serve: I was fain to give place to Robin Hood's men! It is no laughing matter, my friends; it is weeping matter, a heavy matter! Under the pretence for gathering for Robin Hood, a traitor and a thief, to put out a preacher, to have his office less esteemed, to prefer Robin Hood before the ministration of God's word; and all this hath come of unpreaching prelates."

One can well understand the hatred which the good bishop would bear towards the name and memory of an outlaw who had set himself to oppose the authority of the priesthood, and who was associated in the minds of the people with the repression of the tyrannies of religion and government. Fordun, who died in 1385, alluded to the outlaw as "that most notorious cut-throat," which was a somewhat unromantic way of mentioning the popular hero. Major styled Robin Hood and Little John "most famous robbers." Furthermore, Major said that Robin "was the most humane and the prince of all robbers:" the belief being that the outlaw robbed only the rich while he gave largely to the poor; that he never killed any person, unless attacked or resisted, and that he was particularly careful never to ill-treat a woman. So chivalrous a robber was well calculated to inspire admiration in a time such as that in which he lived. His special abhorrence were bishops, abbots, priests, and monks, and he was never so happy as when relieving some member of these holy orders of what he conceived to be their ill-gotten gains. His band at one time formed a numerous company. He had a hundred archers who all dressed in Lincoln green; "men," says Major, "most skilful in battle, whom four times that number of the boldest fellows durst not attack." In recruiting for his outlaw band he used to adopt a rather singular course. "Wheresoever he heard of any that were of unusual strength and hardiness," says an old writer, "he would disguise himself, and, rather than fail, go like a beggar to become acquainted with them; and, after he had tried them with fighting, never give them over till he had used means to draw them to live after his fashion." In shooting with the long bow, Robin Hood's archers are said to have "excelled all the land."

As to who Robin Hood really was, or at what exact period he lived, there have been many conjectures. It is generally believed, however, that he was born at Loxley Chase, near Sheffield, either at the close of the reign of Henry II., or in the reign of Henry III., towards the year 1230. He was probably reared on the lands that had belonged to Earl Waltheof, the last great resistant of the Norman *régime*, and, from an inherited antipathy to the Norman kings, took his stand on the popular side under Simon de Montfort, as did Little John, and on being defeated at the battle of Evesham, in 1265, the two formed a companionship and organised a band of sympathisers, and sought refuge and subsistence in the woods, dales, and cloughs of Nottinghamshire, West Yorkshire, Derbyshire, and other places. In this way Robin Hood would come to personify "to thousands in England," as Professor Morley observes, "the spirit of liberty in arms against the cruel forest laws, against all tyrannies of the strong in Church and State, against all luxury fed on the spoils of labour." Ritson argues that Robin Hood's true name was Robert Fitzooth, which vulgar pronunciation easily corrupted into Robin Hood. He was frequently styled Earl of Huntingdon, and was generally understood to have a claim to that title, but being outlawed by the king he sought the asylum of the woods and forests, and thenceforward lived by robbery. Dr. Spencer T. Hall, "the Sherwood Forester," has advanced the ingenious theory that the name Robin Hood was merely an elisional pronunciation of the appellation "Robin o' th' Wood," which might be a mythical title "assumed by or given to any great woodland outlaw of the hour;" he leans to the opinion, however, that there was one man who bore the name with more dignity than all the rest, and that this person was the outlaw hero who lived in the 13th century, and was popularly believed to be the Earl of Huntingdon. Dr. Stukeley, in his "Palæographia Britannica," goes so far as to give the pedigree of Robin Hood, as follows :—

"Gilbert de Gaunt, Earl of Lincoln, and his wife, Avis, had two daughters, Alice and Maud.

Alice married an Earl of Huntingdon ; Maud married Ralph Fitzooth, a Norman Lord of Kyme.

Alice died, childless, in 1184. John, Earl of Huntingdon by another line, died childless, in 1237.

Maud had by her husband, Ralph Fitzooth, a son, Walter, who was brought up by Robert, Earl of Oxford, as his son.

That Walter married a daughter of Payn Beauchamp and Lady Roisia de Vere. The hero of popular legend was their son Robert, grandson of Ralph."

There is one more reference to Robin Hood's birth, which, though it will not tally with the statements of Dr. Stukeley, still bears out the notion that the outlaw was of noble birth. In the ballad of "The Birth of Robin Hood," printed by Jamieson from the recitation of Mrs. Brown, it is related how Willie and Earl Richard's daughter go to "the gude greenwood,"

> "And ere the night was done
> She's born to him a bonny young son,
> Among the leaves sae green."

This son, it is stated, is Robin Hood. The ballad, however, does not belong to the famous Robin Hood series.

As bearing upon this question of the nobility of extraction of Robin Hood, may be mentioned Anthony Munday's popular play, originally called *The Downfall of Robert, Earle of Huntington*, but subsequently presented under the more amplified title of *Robin Hood of Merrie Sherwodde ; with his love to chast Matilda, the Lord Fitzwater's daughter, afterwards his faire maide Marian.* This play was first printed in 1601, and was for a long time attributed to Thomas Heywood. Munday also wrote a companion play, *The Death of Robert, Earl of Huntington.*

So much for the evidence as to the name and origin of the famous outlaw. We will now make an attempt to arrive at some idea of the composition of Robin Hood's band, and the style of living adopted by them. The parts of the country most affected by the outlaws seem to have been Barnsdale, in Yorkshire, and Sherwood Forest in Nottinghamshire. The district of Barnsdale comprised a large tract of country between Doncaster and Pontefract, and was in Robin Hood's time covered with forest. Fordun, in his "Scotichronicon," says that Robin Hood was attending mass in Barnsdale when he heard that his enemies were upon him, and that he would not defend himself until the mass was done ; then triumphed easily, and ever after held masses in greater veneration. Sherwood Forest covered the central portion of the county of Nottingham to Mansfield, and extended twenty miles from north to south, and from five to seven miles from east to west. According to the survey of 1609, Sherwood Forest consisted of 95,000 acres. Ranging these forests with his "merrie men," Robin Hood for many years appears to have held a sort of independent sovereignty, defying the law and being to some extent abetted by the peasantry in the neighbourhood of his haunts. Robin's character, as set forth in the ancient ballads, was that of a bluff, strong, brave fellow, with a hearty relish of fighting and fun, and a healthy contempt for all that was mean or cowardly, a love of manly independence and courage, and a fervent hatred of all oppressors, clerical and lay. His chief followers and favourites appear to have been Little John, who was said to be six feet four in height, and whose real name was Nailor; William Scathelock, Seadlock, or Scarlet (more popularly known as Will Scarlet); George-a-Green, "the jolly pinder of Wakefield;" Much, or Moche, a miller's son; and Friar Tuck. Thus Drayton, in his *Polyolbion*, published early in the 17th century, describes the doings of the outlaw band, determining to sing of

> Lusty Robin Hood, who long time like a king
> Within her compass lived, and when he list to range
> For some rich booty set, or else his air to change,
> To Sherwood still retired, his only standing court,
> Whose praise the Forest thus doth pleasantly report :
> " The merry pranks he played would ask an age to tell,
> And the adventures strange that Robin Hood befel,
> When Mansfield many a time for Robin hath been laid,
> How he hath cozened them that him would have betrayed ;
> How often he hath come to Nottingham disguised,
> And cunningly escaped, being set to be surprised.
> In this our spacious isle, I think there is not one,
> But he hath heard some talk of him and Little John ;
> And to the end of time the tales shall ne'er be done
> Of Scarlock, George-a-Green, and Much, the miller's son ;
> Of Tuck, the merry friar, which many a sermon made

In praise of Robin Hood, his outlaws, and their trade.
An hundred valiant men had this brave Robin Hood,
Still ready at his call, that bowmen were right good ;
All clad in Lincoln green, with caps of red and blue,
His fellow's winded horn not one of them but knew,
When setting to their lips their little bugles shrill,
The warbling echoes waked from every dale and hill ;
Their baldricks set with studs, athwart their shoulders cast,
To which, under their arms, their sheafs were buckled fast ;
A short sword at their belt, a buckler scarce a span,
Who struck below the knee not counted then a man.
All made of Spanish yew, their bows were wondrous strong ;
They not an arrow drew but was a cloth-yard long.
Of archery they had the very perfect craft,
With broad-arrow, or butt, or prick, or roving shaft.
At marks full fifty score they used to prick and rove,
Yet higher than the breast, for compass never strove.
Yet at the farthest mark a foot could hardly win,
At long butts, short, and hoyles, each one could cleave the pin ;
Their arrows finely paired for timber and for feather,
With birch and brazil pieced, to fly in any weather ;
And shot they with the round, the square, or forked pile,
The loose gave such a twang, as might be heard a mile.
And of those archers brave, there was not anyone
But he could kill a deer his swiftest speed upon,
Which they did boil and roast in many a mighty wood,
Sharp hunger the fine sauce to their more kingly food.
Then taking them to rest, his merry men and he
Slept many a summer's night under the greenwood tree.
From wealthy abbot's chests, and churl's abundant store,
What oftentimes he took he shared amongst the poor ;
No lordly bishop came in lusty Robin's way,
To him before he went, but for his pass must pay.
The widow in distress he graciously relieved,
And remedied the wrongs of many a virgin grieved.
He from the husband's bed no married woman wan,
But to his mistress dear, his loved Marian,
Was ever constant known, which wheresoe'er she came
Was sovereign of the woods, chief lady of the game :
Her clothes tucked to the knee, and dainty braided hair,
With bow and quiver armed, she wandered here and there,
Amongst the forests wild ; Diana never knew
Such pleasures, nor such hearts as Mariana slew."

Little John's devotion to his master is something remarkable. He was ever at hand to aid Robin Hood in
time of trial or danger, and in point of daring even sometimes excelled his chief. When Robin was set upon by the
Sheriff of Nottingham and his men, his first thought was,

"Now miss I Little John;"

and, as we have seen, Little John was with Robin Hood at
Kirklees when the latter died, and thirsted to avenge his
master's death by burning down the priory. It is related
that Robin Hood first encountered Little John in Sherwood Forest. They met upon a narrow wooden bridge
which spanned a deep brook. There was not room for two
to pass, and neither would give way, so they got threatening
each other with violence, and Robin threatened the stranger
that if he did not make way for him he would "show him
right Nottingham play." As he spoke, Robin drew an arrow
from his quiver, and was about to place it on his bowstring,
when the stranger vowed that he would "liquor his hide"
if he attempted to touch the string. "Thou dost prate like
an ass," quoth Robin, "for if I were to bend my bow, I
could send an arrow through thy proud heart before thou
could'st strike me a single blow." "Thou talkest like a
coward," replied the stranger; "thou standest there, armed
with a long bow to shoot at my breast, while I have nothing
in my hand but a simple staff." "I scorn the name of a
coward," cried bold Robin, laying aside his bow, "therefore,
I'll lay by my long bow, and get myself a staff, and then I
will try the truth of thy manhood." On these terms they
then had a set-to, and, after a long struggle, Robin was
hurled headlong into the brook. Robin acknowledged
himself vanquished, but scrambling to the bank he blew a
loud blast upon his horn, and a troop of stout bowmen
quickly made their appearance. Robin's men, on learning
what had occurred, would fain have chastised the tall
stranger, but their master bade them desist, and declaring

himself to be the outlaw chieftain, asked the stranger to join their band. "Speak up, jolly blade, and never fear," said Robin, "I'll teach thee the use of the bow, and thou shall shoot at the fallow deer." "With all my heart," said the stranger. "My name is John Little, and you need never fear but that I shall play my part well." After that, they prepared a right merry feast. John was taken into the brotherhood, and transposing his name, he was christened Little John. In nearly all the Robin Hood ballads Little John plays a part only second to that of his chief. There is little record of him apart from his connection with Robin Hood. His real surname, tradition says, was Nailor. What became of him after the dispersal of Robin Hood's band is not clearly known. The *Ashmole MSS.* contain the following note in reference to his burial: "Little John lyes buried in Hatherseech (Hathersage) Churchyard, within three miles fro Castleton in High Peake, with one Stone set up at his Head and another at his Feete, but a long distance between them. They say a piece of his bow hangs up in the said church." The cottage in which he resided, and the place where he was buried, are still pointed out to visitors. Of Will Scarlet not much is recorded, except that he was one of Robin Hood's most trusty lieutenants. In Munday's plays Scarlet and Scathlock are two persons,—brothers. George-a-Green, "the pinder of Wakefield," was well known for his lusty courage, and his fame having reached the ears of Robin Hood, the outlaw captain determined to win him over to join his company. As the old ballad—twice alluded to by Shakespeare—tells us, "Robin Hood, Scarlet, and John" wended their way to Wakefield, and

———— espy'd the jolly pinder,
As he sat under a thorn.

"Now, turn again, turn again," said the pinder,
"For a wrong way you have gone;
For you have forsaken the king's highway,
And made a path over the corn."

" O that were a shame," said jolly Robin,
  " We being three, and thou but one."
The pinder leapt back then thirty good foot,
  'Twas thirty good foot and one.

He leaned his back fast unto a thorn,
  And his foot against a stone,
And there he fought a long summer's day,
  A summer's day so long ;
Till that their swords on their broad bucklers
  Were broke fast into their hands.

After that, Robin, of course, offered him the right hand
of fellowship, and invited the pinder to join his band,
which he subsequently did. *George-a-Green, the Pinner of
Wakefield*, is the title of one of Robert Green's plays.
Friar Tuck was Robin Hood's father-confessor, the "curtal
friar of Fountains Abbey," and the holy clerk of Copman-
hurst of Scott's *Ivanhoe.* He is always represented as a
sort of clerical Falstaff, and had great skill in archery.
Robin Hood, we are told, "tooke a solemne oath" one day
"that he would neither eate nor drink till the fryer he did
see," and he forthwith started off to " Fountaine Dale," and
spying the friar beside the river, he called to the holy man
to carry him across.

The fryer tooke Robin Hood on his backe,
  Deepe water he did bestride,
And spake neither good word nor bad,
  Till he came at the other side.

Lightly leapt Robin offe the fryer's backe ;
  The fryer said to him againe,
" Carry me over this water, thou fine fellow,
  Or it shall breed thy paine."

Robin Hood took the friar on his backe,
  Deep water he did bestride,
And spake neither good word nor bad,
  Till he came at the other side.

Robin then commands the fryer to carry him across once more, and the monk obeys, but,

—— comming to the middle streame,
There he threw Robin in ;
" And chuse thee, chuse thee, fine fellow,
Whether thou wilt sink or swim."

A fierce encounter ensues, as a matter of course, and the Friar is ultimately defeated, and agrees to join Robin Hood's band. Tuck is from that time the apologist of the outlaw, as well as his boon companion, and many are the sermons he is represented as having preached to prove that Robin Hood's sovereignty was morally as lawful as that of the King. Thomas Love Peacock, the novelist, in his novel, *Maid Marian*, has cleverly illustrated (in imagination) this aspect of the Friar's character. The following passage is worth quoting, fiction though it be :—

"Truly," said the friar, "I have a chapel here hard by, in the shape of a hollow tree, where I put up my prayers for travellers ; and Little John holds the plate at the door, for good praying deserves good paying." "I am in pure company," said the baron. "In the very best of company," said the friar ; "in the high court of Nature, and in the midst of her own nobility. Is it not so? This goodly forest is our palace ; the oak and the beech are its colonnade and its canopy ; the sun, and the moon, and the stars are its everlasting lamps ; the grass, and the daisy, and the primrose, and the violet are its many-coloured floors of green, white, yellow, and blue ; the May-flower, and the woodbine, and the eglantine and the ivy are its decorations, its curtains, and its tapestry ; the lark, and the thrush, and the linnet, and the nightingale are its unhired minstrels and musicians. Robin Hood is king of the forest, both by dignity of birth and by virtue of standing army, to say nothing of the free choice of his people, which he has indeed. . . . He holds his dominion over the forest, and its horned multitude of citizen-deer, and its swinish multitude or peasantry of wild boars, by right of conquest and force of arms. He levies contributions amongst them by the free consent of his archers, their virtual representatives. . . . What title had William of Normandy to England that Robin of Locksley has not to merry Sherwood? William fought for his claim. So does Robin. With whom both? With any that would will or dispute it. William raised contributions. So does Robin. From whom both? From all that they could or can make pay them! Why did any pay them to William? Why do any pay them to Robin? For the same reason to both—because they could not or cannot help it. They differ, indeed, in this, that William took from the poor and gave to the rich, and Robin takes from the rich and gives to the poor; and therein is Robin illegitimate, though in all else he is the true prince. Scarlet and John, are they not peers of the forest?—lords temporal of Sherwood? Am not I lord spiritual? Am I not Archbishop? Am I not Pope? Do I not consecrate their banner and absolve their sins? Are not they State, and am not I Church? Are not they State monarchical, and am not I Church militant?"

This is an excellent plausible sermon, much better, doubtless, than the real Friar Tuck would have been capable of delivering, though it is worth noting because of its embodying so many of the sentiments of the poorer classes as regards government and authority in the feudal period.

Arthur-a-Bland, "the jolly tanner of Nottingham," was gained over to the ranks of the outlaws much in the same way as Little John and George-a-Green were won. Robin Hood had an encounter with the tanner, and found him so doughty an opponent that he took steps at once to enlist him a member of his band. Arthur, the tanner, was a kinsman of Little John's, and, on this being discovered, the three men (again the old ballad is our authority) danced round an old oak tree that was near, and sang in chorus,

> "For three merry men, and three merry men,
>   And three merry men be we,
> And ever hereafter, as long as we live,
>   We three will be as one;
> The wood it shall ring, and the old wife sing,
>   Of Robin Hood, Arthur, and John."

Much, or Midge, the miller's son, was another of Robin Hood's trusty companions.

Allin-a-Dale, or Allan-a-Dale, is another name that stands prominently forth in the Robin Hood legends. Allan is made the hero of one of the Robin Hood ballads. The story is that Allan was to be married to a damsel whose parents were opposed to him, they having in view a wealthy old knight as a husband for their daughter. Robin Hood disguised himself as a minstrel, and went to the church where the wedding was to take place, and when the old knight and the young damsel advanced into the church, Robin Hood exclaimed, "This is not a fit match

> That you do seem to make here ;
> For since we are come into the church,
> The bride shall chuse her own dear."

Then he blows a blast upon his horn, and four-and-twenty bowmen answer the well-known summons. The bishop, however, declined to marry the "finikin lass" to Allan until the banns had been asked three times, whereupon Robin divested the bishop of his gown, and put it upon Little John, who asked the banns seven times, and the wedding was performed. Allan, of course, repaid this service by becoming one of Robin Hood's men, but, beyond the ballad in question, there is little recorded of him. Scott, however, makes him one of his characters in *Ivanhoe*.

It is now necessary that something should be said about the lady who cut so prominent a figure amongst this band of outlaws—Maid Marian. We have seen what Drayton has said of her; how glowingly he described her charms, and how warmly he praises her constancy. Tradition says that she was the daughter of Robert, Lord Fitzwalter, and remained the faithful wife or mistress of Robin Hood for many years during the period of his outlawry. Matilda is understood to have been her real name, but, on casting in her lot with that of the outlaw captain, she assumed the

P

name of Marian. She has no place, however, in the older
ballads; the only ballad in which she is particularly mentioned is one that in all probability was not written until
about four hundred years after the period in which Robin
Hood and his merry men flourished. It is stated by some
that she was ultimately poisoned with a poached egg at
Dunmow Priory by a messenger sent by King John, whose
love she had rejected.

How many years Robin Hood lived the life of an
outlaw is not recorded. The ancient ballads deal more
with deeds than dates. The oldest of these ballads shows
how Robin Hood lent his aid to an impoverished knight,
who was thereby enabled to redeem his property, which
had been mortgaged to the Abbot of St. Mary's, of York.
Then we read how Little John entered the service of the
Sheriff of Nottingham, and by various crafty devices robbed
him, and eventually betrayed him to Robin Hood, who
made him swear on his "bright brand" that he would
never waylay the outlaw, and that if he should find any of
his men, either by night or by day, he would help them as
much as should be in his power. In another ballad we
learn of a famous adventure which Robin Hood had with
the high cellarer of St. Mary's Abbey, from whom he
obtained a large sum of money, after which he declined
to accept from the before-mentioned knight the money he
had twelve months before paid for him to the Abbot of
St. Mary's. Then we are told of a shooting match at
Nottingham, in which Robin wins the prize; and the sheriff,
proving unfaithful to his oath, attempts to capture the
outlaw and his band, and a desperate fray ensues, ending
in Robin Hood and his men taking refuge in the castle of
Sir Richard of the Lea. After that the sheriff besieges the
knight's castle, and Sir Richard appeals to the King
(Edward) who, with five knights, all disguised as monks,
goes to Sherwood Forest and seeks out Robin Hood, who

receives them and entertains them right merrily. Ultimately the King is discovered, and His Majesty generously pardons the outlaw and invites him to Court. Robin accepts the invitation, and afterwards returns with greater affection than ever for his old mode of life. It may be mentioned, however, that ere the arrival of the King in Sherwood Forest, Robin had rescued Sir Richard of the Lea, who had been captured by the sheriff on returning from London, and had slain the sheriff. A further ballad relates how Sir Guy of Gisborne had sworn to take Robin Hood, how the knight and the outlaw meet in the forest, how Sir Guy is struck dead at a blow, and how the sheriff and his men, who have set on and bound Little John, are made to fly by Robin and his bold archers. The ballad which relates how Robin Hood played certain pranks with the Bishop of Hereford is very amusing. The ballad of "Robin Hood's Death and Burial" we have already referred to. "Trusting in his last illness to the sympathy of his cousin," says Mr. Robert Bell, "who was prioress of Kirkley Nunnery, in Yorkshire, religious women in those days being well skilled in the medical art, he placed himself freely in her hands, and she treacherously made away with him, by shutting him up in a room and leaving him to bleed to death. The prioress may have been tempted to commit this foul deed by way of exacting retribution for the sins of his life ; or it may be, as some of the commentators affirm, that she was incited to despatch her kinsman by one Sir Roger, of Doncaster, who had a grudge against him. The fact is piteous enough, either way, that he who escaped unhurt through so many desperate raids and combats, who broke prison and evaded the sheriff so often and so successfully, and who succoured so many lovers and widows, and punished so many hard-hearted law-officers and dignitaries of the Church, should come to so miserable an end by the hand of a woman. The incidents of the closing scene, the tenderness which Robin Hood shows towards women to the last, and his calling for an arrow to mark the spot where he was to be laid, terminate his life in a spirit appropriate to its wild and poetical character." Ritson gives the date of his death as the 18th November, 1247, but the inscription before referred to gives it as the 24th December, 1247. The outlaw is supposed to have been in his eighty-seventh year at the time of his death.

There is probably no other character in the whole range of English history that has been so great a favourite with literary men. Sir Walter Scott introduces him both in *Ivanhoe* and *The Talisman*, and numerous plays and operas, in which he is the hero, have been written. In 1741 Dr. Arne and Burney composed an opera on the subject; in 1787 O'Keefe and Shield collaberated on the same theme; and in our own time Mr. Macfarren has given the outlaw's life a fresh operatic setting. Mr. T. Love Peacock and Pierce Egan have both written fictions on the subject of Robin Hood.

THE STORY OF THE ELLAND TRAGEDY.

IN or about the fourteenth year of the reign of Edward III., as the ancient ballad tells us,

> "At Eland Sir John Eland dwelt
> Within the manor hall,
> The town his own, the parish held
> Most part upon him all."

Sir John Elland was one of the most powerful of the lesser order of barons, and his influence in West Yorkshire was very great. His family had possessed the manor from prior to the Conquest; and, strange as it may now appear, Elland was in Sir John Elland's day a formidable rival to Halifax, and had enjoyed the privileges of a weekly market for many years, under a charter granted by Edward II.

Like many other barons of old, Sir John Elland was a man of strong and determined purpose, and could ill brook opposition of any kind. His will was law, and woe to the unfortunate being who incurred his displeasure! The Elland race were renowned for their bravery and for their proneness to quarrel, and were held greatly in awe by the neighbouring gentry and peasantry.

Tradition told a curious story in regard to the Ellands who held the manor in the time of Edward the Confessor. It was said that a young Norman, named Hugo Beaulay, of great personal beauty but of poor condition, had come over to this country in the train of the King, and that, coming to

Yorkshire with one of the sons of Earl Godwin, and being overtaken by a storm, he had taken shelter under the roof of the then lord of Elland, and had then and there fallen in love with the lady of the house, a young and remarkably beautiful woman. Hugo Beaulay lingered at Elland manor-house far beyond the time which hospitality or courtesy would ordinarily prescribe, and at length it dawned upon Wilfrid of Elland that the wife of his bosom was false to him, and regarded the handsome young Norman with feelings of affection. Thereupon the lord of Elland challenged his guest to combat, and they fought with furious intent in the great hall of the mansion. The guilty wife was present, and, it was darkly hinted, rendered assistance to her paramour, who smote his opponent mortally in the breast with his dagger. When the house-knaves, hearing the sounds of the combat, forced their way into the hall; their master was lying on the floor with his life-blood oozing from him. The dying man rose upon his arm, and, dipping his hand in his blood, cast some drops upon Beaulay, and gasped, " Even as thou hast won this heritage, by such means it shall go from thee and all thy house." Saying which, Wilfrid of Elland fell back dead, and Hugo de Beaulay took possession of the Elland estates and name, and took to wife the woman whose beauty had caused this unhappy bloodshed.

Hugo of Elland fought hard for the Norman William, when the latter came over and assumed the English crown, and for his services was requited with the knightly dignity and the gift of large estates. But Sir Hugo perished miserably in 1069, in the great Saxon uprising, being slain by one whom he had dispossessed of his lands.

Thus far we have the record of tradition merely ; but when Sir John Elland comes upon the scene, we find ourselves in the region of reliable historical evidence. The descent from Hugo Beaulay to Sir John Elland is supposed to have been direct, though no authoritative proof thereof is extant. We know that Sir John's father was on the side of the Earl of Lancaster, in the disputes between Edward II. and that powerful noble, and that he had been taken prisoner and hanged soon after his leader's head was severed at Pontefract Castle, but of the history of the house of Elland from the time of Sir Hugo Elland's death in 1069, to the time of Sir John Elland's father, we know nothing.

The Sir John Elland with whom our story has mainly to do, distinguished himself against the Scots, and grew into high favour with Edward III. He was a broadly-built, huge man, skilled in the use of all warlike weapons, and remarkable no less for his furious passions than for his physical strength. He was a "good hater" and of a very revengeful disposition. The man who thwarted him was sure to be made to feel his vengeance. Sir John was wont to say that "he feared neither man, nor God, nor devil."

The story goes that from the time when the dying Wilfrid of Elland marked Hugo Beaulay with his blood, every member of the Elland race had borne upon his forehead three red spots, and it was said that the Sir John Elland of whom we now speak was no exception in this respect.

Be that as it may, Sir John Elland was a knight of dark deeds and unholy passions. He had been thrice married. First, to Alice, daughter of Sir Robert Lathom, who bore him several children; secondly, to Ann, daughter of——— Rygate, by whom he had no issue; and thirdly, to Olive ———, by whom he had a son Robert, who married Alice, daughter of Fitz-Eustace.

Sir John Elland was all-powerful within his own domain, and looked with a jealous eye upon such neighbouring lords as rivalled him in wealth. Sir Robert Beaumont, of Crossland Hall, was one of the most formidable of these rivals, and upon him accordingly Sir John Elland fastened his hatred, and strove with all his craft to work him some ill. Sir Robert was related by blood or marriage, with Hugh of Quarmby, and Lockwood of Lockwood, who both held manors in the neighbourhood, and were respected for their bravery. For some reason or other, Sir John Elland took it into his head to include the Beaumont, Quarmby, and Lockwood families in an atrocious scheme of violence. It has been suggested that Beaumont and his friends had inherited amongst them certain estates which Sir John had thought to obtain for himself, and that being disappointed in this he had sought to avenge himself upon them. The ballad before referred to makes another suggestion in regard to the cause of Sir John's wrath.

> "Some say that Eland sheriff was
> By Beaumont disobey'd,
> Which might him make for that trespass
> With him the worse appaid."

But let the reason be what it might, Sir John Elland one night summoned a number of friends and retainers, turbulent spirits and strong, and with them set out for Quarmby Hall, which place they assaulted and took possession of, and ruthlessly slew Hugh of Quarmby. This cruel deed done, they hurried on to Lockwood, and murdered Lockwood of Lockwood. They then marched across, in the dark night, to Crossland Hall, with intent to take the life of Sir Robert Beaumont; but the task was not so easy, for the ancestral mansion of the Beaumonts, unlike those of the Quarmbys and the Lockwoods, was surrounded by a moat, and the drawbridge was up, now that it was night. For a time they crept noiselessly about seeking for means of ingress, and after a while they chanced to see a serving-wench leave the hall to pay a secret visit to the neighbouring village, where probably she had a lover to meet. The girl let down the bridge and crossed it, and no sooner had she done so than Sir John Elland and his armed ruffians rushed forward, made their way over, and attacked the hall, bursting open the doors, and making fearful wreck wherever they went.

Sir Robert Beaumont and his lady were in their sleeping chamber, having retired for the night, but Sir John unceremoniously invaded their privacy, and, in spite of the screams and protestations of the affrighted wife, seized Sir Robert and dragged him down into the large hall. Meanwhile, the servants had all been roused from their slumbers, and hastily attiring and arming themselves, valiantly defended their master from the savage onslaughts of his enemy. A terrible struggle ensued, and as the torchlights threw their fitful flames hither and thither, many a brave retainer's blood was seen to besprinkle the floor. At length, Sir John Elland and his band overpowered their opponents, and binding Sir Robert Beaumont, they cut off his head in the presence of his innocent wife and children.

When this foul deed had been accomplished, Sir John Elland and his myrmidons sat down and compelled the servants of the house of Beaumont to bring them wine, and bread, and ale, and then they feasted themselves right merrily. The young and beautiful lady, whom they had so cruelly widowed, was forced to hand Sir John a tankard of wine, and he toasted her, and jested with her sorrows. Sir John also commanded the two young sons of Sir Robert Beaumont to eat with him ; and Adam, the eldest, who was about five years of age, would neither eat nor drink, but when Sir John offered him bread, the child threw it at the knight with disdain; at which Sir John waxed angry, and swore he would weed out the offspring of Sir Robert Beaumont's blood, as they weed out the weeds from the corn.

They feasted themselves far into the night, and then Sir John Elland and his band, after having committed these atrocious and horrible murders, wended their way back in the midnight darkness to Elland Hall, leaving desolate and wretched three homes, which but a few hours before had been peaceful and happy.

For many days afterwards, the country side rang with the news of the terrible deeds which the lord of Elland had wrought; but Sir John Elland was so much feared by his neighbours that none dared to move in the matter, and thus provoke his hostility. Not even the law was set in motion to bring the knight to answer for his murderous work.

Lady Beaumont, in sore anguish and distress, despatched two trusty messengers to Lancashire, to her relatives there, the Townleys and Breretons, to inform them of the sad thing that had happened, and she and her children, as well as the bereaved members of the Quarmby and Lockwood families, were received into the hospitable halls at Townley and Brereton, and continued to reside there in safety for many years.

As the heirs of the respective houses of Beaumont, Quarmby, and Lockwood grew up to manhood, they familiarised themselves with, and became great adepts in using, warlike weapons. They were all fine, stalwart fellows, and were of high courage and bold of speech. Often and often did they converse together on the wrongs which had been inflicted on their families by Sir John Elland; and many were the plans of revenge which they concerted from time to time.

All this while the Lord of Elland seemed to flourish with his ill-gotten wealth, and troubled himself little with thinking of what had become of the younger branches of the Beaumont, Quarmby, and Lockwood families. He was still sheriff, and held great sway in the county. His eldest son was a tall, handsome young fellow, and was already married, and had a son; and Sir John's eldest daughter had contracted marriage with one of the Saviles, of Howley Hall.

Nineteen years had passed away since the fatal day

when the halls of the Beaumonts, the Quarmbys, and the Lockwoods had been dyed with blood; and one day, as the three young men who now represented those houses, were walking together by the river at Townley, young Lockwood said to his companions, "It is time that we now betook ourselves to the country of our fathers, there to revenge us upon him who shed their blood." Adam of Beaumont, and his kinsman Quarmby, concurred in this, and straightway they set about planning some means of revenge, and put themselves in communication with certain persons favourable to their schemes, who lived in the neighbourhood of Quarmby.

Not long afterwards, two men named Haigh and Dawson, visited Townley Hall, and informed young Beaumont, Quarmby, and Lockwood of the doings of Sir John Elland. They were told that the knight kept his Sheriff's Turn at Brighouse, on an appointed day, and that on his way home he would have to pass Cromwelbottom wood, a lonely spot where he could be easily surprised.

Accordingly, by the day named, Haigh and Dawson had conducted the three young lords from Lancashire to the place of ambush, where they were to wait the coming of the sheriff. They waited long and patiently "beneath Brookfoot, a hill there is to Brighouse in the way,"

"Forth came they to the top of this,
There prying for their prey."

Presently, they spied Sir John riding forward up the lane towards them, and they suddenly confronted him. Sir John was startled somewhat at their appearance, but doffed his bonnet to them in courtesy, and was about to proceed.

"Thy courtesy avails thee not, Sir knight," said Adam of Beaumont, stepping forward and stopping Sir John's progress.

"Who are ye?" asked Sir John, fiercely. "Thieves— or assassins?"

"Neither thieves nor assassins, Sir John Elland, of Elland," said young Beaumont, "but the avengers of blood."

Sir John turned pale.

"Who are ye, I say?" he repeated, excitedly.

"I am the son of that Sir Robert Beaumont who was slain by thee," said Adam of Beaumont; "and these two are my kinsmen come to revenge themselves upon thee for the murder of Hugh of Quarmby, and Lockwood of Lockwood, their fathers."

"This is the chick who cast the bread in my face," muttered Sir John to himself, as he looked on the determined countenance of the heir of the Beaumonts. "Why did I not exterminate the whole brood?" Then he retreated a step, and, something of his old ferocity coming to his aid, he said, "Beware what ye do, young men; there are those who will inflict full and swift punishment upon you, if you work me any ill."

"We reck not what others may do," cried Quarmby; "our reckoning is with thee."

"Have at him," urged Lockwood.

That moment Sir John sprang like a tiger towards Adam of Beaumont, and would have cloven his head with his sword, but for the swift interference of Quarmby and Lockwood, the latter of whom struck the weapon from the knight's hand, while the former seized and pinioned his arms. Then they set up their fathers' murderer, their swords pierced him through and through, and he fell dead at their feet.

And now that Sir John Elland was done to death, his slayers mounted themselves upon their horses and fled to the fells of Furness, and there they remained for a considerable time. Their thirst for revenge was not yet satisfied, however; they had made up their minds to wipe the race of Elland from the face of the earth.

There was now another Lord of Elland instated at Elland Hall—the eldest son of the dead Sir John—he who had married a daughter of the house of Savile. He also was Sir John, but of a much different disposition to the one who was deceased. Young Sir John and his lady were greatly beloved for their benevolence and kindness, and their neighbours looked upon them with much favour.

On the Palm Sunday evening that followed the murder of Sir John the father, Adam of Beaumont, Quarmby of Quarmby, and Lockwood of Lockwood, reappeared in the neighbourhood, along with their companion Lacy, taking themselves "about the mirke midnight" to "Eland miln." They broke into the mill house and lay concealed there until the morning, when they were discovered by the miller's wife, who had come thither in haste for some corn. They seized and bound her; and after a while the miller himself, impatient of his wife's delay, came with a cudgel to look for her, and they seized and bound him also.

Beaumont, Quarmby, Lockwood, and Lacy, were now prepared for the arrival of the young knight, who would be compelled to pass that way on his return from Bothom Hall, whither he went by Savile Gate twice a year.

> "The drought had made the water small,
>   The stakes appeared dry;
> The knight, his wife, and servants all,
>   Came down the dam thereby."

As soon as the party came near, Adam of Beaumont rushed forth from the mill, bow in hand, and shot at the knight, hitting him in the breast-plate.

"Cousin, you shoot wide," exclaimed Lockwood, as he himself let fly an arrow at Sir John, but was no more successful than Beaumont had been. Another shot followed quickly from the same bow, however, and this time the arrow passed through the young knight's head, and he was killed. His little son was also so wounded, that he lived not many hours.

Beaumont and his fellow-murderers now took flight again; going by Whittle Lane End, to the old Earth Gate. Then they made their way to Annely Wood, and there hid themselves.

As soon as the people of Elland heard of the murderous deeds that had been done, they roused themselves and followed in fierce pursuit of the fugitives. They armed themselves with "bows and shafts," and clubs, and "rusty bills, that saw no sun that year." Beaumont, Quarmby, and Lockwood saw their pursuers coming, and valiantly prepared to defend themselves, and so desperately did they fight, that they were able to stave their opponents off, and make further flight. They now held their way towards Huddersfield, all but Quarmby, who was found nearly dead in Annely Wood. There he was slain outright. Lockwood retired to a solitary place called Camel, near Cawthorn (now Cannon Hall), where, after a desperate resistance, he was subsequently taken by the sheriff and his men, and cruelly put to death, to the utter extirpation of the ancient family of Lockwood of Lockwood. Adam of Beaumont was more fortunate. He escaped to France, and by some means or other got into the service of the knights of Rhodes. He resided sometimes at Rhodes with the knights, and sometimes in Hungary, where, in one of the engagements against the Turks, he honourably terminated his life.

The Elland estates, which had been gained and kept by so many crimes, passed into the possession of the Saviles.

THE STORY OF PROPHET WROE.

SOMETIME during the first decade of the present century, a Spanish gentleman named Don Manuel Alvarez Espriella paid a visit to this country, and, being a man of observation and ability, was prompted when he returned to his native land to publish an account of the many strange and wonderful things he had seen in our "tight little island." The thing that seemed to give Don Manuel the most astonishment was that in England, "where Catholic Christians were so heartily despised for superstition; in England, where the people think themselves so highly enlightened,—in this country of reason and philosophy, and free inquiry," it should have been possible to have got together a large and influential following who believed in and pledged themselves to support the wild doctrines preached by Joanna Southcott. "This phrensy would have been speedily cured in our country," says the Spaniard; "bread and water, a solitary cell, and a little wholesome discipline, are specifics in such cases."

It is certain, however, that "this phrensy" was not "speedily cured" in England. Joanna Southcott failed to fulfil the prophecies she uttered concerning herself—she neither gave birth to the promised Shiloh, nor asserted her power to live for ever—but the infatuated people who had been deluded by her visions and prophecies still believed in her teachings, and found excuses for the disappointment she had landed them in by her dying childless. Now that Joanna was dead, the prophets who succeeded her proclaimed to their brethren that there would one day be a resurrection of Joanna's body, and that she would still be the mother of the promised Shiloh. Such, it may be presumed, is the dream of the small remnant of Southcottians which still holds together, and worships in peaceful seclusion, some in the "Mansion" erected for Prophet Wroe, near Wakefield, some in Rossendale, and some in other remote places. But the sect is gradually dying out, it would appear; they have no prophet or prophetess to-day who is bold enough to go forth amongst the people and declare the Gospel according to Joanna.

It was given to the West Riding of Yorkshire, however, to produce a successor worthy of the great Joanna, in the person of John Wroe, who was born at Bowling, and baptised in the Bradford Parish Church in the year 1782. When Joanna Southcott died, in 1814, Wroe would be thirty-two years of age. He was to some extent acquainted with the doctrines of the Joannas, but it was not until some five years after the death of Joanna that Wroe began to aspire to the mantle of the prophetess. But John was about that time "at his wit's end" what to do in order to pick up an easy livelihood; trade had turned its back upon him, or *vice versa*, and it was necessary that he should direct his attention to something fresh. John had been in partnership with his father for some time, as worsted manufacturer, coal proprietor, and farmer; but the father, for some reason or other, had found it necessary to oust his son from the firm, and quarrels had ensued. Subsequently, John took to wool-combing, and engaged apprentices, but before long he found himself in the Bankruptcy Court, and knew not which way to turn.

Wroe had been married several years at this date, he

having found a wife in the daughter of Benjamin Appleby, of Farsley Mills, near Leeds. Mrs. Wroe was a good-looking woman, and proved a valuable helpmeet to John, not only in his pre-Joannian days, but after he assumed the rôle of the prophet. In 1819 Wroe was attacked by fever, and Dr. Field, who attended him, advised Mrs. Wroe to prevail on him to seek spiritual comfort, and settle his affairs. At first Wroe asked for some Methodist preachers to be sent to him, but although his wife invited four of them to come, they all declined. Mrs. Wroe then asked her husband to see a clergyman of the Church; but he begged her to read him some chapters from the Bible, "and," said he, " I will see what I can do for myself."

He now began to recover, but as he lay on his sick bed thinking of the worldly surroundings which would be his on reaching convalescence, he communed much with his spirit, and gradually shaped out a new career for himself. As soon as he was able to walk about he was to be seen wandering in the fields and lanes with his Bible in his hand, spelling out the prophetic books as well as he could, and filling his mind with those scriptural texts and phrases which he was afterwards to turn to profitable account. His habits became nocturnal, he rambled in the fields in the night-time, and saw visions. He was seized with many epileptic fits about this time, and used to lie in a state of trance for many hours at a stretch. The first of these trances, he tells us, came on about two o'clock in the morning of November 12th, 1819, as he walked in the fields, "when," he says, "a woman came to me and tossed me up and down in the field. I endeavoured to lay hold of her, but could not; I therefore knew it was a spirit." It has been suggested that the "spirit" in question might have been his wife, who, it is natural to suppose, would resent this kind of night rambling; but is it not more likely that the "spirit" was some bovine creature angered at the

Q

unctuous intrusion of the prophet upon his domain?   After this, Wroe remained in bed twelve hours, and saw more visions.

Six days later he had another fit, and lost his sight and power of speech.   On regaining consciousness he was moved to write on a black board the particulars of the vision he had had.   He said he had walked about a mile down a lane where there were large numbers of oxen, who tossed their horns and frightened him to tears.   "An angel met me," he says, "and he took me to a large place, where I saw a great number of books, placed on their edges, having gilt letters.   There also appeared large altars, full of letters, but I could not read them.   I begged that I might be enabled to read and understand what I had seen; and there appeared another, the letters of which were black print or Old English, with the word Jeremiah on the top of it, and the letter L.   I wrote on the wall with my fingers at the time, as I lay in bed; the people who were present observing me, concluded that I wished to write (I was dumb, for my tongue was fastened in my mouth as before); they gave me a piece of board and chalk, and I wrote Jeremiah, 50th chapter.   I had never read this chapter, or heard it read, or seen it before, to my recollection; but when I came to myself I could, without looking at it, repeat nearly every word in it."

On the 29th of November, and again on the 14th December, he had other fits, accompanied by visions.   On the latter occasion, he says, "I was again struck blind at about ten o'clock in the forenoon, and remained more like a corpse than a living man for twenty-four hours, when I came to myself by degrees, but continued blind for five days.   After many things, the angel said to me, 'Thou shalt be blind for six days, and on the seventh day thy father shall come to thee, and many people with him; he shall lay his right thumb on thy right eye, and his fourth finger on thy left, as a token that he remembers his former sins and wickedness; and if not, it will be a witness against him at the Day of Judgment, and thou shalt receive thy sight.' During the six days that I was blind my wife at one time was reading a hymn for me; when she had read it I desired her to read it again, but before she had done so I fainted, and saw the elements separated, and there appeared before me a large open square. I saw our Saviour nailed on the Cross, and the tears trickling down His face, and at that time I thought He was weeping for the wicked people upon earth. An angel then appeared, holding a man by a single hair of his head, who had a very large sword in his hand, which he waved backward and forward. I then saw a pair of scales let down to the earth, and a great bundle, which was placed in one side of the scales, which I thought represented the sins of the people, and then saw a great number of weights placed in the other; but the bundle was so much heavier that the weights bounced out and the scales were drawn up into heaven. Then the man that was held by the hair of his head by the angel brandished his sword six or seven times, as formerly, and disappeared. I afterwards saw Moses and Aaron, accompanied by a great number of people, attended by angels, and I heard such delightful music as it would be impossible to describe. There was darkness over the place soon after, and I lost sight of all in a moment."

It is related that Wroe continued with his eyes closed for six days, and on the seventh his father came and placed his thumb on his right eye, and his fourth finger on his left, and John opened his eyes and fainted. John's cousin asked him how he felt before his sight was restored? and John answered, "I got a glance of that glorious place, and at that instant my sight returned."

Wroe now felt, or pretended to feel, that he had been selected by the Almighty for the working out of some divine mission, but it was a considerable time before he could discover the precise nature of that mission. One night, however, as he lay in bed, he awoke and saw the words, " A. A. Rabbi, Rabbi, Rabbi," written in gilt letters on a black board, and placed on the tester of his bedstead. He then concluded that he was meant to be sent amongst the Jews, and conceived the notion that he had been commanded to "testify" in England for three years, "with his hat on his head," after which he was to join the Jews altogether. He now visited Huddersfield, Manchester, and Liverpool, and mixed amongst the Jews of those towns, but without making any deep impression. This was in 1820. Meanwhile, he went on with his visions, and began to utter predictions in regard to many things. Of course, some of his predictions came true—it could not be otherwise—and the more ignorant and superstitious of the people began to believe that John was endowed with supernatural power. His wife's brother was ill in bed, and John sent his wife to tell him he would die; and die the brother did, in a few days afterwards. On another occasion, John's cousin and employer refused to give him any more work, telling him he was more fit to be a preacher than a woolcomber; thereupon the prophet swooned away, and on recovering himself, pointed to the son of his employer and said in a solemn voice: "Take notice of that young man: he will never do any more work; he will never pay another man his wages." The young man was immediately afterwards taken ill and died.

Wroe's reputation spread, and he set about finding a sufficient field for the employment of his prophetic power. He sought to ally himself with the followers of Joanna Southcott. George Turner had succeeded Joanna as the head of the sect, and on Turner visiting Bradford in 1820, Wroe and he came to an arrangement whereby Wroe was to confine his labours to the conversion of the public, while Turner kept exclusively to the elect.

The year 1822 was an eventful one for Wroe. He had by this time obtained a complete ascendancy over the Bradford Joannas, and with the audacity that generally characterised his actions presumed to give forth a prophecy in direct opposition to the prophetic utterances of Turner, the head of their church. Turner had announced that on the 14th of October in that year, the anniversary of Joanna Southcott's death, they would witness the advent of the promised Shiloh. Wroe knew better than to pin himself down to an early date like this, and knew, moreover, that the failure of the prediction would bring discredit upon Turner, so on the 25th August he went down, full of prophecy and fervour, to the meeting-house of the Joannas in Aldermanbury, Bradford, and thus delivered himself :— " You are expecting Shiloh to appear and be amongst you on a certain day ; but I tell you He will not ; and many of the believers will fall off, not merely one or two in a society, but whole societies will fall away. Yet I do not doubt that the visitation to George Turner is of God ; and as a testimony of which, I will give in my name among you."

There was great commotion amongst the Bradford Joannas at this astounding declaration, but the community as a body were not disposed to accept Wroe as their prophet. The next Sunday evening he went to the meeting again, and fell into a trance before the eyes of the whole assembly. On awaking he told the doubting congregation that an angel had appeared to him and commanded him to act as their prophet, but only two persons could be got to give in their adhesion to him even then. Wroe was not to be easily thwarted in his purpose, however, so on the succeeding Sunday night he hit upon a new method of winning the brethren over to his side. He caused two men to take their stand, one on each side of the archway leading into the second room of the meeting-house. Each of the two men held a sword, and the swords were united at the points, so that the congregation, to enter, had to pass under the swords. Wroe entered last of all. Then the men pointed their swords at his breast, saying, "The sword of the Lord is against thee." Wroe instantly fell on his knees, and prayed aloud that if his mission were not divine, the swords might fall and smite him asunder. Wroe then stood up and walked to the second archway, the men with the swords stepping backwards before him, still with their swords at his breast. In this strange position he stood and addressed the congregation on the high and holy nature of his mission, and, when when all was over, he desired all who believed in him to pass under the swords, and the great majority of the people obeyed.

From this time forward, Wroe assumed the leadership of the Bradford Joannas; and members of the sect at Ashton-under-Lyne, Stockport, Sheffield, Colne, and other places, subsequently became converted to Wroe's mission.

Wroe now employed himself solely in the work of the mission, and doubtless found it more profitable, from a pecuniary point of view, than anything he had had in hand for a long time. Mrs. Wroe assisted him in his ministrations, and is said to have been a superior preacher to the prophet. Wroe was continually seeing fresh visions, and giving the details thereof in penny tracts. He did not, so far as we know, emulate the founder of the sect in the manner of delivering his prophetic messages in rhyme. She used to intersperse her visionary maunderings with scraps of doggerel rhyme. Wroe stuck to plain—very plain—prose.

Wroe was about as illiterate as Joanna; neither of them could write a grammatical sentence; reading was a difficulty to both. Wroe spoke in the Yorkshire dialect, and pretty broadly too, but his mind was so full of his subject that he could hold forth at great length on the promised Southcottian millennium, and never failed to unfold the prophecies and open the seals of the Apocalypse. His denunciations of his Satanic Majesty, too, were something marvellous in their way; and after he had blackened the character of the Father of Lies to his heart's content, he would speak in glowing terms of the thousand years during which Satan would be bound. John was a hale and stalwart man at this time, and dressed, and commanded his followers to dress, in a style that rendered them peculiarly conspicuous. The prophet wore a blue coat, drab pantaloons, and a slouch hat; and the fact that the male Joannas wore their beards at a time when beards were altogether out of fashion, caused them to be much noticed, not only by the hordes of boys who used to shout after them, but by everybody. These were the people who maintained that Joanna Southcott was the woman mentioned in the Revelation, with the moon under her feet, and on her head a crown of twelve stars. Almost as odd a character as John was a preaching companion of his, named Tillotson. John often took Tillotson with him on his preaching rounds, and when the crowd gathered to hear them happened to be very large, the preachers separated, Wroe addressing one portion of the assembly and Tillotson the other. At the conclusion of the service the ample bonnet of John never failed to be taken round as a collection-box. There was probably some special virtue in John's hat, for he would not permit any other person's head-covering to be sent round. John professed a certain contempt for money, for all that, and did not carry any about with him. His wife or an attendant paid all dues and demands, tolls, &c., and John only condescended to bring his mind down to money matters when collection time came round.

As soon as John had made himself sure of the fidelity of his followers, he began to announce his intention of proceeding upon his mission to the Jews. Large sums of money were raised for him, and on the 27th of April he embarked at Liverpool, in the brig Doris, for Gibraltar, in company with Robert Harling, of Thornhill.   They reached Gibraltar on the 20th May, and on the day following the ship returned to England, and Harling with it, the prospect of the mission not being to Robert's liking.   On the 31st of May Wroe appeared in the synagogue of the Jews and delivered his testimony to them, but they turned him out, and the Governor of Gibraltar had to forbid him to preach in public.   He was offered a free passage to England, however, on condition that he would depart at once, and John accepted the offer, and returned home, not, however, before he had invaded the Roman Catholic churches and left on their altars copies of his prophecies.   One of these prophecies ran thus :—

"I, Jesus from heaven, command thee, John Wroe, to warn the kingdom of Spain that if they return not from their wicked ways of worshipping images made with men's hands, and bowing before them, I will draw my two-edged sword against them, and it shall turn every way until I have destroyed them.   But who is this that has caused them to err? They have hearkened unto their priests instead of hearkening unto me.   Now, I will tell you what I will do unto your priests: I will chase them as hounds chase a fox, until I utterly destroy them, and the remnant that is left shall slay your king, and they shall know that I have sent this unto them by my servant."

During his two months' stay at Gibraltar he excited a good deal of enmity by his strange proceedings.   He began to address the Irish Roman Catholic soldiers, but the adjutant turned him out, and the priests had to thrust him from their cathedral and lock the doors behind him.   He was several times threatened with a pistol, and one day an enraged woman threw a pitcher out of a window at his head, but missed him.

On the 23rd of August Wroe landed at Liverpool again, and for the next few weeks employed himself with visiting the Southcottian flocks at Ashton-under-Lyne and Birmingham. On the 12th of October, in company with William Lees, he sailed for the continent, and reached Paris on the 16th, and began to preach in the Yorkshire dialect to the Parisians in the Palais Royal. From Paris the wandering Joannas went to Strasburg, then to Vienna, and over the Sommering Pass to Trieste. After this, they proceeded to Venice, Verona, Vicenza, and Milan, at each of which places they astonished the people by "testifying" to them. On leaving Milan they made their way back to Paris, and came home by way of Amiens and Calais. At the latter place they were arrested, by order of the Minister of the Interior, and the police overhauled their boxes, but finding nothing but tracts on religious subjects, they were allowed to depart. John was probably tired of tract distributing by this time, for he received a "command" to tear the whole of his collection of tracts, prophecies, and denunciations into small pieces, and scatter them contemptuously about the streets of Calais.

John and William had a very rough passage across the channel, and William became much depressed, but the prophet cheered him up by telling him that before they reached home he would see the young woman who was to be his wife. Truly enough, at Gravesend, where Wroe and Lees stayed to preach, Lees met for the first time "the enchanting Cordelia Chenne," whom he subsequently married.

In the early part of 1824 Prophet Wroe was again busy amongst the faithful in Bradford. In January of that year he received a communication from "the Spirit," directing him to spend forty days in a dark hole, and eat nothing but butter and honey, and drink nothing but milk. How he acquitted himself in this ordeal is not recorded, but he always contrived to satisfy his followers. The popular mind, however, could see nothing but fanatical foolery in John's trances and prophecies, and he was not treated with the reverence and respect which a prophet ought to be capable of inspiring. The boys used to call him "Pudding Wroe," and shouted the name after him as he passed along the streets. It was said that on awaking from one of his long trances and being asked what he could eat or fancy, his invariable answer was, "Nowt but puddin'." One day, after having this phrase dinned into his ears to a provoking degree, he went home in a bad temper. The table was laid for dinner, and his wife and children were ready in their places. "What is there for dinner to-day?" asked the prophet. "Nowt but puddin'," shouted the unthinking children. Wroe flew into a passion, and said to his wife, "I'll tell tha what, lass, I weant have yond stuff called puddin' onny more." "Whah, lad, what is t' barns to call it, then?" said Mrs. Wroe. "They mun call it *soft meyt*," answered John.

In February, 1824, the prophet gave it forth that he would be baptised in the River Aire, at Apperley Bridge, and that he would on that occasion be endowed with miraculous power, and would divide the water and walk across the river dryshod. The following is a copy of the placard which Wroe caused to be posted in the neighbourhood of Bradford at that time :—

The public are respectfully informed
that
JOHN WROE,
the Prophet of the Lord,
will be
Publicly Baptised in the River Aire,
near Idle Thorpe,
At half-past one o'clock,
on Sunday, the 29th day of the 2nd month, 1824, at which holy ordinance appropriate hymns (accompanied by a select band of music) will be sung, and immediately after
WILLIAM TWIGG,
one of the witnesses mentioned in Revelation, chap. ii., will preach the everlasting Gospel, as revealed by the Redeemer of the World.

On the day named, Wroe and his band of followers assembled at the house of William Smith, at Thorp Garth, Idle, and walked in procession, headed by a band of music, to the place indicated. Thirty thousand people assembled that cold February day to witness the prophet's performance.

"Both sides of the river," says a contemporary record, "were lined with persons of various ages and denominations. The Spirit had given John a sign that on his entering the water the sun should shine; for during the two preceding days the weather was extremely cold, with severe frost accompanied with snow. The Sunday forenoon on which the ceremony was to take place continued very wet till noon, and when Wroe arrived at the brink of the river the sun was still veiled. He walked down the river side, intending to delay till the clouds broke; but the people, thinking that he was afraid of the cold water, roared at him, 'He durs'n't go in! He's runnin' away!' They were all disposed to view the fun, and they endeavoured to stop Wroe's further progress. Some friends followed him, urging him not to disappoint the crowd, and he found that he had better put a bold face on it, and go in. The sun just then shone forth with a degree of warmth most unusual at that season of the year. The musicians and singers began to play and sing, and he descended into the water. But when preparing to do so, a cry was raised by the multitude, 'Drown him!' The same words were uttered by some young men who had placed themselves on the branches of a tree adjacent to the river. John commanded them, in the name of the Lord, to come down. One of them, named Hudson, who was formerly John's apprentice, cursed him. Immediately that part of the bank on which the tree grew gave way, and all were precipitated into the river. None of them were drowned, but some had five or six miles to travel home in their wet clothes; and Hudson, who had cursed John, died within a few days after. When

John came out of the water the musicians and singers again performed."

But the crowd felt they had been trifled with ; they had come to see John divide the waters, and the river had continued to flow on in its usual course. They, therefore, set upon the prophet, and pelted him and his flock with mud, making them beat an ignominious retreat.

On the 17th of April following, Wroe made himself conspicuous at Ashton-under-Lyne, where, at a meeting-house of the Joannas, he was publicly "circumcised," in the presence of the congregation, the exhibition being prefaced by the usual musical performances. The report now got abroad that the prophet enjoined circumcision on all his male adherents, and several children were said to have died in consequence. Wroe denied the reports as to these deaths, "with one exception," and that was in regard to the child of Robert Grimshaw, of Hurst Brook, near Ashton. The child died, and Henry Lees, the operator, was tried at the assizes for manslaughter, but acquitted, the evidence not being conclusive as to Lees having caused the child's death.

On the 30th of August, Wroe was again baptised in the river Medlock, near Park Bridge, on which occasion he was left unmolested by the mob. On leaving the river he stood with one foot in the water, and the other on the land, raised his hands to heaven, and swore that there should be no more time—in imitation of the angel described in Revelation x. 5, 6.

On the 11th September the prophet received a command to wander in the fields for fourteen days, and live on nuts, wheat, blackberries, hips, herbs, and water, and this "command" he professed to execute. On completing his fourteen days' wanderings he told his wife that "he had had a command from God that she should destroy all pictures, portraits, or likenesses of anything He had created or caused to grow, whether of iron, stone, wood, cloth, or paper, and everything of a black colour that could be found within the house." His wife immediately obeyed.

On Sunday, the 26th September, Wroe was again at Bradford. He had done so many strange things to take the attention of the public about this time, that an immense crowd of people assembled to hear him, and so much were they opposed to his doctrines, that they assaulted him and some of his principal followers when the service was over. John left the meeting-house accompanied by Mary Brear and Elizabeth Elsworth, and before they had proceeded many yards they were pushed and hustled by the crowd. They made their way to the New Inn, however, where horses were waiting in readiness for the prophet and a companion (Joseph Brear), but the mob pushed forward, and John had to make his escape by the back door. Wroe was seen as soon as he got into Great Horton-road, and the cry was raised, "Kill him! kill him!" Thousands of persons pursued him, and he was surrounded. "That's the devil who says he's been living o' hips an' haws, an' wheat an' nuts, for fourteen days!" shouted the ironical crowd. They pulled the prophet from his horse, struck him, threw stones at him, tore his clothes, and used him very badly. If it had not been for a storm of rain coming on and dispersing the crowd, he might never have escaped alive; as it was, he reached the house of his friend Moses Elsworth, at Horton, in a pitiable condition; "nearly his whole body was black; he had also one of his eyes much discoloured, and received a cut on his face from a stone." The next day, John obtained warrants against nineteen of the rioters, and they were severally bound over to keep the peace for twelve months.

Yorkshire was becoming rather a hot place for the prophet, so he had a revelation to the following purport:— "Go thou to Tozer, and stand before him, and prophesy, with thy rod in thy hand, and say, 'Thus saith the Lord, the Lord thy God has showed thee many things; and for this end wast thou born. The seal thou hast received thou shalt be able to retain; but thy body shall go to the dust, and thou shalt put on incorruption at the first resurrection. . . . Thou shalt be a witness for Joanna, and thou shalt come with her, and at that day thou shalt be great unto the ends of the earth.'"

In obedience to this command, John, with his faithful friend William Lees, went to London, and presented himself before the congregation of Mr. Lindsay, the chief prophet of the sect in the metropolis. Tozer was Lindsay's head man, and claimed to be "The man clothed in linen, with the writer's inkhorn," spoken of by the prophet Ezekiel. Now when William Lees appeared before Tozer with a white surplice on and an ink-bottle at his side, Tozer felt that the Yorkshireman meant mischief. After wrestling in prayer for a brief space, Wroe stood up and said, "Thus saith the Lord, There are in this place those whose places shall be taken by others who have mocked and despised them. None shall enter but such as are circumcised or married." Lindsay was confused, and knocked over his inkstand, and Tozer made a little speech of conciliation. In the afternoon Wroe was at Lindsay's chapel again, and the rival prophets got challenging and defying each other. "I say, in the name of the Lord, you shall shave!" cried Lindsay against Wroe. Then Wroe took his prophetic rod, and thrusting it towards Lindsay, thundered forth, "Dost thou come to defy Israel? The Lord rebuke thee, Satan."

But Wroe was the master of Lindsay in the art of prophecy, and in the end he became the recognised head of the whole of the Southcottian brethren. John then told his people that his mission would last forty years, and that at the end of that time Shiloh would come. The forty years have now more than elapsed, and the prophet is dead, and the promised Shiloh is still to come.

In 1830 John told his followers that he had received orders from heaven that seven virgins should be delivered to him, to comfort and cherish him. "Three of his believers at once gave him up their daughters," says Mr. Baring Gould. "With these poor girls and some married women, Wroe wandered from place to place. They were with him in Kent, in Devonshire, in Lancashire, and Yorkshire—wherever Wroe pretended that he was called. The matter became scandalous, and the confidence of several of the members of the community was shaken. The girls were questioned, and made shocking disclosures. Two of the society, named Masterman and Walker, rose in the congregation at Ashton, on February 27th, 1831, and charged him with profligacy. Wroe could not stand against the storm; he escaped through a trap-door in the orchestra, amidst cat-calls, jeers, and howls. He remained secreted in Ashton a few days, and then left the place for ever."

Shortly after this the prophet informed his faithful adherent Lees, that he was called by the Spirit on a mission, but that he had no funds. Lees thereupon called a covenant-meeting, and a sum of £80 was raised, and placed at the prophet's disposal. Wroe now disappeared on his "mission." A short time afterwards, Lees met a friend who asked him what had become of the prophet? "He has gone on a mission," replied Lees. "Come with me to Manchester, and I will show you what sort of a 'mission' he's gone upon," said Lees' friend. Lees was thus persuaded to go to Manchester, and was taken to a public-house, where the prophet was revealed to him sitting by the fire in his low-crowned hat and long coat, between two common women, with whom he was drinking hot whisky and water. The landlord said Wroe had been there several days. This resulted in Lees renouncing the prophet and all his works. He went home, burned his white robe, destroyed all his books and tracts belonging to the society, shaved off his beard, and the very next Sunday was worshipping at his parish church. But a further cause of anger against the prophet was to follow. Lees' daughter gave promise of becoming a mother by Wroe. The prophet declared that the child that would be born would be the promised Shiloh, but Lees was not to be appeased by such mockeries any longer, so he turned Wroe out of his house. The child proved to be a girl. Lees afterwards took a gun and attempted to shoot Wroe, but the ball missed its mark.

These scandals getting abroad, led to the prophet receiving a warm reception when he next set foot in Bradford. The mob broke into his tabernacle, smashed the windows and benches, and would have maltreated Wroe, but he took care to escape.

At Pudsey, when he was supposed to be on a fourteen days' mission, and was thought to be fasting and praying, he was discovered in the middle of a corn-field, eating new potatoes and mutton chops, and drinking wine which his wife had secretly brought to him. The Pudseyites could not stand this, but seized him, carried him in triumph through the village, set him on a donkey, tied a rope round his body, and ducked him in a horse-pond. Another time, when he was supposed to be in a trance at home, at Bowling, some one discovered him at night, when the house was closed against all comers, sitting up eating beefsteak, pickled cabbage, and oat-cake.

In 1854 the prophet informed his followers that he was commanded by the Lord to build a mansion, and the elders of the Church sat in council, and determined to let Wroe have what they called the Flying Roll money, for the building of his mansion. This fund was contributed to by all the " sealed " members, and at that time amounted to over £2,000. It was estimated that the full number of members would then be about 6,000, of whom 700 were in Ireland.

Wroe now set about collecting additional funds. Subscription books were sent to all the sanctuaries, and every member was to give not less than 10 per cent. of his income. A piece of land was bought near Wakefield, and the building of the house was begun, no architect being employed. It was to be "built as the Spirit directed." The Melbourne Town Hall seems to have been imitated, however; Wroe having been impressed with that building while on a visit to Australia, which continent he visited four times—in 1850, 1854, 1859, and 1862. The mansion was completed according to the directions of Mr. Thorpe, a Wakefield architect, and the original idea was much extended when John saw that he was getting much more money than he had ever expected. John bought a farm of upwards of 100 acres, which was added to the estate. The prophet had this conveyed to himself direct: a proceeding which caused some uneasiness amongst the community, and drew forth a protest from them. Wroe then drew up a will conveying the estate to the society, but a fortnight afterwards this disposition was secretly revoked by another will.

Wroe had always some plausible way of getting over the objections of his flock, however, and when he died, in 1862, in Australia, it was found that the houses and lands which they had subscribed for, were willed and disposed of as his own. The mansion and ninety-eight acres of land were devised to his grandson, James Wroe, who now owns the property, but lets it to the society at a good rental.

Wroe found many adherents both in Australia and America. He paid four visits to each continent, and no doubt derived both pleasure and profit from his trips. He visited America in 1840, 1848, 1853, and 1859. His

R

wife died, at the age of seventy-four, just a fortnight after he set sail for America in 1853. During his travels he assumed various names and titles. At one time he called himself Johanan Asreal; at another time he went by the name of Yokkow, or Yockaman—a corruption, probably, of the word Yorkshireman.

While on his last voyage to Australia, John had a fall on the deck of the ship, and dislocated his shoulder, which was never right again. He took with him to Australia, as companion and secretary, a person named Benjamin Eddowes, and the two made the tour of many of the principal Australian cities. During their stay at Fitzroy, Wroe was seized with sudden illness on returning from a walk, fell forward on the floor, and was taken up a corpse. Eddowes was now left to settle the prophet's affairs, which was a rather difficult matter; the Melbourne members demanding their subscriptions back, because Wroe had falsified one of his own prophecies by dying, he having declared that he would live for ever. The secretary felt it prudent to make his escape, and whether he brought back with him much or little money, or to what purpose he put it when he got back to England, we have no means of knowing.

It is hardly credible that, after so many failures on the part of Joanna Southcott, Wroe, and other leaders of the sect, to fulfil in their own persons, or to point to the fulfilment in any other form, of the many prophecies they uttered concerning themselves and the world in general, there should still remain in existence the least remnant of the faith of the Joannas; but there is still a little band of followers clinging to this strange belief, and holding regular worship in the "mansion," but very few elsewhere. A superstitious belief of this kind seems altogether out of place in modern times, and the wonder is that it has survived all the vicissitudes it has had to bear with.

THE STORY OF BOLD NEVISON, THE
HIGHWAYMAN.

IT is still a common thing in the country districts of Yorkshire, to hear an angered dame allude to an offending youngster as a "regular Nevison." This is a term of comparison and reproach that has survived from the middle of the seventeenth century, and it is not likely that those who use it are fully aware of its import —it probably never occurs to them that the original Nevison was one of the most notorious highwaymen who ever stopped a coach or purloined a purse. Such, however, was the case, and to Yorkshire belonged the honour or dishonour of having given him birth. Living at a time when highwaymen were numerous, and when their intrepidity and daring formed a daily subject of conversation amongst all classes, William Nevison found the period peculiarly suited to his taste and capabilities. Not Claude Duval himself, that naughtiest of pages and most courteous of robbers, could excel Nevison in gallantry and suavity of demeanour: the great Dick Turpin was not a more adroit horseman. The prominent part which Nevison played during the latter portion of the reign of Charles II., on the highways of the North, is testified by Macaulay in his "History of England." "It was related of William Nevison, the great Yorkshire robber," says the historian, "that he levied a quarterly tribute on all the northern drovers, and, in return, not only spared them himself, but protected them against all other thieves; that he demanded purses in the most courteous manner; that he gave largely to the poor, what he had taken from the rich; and that his life was once spared by the Royal clemency."

This notorious ruffian was born in Pontefract, in the year 1639, of "well-reputed, honest, and reasonably estated parents," we are told. Up to the age of fourteen, he was considered an intelligent, hopeful, honest lad, and went to school, and made such progress in learning as satisfied his parents, and gave promise for the future. The bad propensities which so distinguished his after career, however, now began to be manifested, and Nevison made the acquaintance of a number of disreputable youths of his own age, in whose company he spent much time and wrought much mischief. His first act of robbery was committed at his own home, from whence he stole a silver spoon. His father discovered the theft, and was so incensed at the act, that he desired the schoolmaster, who had the training of William in hand, to administer to the lad a severe punishment. This the schoolmaster did, and did it so well, that his pupil writhed under the chastisement, and made a desperate resolve to be revenged upon him. The next night, while his parents were fast asleep, Nevison got up before daybreak, crept softly to the paternal bedchamber, took the key of the money cupboard from his father's pocket, stole downstairs, opened the cupboard, and supplied himself with a sum of about ten pounds from his father's savings. This done, Nevison proceeded to a field in the rear of the schoolmaster's house, where the pedagogue's favourite horse was reposing. He took the horse, placed upon it a saddle and bridle he had brought from his father's stable, mounted the animal, and rode off exultant in the direction of London. On the evening of the fourth succeeding day, Nevison found himself nearing the Metropolis, and, under cover of the darkness, he halted, cut the throat of the faithful beast which had brought him thither, and walked forward into the great city, alone and unknown.

Nevison did not at first give himself up to lawlessness and crime, but, changing his name and obtaining a fresh suit of clothes, set himself to procure a situation, and was fortunate enough to get engaged by a brewer. He remained with this gentleman between two and three years, without being suspected of dishonest intentions. Nevison was patient, however, and only waited his opportunity; it was not that he had become reformed in mind. The opportunity at last arrived. The brewer's cashier one night took to imbibing his master's liquor so freely that he became very drunk, and fell asleep, and while he remained in this helpless state of somnolence, Nevison stole into the counting-house, and rifled the cash-box of all the cash it contained, which amounted to not less than £200.

This robbery accomplished, Nevison was rapidly off and away, and the brewer and the emissaries of the law sought high and low for the lusty, but deceitful Yorkshire lad for many days, but all in vain. Nevison dodged here and there in many disguises, and at last made his way to Flanders, where he enlisted as a soldier. Here he served amongst the English volunteers, commanded by the Duke of York, who, about this time, was made Lieutenant-General of the Spanish forces under Don John of Austria. Nevison was engaged in the siege of Dunkirk, and, it is said, acquitted himself with considerable bravery. Military glory, however, was not much in Nevison's line, so he saved what money he could out of his pay, and ultimately took secret leave of his regimental friends, making his way with all possible speed to England.

When Nevison set foot once more on English soil, he

made the resolution to adopt the profession in which he afterwards gained so much notoriety. He resolved that he would gain his livelihood on the road, and with this view, at once possessed himself of a suitable horse, and a proper equipment of arms. Upon what particular highway Nevison first began to practise as a robber, is not stated, but it is probable that he would try his 'prentice hand in the vicinity of the great city. At all events, Nevison was too independent and high-spirited to enter into partnership with anyone else in this business. He would neither share the risks of others, nor put his own life into jeopardy, by entrusting others with his secrets. He would act alone. In this spirit, he took to the road, and for a time was very successful; his audacity and cunning carrying him through exploits that few ruffians would have had the courage to enter upon.

It was not long before Nevison made his way to the North, and began to frequent those roads which had been familiar to him in his more youthful days. One night he was scouring the road in search of a prize, when he met two countrymen, who came up to him in great distress, and entreated him not to proceed further, lest he should be robbed as they had been. About a mile away, they said, they had been set upon by three highwaymen, who robbed them of all their money. "How much have you lost?" asked Nevison. "Forty pounds," they answered. "Turn back with me, then," Nevison said, and show me the way they went, and my life to a farthing I make them return you your money again." The countrymen hesitated for a moment, but their desire to get back their money overcame their irresolution, and away they all three rode in company, at a great speed, until they came within sight of the robbers of whom they were in quest. Nevison now commanded the two countrymen to remain behind, while he rode forward. They did so, and Nevison was soon in parley with one of the highwaymen. "Sir," he said, "by your garb, and the colour of your horse, you should be one of the gentlemen I am looking after; and, if so, my business is to tell you that you borrowed of two friends of mine forty pounds, which they have desired me to demand of you, and which before we part I must ask you to restore." "How!" quoth the highwayman; "forty pounds! Hang you, sir, are you mad?" "So mad," replied Nevison, "as that your life shall answer me if you do not give me better satisfaction." With that, Nevison drew his pistol, and placed it to the robber's breast. At the same time Nevison had taken care to seize his rival's reins, so that he could neither get at his sword nor his pistols. "I yield," said the robber; "my life is at your mercy." "No," said Nevison; "'tis not *that* I seek for, but the money you robbed these two men of, who are riding up to me, which you must refund." The thief complied to the extent of delivering up all he had, and told Nevison that his companions had the rest. Nevison now forced him to dismount, and took away his pistols, which he gave to the countrymen. He then gave his horse to the charge of the countrymen, and jumped upon the highwayman's steed and rode off after the other two robbers, leaving the first one safely secured. The two robbers heard Nevison riding up behind them, but they took him for their companion, and stopped as soon as he approached. They were now in the middle of a common. "How now, Jack," said one of the men, "what made you engage with yon fellow?" "No, gentlemen," said Nevison, "you are mistaken in your man; by the token of your companion's horse and arms, he hath sent me to you for the ransom of his life, which comes to no less than the prize of the day, and if you presently surrender, you may go about your business; if not, I must have a little dispute with you at sword and pistol." No sooner had Nevison said this than one of the men let fly at him, but, missing his aim, received a bullet from Nevison in his right shoulder. Nevison was now about to fire upon the other robber, but the latter called for quarter, and promised to surrender everything. Nevison took all the money they had, which amounted to upwards of £150, and with this booty rode back to the country-men, and released their prisoner. He then presented the men with their £40, and, after cautioning them to look better after it in future, rode away with over £100 in his pocket.

Nevison continued to ply his dishonest trade for a considerable time with success. But the risks were great, and at times he narrowly escaped apprehension. About the year 1661, however, after having relieved a rich country grazier of £450, he made a sudden resolution to retire from the road, and walked quietly back to Pontefract, and presented himself at his father's house, with the intention of thereafter leading an honest and decent life. His father, who had long regarded his son as dead, never having heard of him for many years, was overjoyed at his return. Nevison lived at home unsuspected until his father's death, when he returned to his old courses, and became a greater terror than ever to travellers. It was about this period that he began to levy black-mail upon the carriers and drovers of the northern highways, and they were glad to compound for their safety in this way. He appointed them to leave their tribute at stated times, and at certain specified houses, and if they failed to carry out their agreement, he inevitably avenged the default by robbing them the next time they made their appearance on the road. Many of the wayside innkeepers must in those days have connived with the robbers, who paid royally for refreshment and shelter, and spent their ill-acquired gains with characteristic recklessness. Occasionally the Government would be moved to issue a proclamation against the harbouring of these knights of the road. One of Nevison's hiding-places was at Ringston Hill, near Wakefield, in which locality there still exists a very ancient oak, measuring 27 feet in girth a yard above the ground, in the hollow trunk of which Nevison is said to have concealed his stolen treasures. There was a public-house at Ringsden Hill, in the time of Charles II., and at the Rotherham Sessions, held in 1676, Adam Hawksworth, the landlord, was ordered to have his sign taken down for harbouring Nevison.

There was another inn at Howley. This inn stood near the ruins of the ancient hall of the Saviles, at which Nevison put up occasionally, and was kept by a person named Fletcher. The historic mansion had then only been in ruins a few years, but the situation was a lonely one, and offered the robber the seclusion that he sought. There was also another attraction for Nevison in this neighbourhood. "Like the formidable Samson," says Scatcherd, in his "History of Morley," "he had, at Dunningley, his 'Delilah'—a married woman, I believe, whose offspring and descendants (whether improperly or otherwise I wot not) were long honoured with his name." Certain, however, it is, that Nevison was often travelling to Dunningley and Howley. Many motives, indeed, prompted Nevison to visit this locality. "Here was a lonely spot," says Scatcherd, "near a large wood, many fairs of different kinds, many cross-roads, at a convenient distance from Pontefract (the place of his nativity) and of his father's abode."

A large reward had been offered for the capture of Nevison; and Fletcher, the innkeeper, who had been accustomed to lodge the highwayman, was tempted by it, and determined that the next time Nevison came that way he would entrap him. He called his brother to his aid in the matter, and together they laid their plans for securing the robber. It was not long before the opportunity for putting their scheme into practice occurred. Nevison came riding up one day with his customary assurance and audacity, and after dismounting and giving his horse over to the charge of the ostler, entered the inn, and proceeded to make himself comfortable, as he had done on so many previous occasions. When Nevison had got himself settled down to his refreshment, the Fletchers set about the carrying out of their bold project. They fastened the robber's horse in their stable—that wonderful one-eyed, dusky-brown animal, whose fleetness had so often been the means of freeing its master from danger—and then they pounced upon the unsuspecting highwayman, overcame him, and fastened him up in an upper room. "But Nevison soon forced his way through a window," says Scatcherd, "and making a spring, he alighted upon a heap of manure which was just under it, and took his course towards Morley. An alarm, however, was soon given, and one of the Fletchers pursued him closely on foot. Being a remarkably athletic man—relying upon his strength, and probably fancying he had disarmed his visitor, he called upon him to surrender himself. Nevison, on the other hand, attempted to argue, and reproached the other with his treachery and ingratitude; but the great reward was predominant in the mind of Fletcher, so that he grappled with his customer, and in the struggle which ensued the robber fell undermost. Finding himself again overcome by force, Nevison had recourse to a 'bosom friend'—a short pistol, which firing at the heart of Fletcher, he rolled from his body a lifeless corpse." Some assert that it was a small dagger, and not a pistol, that Nevison used; and it was related that this dagger, all covered with blood, was afterwards found in the thatch of a cottage which stood near the spot where the murder was committed. Be that as it may, there is no doubt that Nevison killed his would-be captor, and there still exists in a field near Howley Hall a small stone of cylindrical shape, bearing the inscription. "Here Nevison killed Fletcher, 1684." As soon as Nevison had quietened Fletcher, he took the key of the stable from the murdered man's pocket, regained his horse, and "rode to York, at a rate so incredibly swift that upon his trial afterwards he established an *alibi*, by proving himself to have been upon the Bowling Green there at an early hour of the same day."

Much of the equestrian ability of this daring ruffian seems to have been tacked on to the career of Dick Turpin by a later generation. There is a place at Ferry-bridge which bears the title of Nevison's Leap. It is a cutting in the road, across which the thief once leapt his horse and escaped his pursuers, who were afraid to trust their steeds to follow him over this dangerous chasm.

For many years Nevison appeared to bear a charmed life. He had many hair-breadth escapes, but, thanks to his brave horse, and the connivance of his friends the inn-keepers and drovers, he was able to pursue his evil ways with impunity for a considerable period. On two or three occasions, however, his good luck seemed to desert him, and he was captured by the representatives of the law and borne off to gaol. Once he was taken and committed to Leicester gaol, where he was so narrowly watched, and so strongly ironed, that he could scarcely stir. He did not give up all hope, however, but by a cunning stratagem resolved to effect his release. He feigned to be ill almost to the verge of death, and asked for one or two trusty friends to be sent to him to console him in his dying moments. The friends were permitted to come, and one of them, a physician, reported that the robber was sick of a pestilential fever, and that if he had not the benefit of the open air, he would infect the whole gaol with the disease, and all the inmates would die. The gaoler, alarmed at this statement took off Nevison's fetters and removed him to another room, where he was kept to himself. In the meantime, a nurse had been provided, and the physician came two or three times a day to visit the prisoner-patient. After a short while, the physician gave it out that Nevison's life could not be spared, and that his distemper was extremely contagious. The gaoler's wife would not permit her husband or any of the servants to go nearer than the door of Nevison's cell, and thus the robber's confederates were able to prosecute their deception without interruption. One day they painted Nevison's breast and face and body with blue spots, resembling those that made their appearance on persons afflicted with the plague, and were regarded as the certain fore-runners of death. This done, the physician administered a dose to Nevison that rendered him insensible and deathlike for a couple of hours, and the gaoler was then informed that the unfortunate highwayman had cheated the hangman by dying of the plague. Nevison's friends now demanded the body, and brought a coffin to carry him away in. A jury was summoned with all speed to examine into the cause of death; but, fearing the contagion, they did not prolong their inquiry, but after observing the spots and marks of death, the set eyes, and the rigid jaws, they brought in their verdict that Nevison had died of the plague, whereupon the body was hurried into the coffin, and immediately carried away.

The innkeepers, drovers, and carriers were greatly surprised when they saw Nevison on the road again, and it was reported that the highwayman's ghost had taken to the traffic which Nevison had so successfully engaged in while in the flesh. When the drovers and carriers were called upon, however, to make good to the robber what he calculated he had lost during his imprisonment, they were convinced enough of his living entity, and compounded with him as before, for their own safety's sake. When the Leicester gaoler came to learn the trick that had been played upon him he was greatly incensed, and the authorities were so enraged that they ordered the gaoler to recapture the robber at his peril.

How much of this story of the escape from Leicester gaol is apocryphal we have no means of ascertaining, but it will probably be well to take it *cum grano salis.* It is certain, however, that shortly after the murder of Fletcher, Nevison was captured at Sandal. Captain Hardcastle is generally accredited with having been the person to accomplish this feat. Scatcherd, however, with his usual perversity, says, "that person, instead of a Captain Hardcastle, was a valiant tailor, who finding him asleep on the bench of a house, the sign of the Magpie, at Sandal, and one of the then three inns called 'Sandal Three Houses,' pinioned his arms and procured assistance." A note from the records of the Wakefield Sessions, however, somewhat upsets Scatcherd's statement. The entry runs thus :— "Wakefield Sessions, 9th Octr., 1684. Order for constable of Sandal to pay John Ramsden 10s. 6d., for the constable of Sandal, and William Hardcastle, gentleman, three days conveying one Nevison, a highwayman, to the Castle of York, and 2s. 6d. for obtaining the order." Nevison was expected at Sandal Three Houses, and was "seized by Captain Hardcastle as he entered the house on the southern side of Castle Lane," says Mr. W. S. Banks, in his "Walks in Yorkshire."

Nevison's desperate career was now nearing its end. He was tried at York, and shortly afterwards executed, at the age of forty years. The terror with which he was regarded during the period he held such sway on the northern highways, is amply testified by the fact that his name has been preserved as a by-word for all that is wicked and reckless in the quiet country places of Yorkshire for two hundred years.

YORKSHIRE GHOST STORIES.

WHAT Yorkshireman has not in his youthful days been struck with terror by the fireside narration of some local ghost story? Such stories abound amongst the hills and dales of our great county, and many localities and habitations, both in the crowded towns and the lonely corners of secluded villages, have been invested, through some ghostly connection, with a supernatural glamour which will never wholly wear away. The "Guytrash," with his cloven feet, and eyes as large as saucers, was, as far as I have been able to learn, a strictly local visitant, and did not prowl about any other county than that of York. There is more kinship than at first sight appears between these uncouth Yorkshire ghosts and the satyrs and fawns of the Hellenic mythology. The "Guytrash," however, only seems to have been an aimless wanderer, whose sole purpose was to frighten people in lonely places on dark nights. I once knew a man who said he "varry near saw it" one night as he was going home to Horton rather late, but that is about as near the "Guytrash" as ever I have been able to get, so it is not much that I can say about this mysterious creature. Of ghosts of the orthodox type there are many tales to tell in this district.

THE BIERLEY GHOST.

In the year 1831, there died at a farm-house at Bierley, a widow named Mrs. Kay, who was buried in the burial-ground of Red Chapel, Cleckheaton. After her death the farm fell into the possession of a Mr. Firth, who lived upon an adjacent farm, and was a distant relation of Mrs. Kay. The deceased lady had been in comfortable circumstances, and the succession of Mr. Firth to the farm which she had held was entirely in accordance with her own wishes, as expressed in her will. Notwithstanding this, the spirit of the old lady could not rest, and for a considerable time she continued to haunt the farm where she had spent so many years of her life, and excited great terror in the neighbourhood. Her presence was seldom manifested except by peculiar noises or signs. Sometimes the sounds were like the sliding of bolts and the rattling of chains; sometimes footsteps would be heard up and down the stairs, stamping three times on every step, and accompanied by the sound of a rustling silk dress; and at other times, the sounds would be like the emptying of sacks of corn upon the floor. Occasionally the ghostlike noises were heard in the cupboard amongst the pots, and sometimes at the windows. For eighteen months were these visitations continued, and the fame of the ghost spread far and near. The room to which the ghost was most partial was on the ground floor, and some few sceptical persons applied for permission to occupy this room, for the purpose of exorcising the disturbed and disturbing spirit. One gentleman, from Leeds, was allowed to sleep in the room, on condition that he paid for his lodgings. In due time he repaired to the room, resolved upon seeing and exposing the ghost. Next morning, the family found, to their surprise, that the room was deserted; their lodger had fled, leaving behind him, however, the payment for his lodgings upon the table of the ghost's apartment. Whether the ghost appeared to him in *propria persona*, or whether the clank of chains, or the sound of rustling silk struck terror to his soul, he never vouchsafed to say; but the experiment was one that he never desired to repeat. There is one occasion, however, which stands out prominently in the history of this ghost. Two Wesleyan ministers sought to discover the mystery of the ghost, and show the benighted villagers how silly they were in their superstition. They therefore obtained permission to occupy what was called the "boggard room," and had not long retired to its solitude before they saw standing in the middle of the room the form of a woman, and so distinct was her appearance, that both gentlemen afterwards agreed in their description of the ghost to each other. They jumped to their feet at once, but the ghost vanished at their approach, and they were left to pass the remainder of the night in fear and trembling. All subsequent efforts in the same direction by others were equally unsuccessful. One man slept in the room for a month, and twice fired a gun in the direction from whence the ghostly sounds proceeded. The Rev. Benjamin Firth, Independent minister, of Hartshead Moor, devoted a good deal of time to the solving of the mystery. On one occasion he thus addressed the ghost, standing with his face towards the place where the strange sounds could be heard—"In the name of the Father, Son, and Holy Ghost, who art thou? If thou be the spirit of the late Mrs. Kay, make thyself known by rapping on the chair." An answering rap was at once given. Thus encouraged, the reverend interrogator proceeded to enquire, "Hast thou the power of speech?" No answer was given to this, nor could anything further be extracted from the ghost at this interview. For eighteen months these ghostly manifestations were continued, and then, with as little reason as had characterised its original outbreak, it ceased from troubling, and began to rest. And what is most surprising, no one has since confessed to having had a hand in the manufacture of these Bierley visitations. But, after all, it was a most commonplace ghost, and showed neither use nor originality.

THE SCOTTISH PEDLAR.

Sometime towards the close of the last century, a Scottish pedlar, of the name of Alexander McLaren, used to travel with his pack through some of the remote valleys and hills around Ripon. He was known to the country people as "Sandy," and was held in great esteem by them, being frequently a welcome guest at their firesides, where he would smoke his pipe, and exchange gossip with the master or mistress of the house in a most friendly manner. He was a man of regular and sober habits, exact and punctual in his dealings, and possessed a never-failing fund of humour. Sandy, after travelling his lonely moorland rounds for many years, mysteriously disappeared, and the greatest concern was manifested in his fate. Suspicions of foul play were entertained. The old man at whose house he had last been seen, was closely questioned, but he was so simple and straightforward in his statements, and bore so good a character, that suspicion did not rest on him at all. This same old man, many years after the mysterious disappearance of Sandy, related all he knew to a visitor, in something like the following words :—" Aye ! this is th' last plaace he was seen alive at, poor fello' ! It's sae monny year sin' cum Martinmus next. Aye, it was a bad job that, for poor Sandy ! I think I see him just noo, as I saw him that neet when he com' into our hoose, wi' his big pack fastened wi' straps ower his shoulders. He'd cum across fra th' Syke, up by th' Gill top tharr, and then ower th' hill to oor hoose. It was a misty, gloomy, sour-lookin' day, but did'nt rain. When he com' in, it was getten on i' th' efternean—mebby

s

four o'clock or sea—an' he leak'd tired, an' down, an' wauf like. I saw he didn't leek reet, as he used to dae, an' I ax'd him if he wasn't weal? an' he sed na', he didn't ail mickle, but he didn't feel easy in hiz mind, as he'd seen summat as he'd com' across th' end o' th' Gill that was vara queer—he believed it was a wraith—that's what we call a *waft for deeath ;* an' it mud be hiz awn, he sed. 'Stuff an' nonsence,' I sez. 'Sandy, don't be doon-hearted at that, man; it's been a crag, or a thorn-bush, seen through th' mist, they leak vara queer, at times ; it's been summat o' that soart, seur eneaf.' 'Na, na,' sez Sandy, 'it wasna, it shifted aboot, yance an' awhile close to my side, then awa' like drift hauf a mile or mair, then back again quite close to my side, mon, then sank into th' grund reet anenst me ; it was no like a crag or bush ava'.' 'Ay, ay, Sandy, sez I, 'it is queer, for seur, to see things ye've nivver seen afore ; but are ye certain it wasn't a Will-by-th'-Whisp ? They are seen tharr at times, I kno', but it's hardly dark eneuf for 'em yet ; sea what it's been ye've seen I can't tell ; bud come, man, don't let yer heart sink, Betty 'll draw ye a sup o' drink, an' it'll cheer ye up a bit.' He had a drop o' drink, bud it didn't cheer him up mitch, nor he didn't talk as he used to dea. Betty an' him began to bargan for a bit o' stuff for a new goon, an' they'd rayther a hardish bout. Betty sed times were hard ; she awlus does when she wants to buy ought ; at last they agreed, an' Sandy pack'd up his traps ready to start. Before he went he shak't hands wi' beath Betty an' me : he sed he mud nivver see us ageean. 'There's a queer beastie,' sez he, 'wons ower yon hill. I ken he is a gursome carle is that, and wears a face I dinna like.' 'He's not a good 'un,' I sez, 'but yet I think ye need not fear him, Sandy ; you've that aboot ye will keep him awa', I think.' 'An' I doot I've that aboot me will bring him on, tea,' says he ; 'howivver, thear's a God aboon—

good-day to ye beath.' These were the last words that he said befoor he went awa', an', indeed, th' last that I ivver did hear him say. We beath leak'd efter him till he crossed th' runner i' th' boddom tharr, an' watch'd him aboot hawf way up yon hill on th' other side, when we could see him nea longer for mist—indeed it seean began to be dark; an' that's th' last time, I believe, that onny-boddy, that will awn to t', ivver saw him alive." A farmer who had not long been in the neighbourhood was suspected of having murdered the pedlar, but nothing but the vaguest suspicion could be urged against him. He took little or no part in the search for Sandy; and when spoken to on the subject, said, " Sandy's maist likely gaen back to Scotland wi' his plunder." Shortly after the pedlar's disappearance, however, this farmer showed signs of increased wealth, his poor-bred cows and worn-out horses were replaced by healthy and useful animals, and the neighbours whispered, " They've been bowt wi' poor Sandy's brass." Everything appeared to prosper with the farmer, however, and his meal-suppers were of the most festive description. Roast beef and plum 'pudding were to be had in abundance, and strong ale followed without stint. Then came the merrymakings—the dancing, singing, and *guyzing*, the latter constituting a kind of rustic panto-mimic performance adapted for the occasion. One of these pieces was entitled " Stealing the Scotchman's pack," and it was selected by the rustics at one of this farmer's celebrated meal-suppers. Why it came to be selected no one knew, but so it was, and while the *guyzed*, or disguised, rustics were performing it at the hour of midnight, the skeleton apparition of a *real* Scotchman walked through the room where they all were. The apparition wore a broad blue bonnet, and a *maund* or plaid like a Scotchman, but flesh it had none. The *guyzing* at once ceased, the dogs howled and trembled with fear, and the feasters tumbled over

each other in the wildest terror. The popular belief was
that it was the murdered Scotchman who had risen from
his unhallowed grave to remind the now prosperous farmer
of his atrocious crime. One thing and another tended to
impress the belief firmly on the villagers that the farmer
was the guilty person, and many hard things were said of
him, but no direct charge was ever brought against him.
Indeed, the pedlar's body does not appear even to have
been recovered. The suspected farmer prospered for a
time, then all his speculations began to fail, and he died,
years afterwards, in poverty, " execrated as a murderer by
some, and lightly esteemed by all."

FAIR 'BECCA.

In the olden time, it is said, there lived on the slopes
of Hollingwood, in Horton, a beautiful young maiden,
named Rebecca, the daughter of a farmer. The girl
attracted the attention of the heir of the neighbouring
farmstead of Bracken Hall, and was betrayed by him.
Various versions of the legend have been given from time
to time, but the one which seems to have lingered most
favourably in the popular mind is that which Mr. Abraham
Holroyd has been able to recall. " The lines have for
many years been on my memory," says Mr. Holroyd, and
thus he gives the ancient ballad :—

> Now lithe and listen, every one,
>   Come listen to my tale ;
> It is of " Fair Rebecca,"
>   Was born in Bradford-dale.
>
> Ten times ten years since then have passed
>   Which makes it just five score ;
> And Hollin wood *was* then a wood,
>   And the Horton hills a moor.

Young Whaley, then a yeoman bold,
  Made Annie Bell his bride;
And ere the spring returned, there slept
  A daughter at her side.

The neighbours still point out the farm
  Where they did then reside,
And blither hearts could not be found
  O'er all the green hill side.

Remote from towns, their harmless lives
  In daily toils were spent;
And happy in each other's love,
  They loved, and were content.

So lithe and listen, every one,
  Come listen to my tale;
It is of " Fair Rebecca,"
  Once dwelt in Bradford-dale.

Now search and seek where'er you would,
  Throughout all Yorkshire ground,
A fairer maid than she was then
  There could nowhere be found.

Swift as the wind the years flew by,
  And statelier grew the maid;
Her cheeks the rose's hue outvied,
  Down in the greenwood shade.

The stalwart youths o'er all the hills
  Of Horton spoke her fame,
And thus, because she had no peer,
  " Fair 'Becca " did her name.

As graceful as a young gazelle,
  Her step light as the fay,
The village lasses on the green,
  Crowned her the " Queen of May."

And good as fair, beloved by all,
  Blithe sped her youthful hours ;
And yearly, when the whitethorn bloomed,
  She wore that crown of flowers.

To take her place no rival came,
  But all her beauty own ;—
Ah ! better had it been for her
  Had she no beauty known.

For scarcely had she seen eighteen,
  Ere love, that tyrant, came ;
With honeyed words, and whispered vows,
  And set her heart aflame.

He came to her in the scarlet garb
  Of a hunter on his steed,
And a handsome youth indeed was he,
  Though of a deceitful breed.

"Fair 'Becca" went out at early morn,
  With her milk-pail on her arm,
When the hunter chanced to pass that way,
  And he met her on the farm.

"Good morrow," said he, "my bonny, bonny maid,
  Good morrow, good morrow to thee ;
I vow and declare a face so fair,
  My eyes they never did see.

"Sweet maiden fair, I vow and declare,
  If thou wilt my true-love be,
Of all the broad lands of which I am heir,
  The mistress thou shalt be.

"I have jewels, and they shall all be thine,
  As rare as ever were worn ;
And I promise thee all thy heart can wish,
  Thy person to adorn.

"Thou costly robes of silk shalt wear,
　Have servants at thy call;
And thou shalt be a rich man's bride,
　And the Lady of my Hall."

"Words are but wind, young man," she said,
　"And they may nought avail;
Besides, thou art a stranger to me,—
　So pray, let go my pail.

"Thy jewels of gold, I covet them not,
　Or servants to come at my call;
And I cannot consent to be thy bride,
　Or the Lady of thy Hall.

"It would ill beseem a yeoman's child
　Thy silken robes to wear,
Or mistress to be o'er all the broad lands
　Of which thou alone art heir.

"My mother, she bids me of men to beware,
　Says many are false, and few are true;
And should I but listen to what you say,
　I yet may sadly, sadly rue.

"So begone from me, and flatter no more,
　There are ladies enow in the land
Would be doubly glad thy wealth to share,
　And the clasp of thy jewelled hand."

　.　　.　　.　　.　　.　　.　　.

It was just about the Michaelmas time,
　That dreary time of the year,
When the trees begin to change their hues,
　And the fields look brown and sere;

When the winds go piping loud and long,
　And whistle among the sheaves;
When in and out, and round about,
　They whirl the autumn leaves.

"Fair 'Becca" went out at early morn,
    With her milk-pail on her arm;
And her lover stood waiting at the stile,
    In the lane that skirts the farm.

"Good morrow," said he, "my own true love,--
    For my true love thou must be;
For I think of thee through all the day,
    And by night I dream of thee.

"I have brought thee a brooch of purest gold,
    Which for my sake thou must wear;
And to gain thy love I would anything do,
    And to keep it would anything dare.'"

Up spake the maid: "To be thy wife,
    I must father and mother leave;
And should thy words be found untrue,·
    It would cause their hearts to grieve.

"O, I wish I were a rich man's child,
    Or thou of a poorer race;
Yet I cannot believe thee false to me,
    When I look upon thy face."

Then he took a gold ring in his hand,
    And he brake the ring in twain;—
"I will ever," said he, "be true to thee,
    'Till these two meet again."

One half he threw in a pit near by,
    The other he bade her keep;
"Hold this," he said, "until we wed,—
    Whether you wake or sleep.

"And now I vow, by all above,
    The words I speak are true;
And here I vow, by all below,
    I none will wed but you."

Then she gave him her hand, and with it her heart,
  And he gave her the first love-kiss;
And fondly she dreamt that happy hour
  Was but the beginning of bliss.

.   .   .   .

Soon the wintry months were over and past,
  And the flowers again in bloom;
But the maiden she sits alone and weeps,
  For a mother she will soon become.

And she seeketh now, with a breaking heart,
  To hide her scalding tears,
And thinks it is hard such trouble should come
  To one so young in years.

"Come hither to me, my mother dear,
  And sit down by my side;
To-morrow will be my wedding-day,
  And I shall be Walter's bride.

"He said he would come at early dawn
  On his steed, and bear me away;
So get ready my gown of spotless white,
  To honour my bridal day.

"The bells in Bradford church will ring,
  To hail the Merry May;—
And a happy time it will be then—
  And it will be my wedding-day.

"But, mother dear, I have had a dream;
  Come, tell me the meaning, I pray;—
I thought I was dead, and that my head
  In a pool of blood did lay.

"And yet where I lay it was not a grave,
  But a something dark and round;
And the waters trickled over me there,
  As though I were under the ground.

"And the moans I made were echoed back,
  And I still could faintly scream ;
Just then I woke, and I saw you here,
  Then I knew it was all a dream."

"The dream, my child, thou hast told me,
  Is but the effect of care ;
Yet I oft have wished you never had met.
  Or that you had been less fair.

"He hath done to thee a cruel wrong,
  And thou art in a snare ;—
But be calm, my child, and if he should come,
  He may all thy wrong repair."

O, scarcely the maiden her prayer had said,
  And sought her pillow again,
Ere she heard her name in a well-known voice,
  And a tap at her window-pane.

"Come out with me, out over the lea,
  I would speak with thee, my dear ;
Now the stars are dim in the silent sky,
  And the moon is shining clear."

Through the whins and heather together they rove,
  For those hills were moorland then ;
Out over the lea, by the black yew tree,—
  Where Ellison hanged hissen.

On the brink of a pit, where an old thorn grew,
  The lovers at last made a stand ;
One hand of his held her girdle fast,
  And the other her lily-white hand.

Alas ! and alas !   Then her dream came true,
  On that sorrowful May Day morn ;
For the beautiful maid was murdered there,
  And so was her child unborn.

There was weeping then at Bracken Hall Farm,
 And wailings loud and wild,—
For a father had lost a daughter dear,—
 And a mother an only child.

And after, for many and many a year,—
 When the neighbours crossed the wold
At dead of night, they have heard a scream,
 Which has made their blood run cold.

And her restless ghost, in spotless white,
 On the stormiest night was seen,
Far out on the heath, all wet and dank,
 Or haunting the village green.

And to all the cottagers, far and near,
 Such a terror she became,
That the loitering school-boy homeward fled
 At the mention of her name.

And whenever a birth or a wedding came on,
 Over all the country side,
The midwife always heard her shriek,—
 And so did the terrified bride.

THE STORY OF A YORKSHIRE STROLLER.

SCATTERED over our literature may be found many interesting pictures of the lights and shadows of a stroller's life, and many are the illustrious names which have been linked with this Bohemian profession. Molière, the father of French comedy, was a stroller for the greater part of his life, and numerous are the instances of players who have achieved fame and fortune on the French stage, after having toiled and struggled for years amongst ragged troupes of wandering Thespians. Mrs. Siddons was at one time a stroller; so was Kemble, and so was Edmund Kean. The strollers have been satirised by Churchill and others in verse, and depicted in all their tawdry picturesqueness by Hogarth. For a century or two they formed part and parcel of the social existence of the time, and though generally regarded by "the authorities" in the light of mere vagabonds and vagrants, their devotion to their profession, through all the trials and vicissitudes which beset them, and their mock-heroic mode of dealing with the ordinary affairs of life, have ever caused them to be held in kindly regard. On the stage they were emperors, kings, queens, heroes, and heroines; and, wretched and poor as they frequently were, they could not bring themselves, when they doffed the sock and buskin, to the level of ordinary mortals. Lowly though they were as to material wealth, they nursed high thoughts and noble sentiments, and took their views of life from a lofty mental altitude. The straits to which they were often reduced, and the multifarious duties which they were called upon to perform, have often attracted notice. Who has not heard of King, the tragedian, who one night performed King Richard, gave two comic songs, played in an interlude, danced a hornpipe, spoke a prologue, and appeared as harlequin, in a sharing company, receiving as his share, at the close of this fatiguing performance, the sum of threepence and two pieces of candle! And who has not heard of the strolling managers who were often compelled to accept meat and provisions from the public in lieu of money for admission. It is related that once upon a time, Jemmy Whiteley, a well-known manager, after pitching his tent in a village on the coast, could get nothing brought to him but fish. After admitting nineteen persons for a shad a-piece, he stopped the twentieth, and said, "I beg your pardon, my darling: I am extremely sorry to refuse you; but if we eat any more fish, by the powers we shall all be turned into mermaids!"

It is my object in the present paper to tell the story of a somewhat notable member of this fraternity— Mr. SAM WILD—who had as many ups and downs as the best of them, and almost endured martyrdom in the pursuit of the profession of which he was for so many years a prominent, if not a distinguished, ornament. Thirty or forty years ago, there was not a town or village in Yorkshire that was not honoured once or twice a year by the presence, at fair or feast, of Wild's famous dramatic establishment, founded by Old Jemmy Wild, subsequently carried on by his widow, and more recently by their sons, Sam and Tom, either conjointly or otherwise. Poor Sam! the hero of a thousand broad-sword combats—the gallant English tar, who has saved hundreds of shipwrecked maidens, and married them afterwards—the Red Indian, who, with his brave dog, Tippoo, could overcome all the

soldiers that the United States could bring against him—
has now succumbed in the final struggle of all. He
resided at the time of his death, in 1881, in a humble
cottage in Caddy Field, Halifax, with a son and daughter,
who worked at the factory, and were in very necessitous
circumstances.

Sam Wild was born at Huddersfield, on the 4th July,
1815. He was the youngest son of James Wild, or, as
he was always familiarly styled, "Old Jemmy Wild." Sam's
father had originally been a collier, and was afterwards
apprenticed to a rope-maker named Wilkinson. Jemmy
was an excellent player on the clarionet, and ultimately
became the leader of the Cleckheaton Old Band. Indeed,
he paid much more attention to the band than to the
rope, and one time, when Kite and Morris's Circus paid
a visit to Cleckheaton, he was persuaded to join their
instrumentalists. He travelled with Kite and Morris's
Circus for a considerable time, soon becoming conductor,
and afterwards marrying Mrs Kite, the senior partner.
His wife died before they had been married long, however, and he was left sole proprietor of the establishment.
There were no children of this first marriage. For his
second wife he married Elizabeth Atkins, of Coventry,
and, during their peregrinations from place to place, six
children were born to them—Elizabeth and James, both
born at Nottingham; Tom, born at Newark; Sam, born
at Huddersfield; Sarah Ann, born at Halifax; and Selina,
born at Hull. These children were all instructed in the
equestrian and acrobatic arts from their infancy, and might
be considered to have earned their own living almost
from the time they were well able to walk. Jemmy Wild
was by this time much more than a clarionet player; he
had exercised himself in the arts of juggling, vaulting, and
slack-rope dancing, and soon became an adept in these
performances. Moreover, he had, like the renowned

Vincent Crummles, a fortune-telling pony, and, for a time, Jemmy Wild's equestrian troupe enjoyed a fair amount of success. One day, however, the authorities pounced upon him, and charged him with keeping more horses and carriages than he had paid tax upon, and they surcharged him to such an extent that he had to submit to be sold up. The Wilds were now left penniless, and were compelled to appear as mountebanks in the open air, and sometimes in a sort of tent, constructed with stakes and ropes. There was no charge made for admission, but tickets were sold, which gave the chance of obtaining certain prizes which were offered, such as sacks of flour, tea-trays, pocket-handkerchiefs, gown pieces, and so forth. But this plan did not answer for long; one day the Chief Constable of Wakefield paid them a visit, and considering their system of giving prizes illegal, caused a summons to be issued against Jemmy Wild, who was committed for three months to the Wakefield House of Correction. The family were now plunged into worse difficulties. "Brother Tom and I," said Sam, "were sent to an aunt in the country, who, in consideration of so much per head per week, undertook, kind creature, to do her duty by us. But mother, poor soul! being unable one week to raise the wind, as we say—it was the first offence, mind—our affectionate relative consigned us to the tender mercies of the workhouse custodians at Alverthorpe." While at this place, Sam and Tom were sent to the village school, but did not take kindly to book-learning, preferring to wander forth into the fields and lanes. Meanwhile, their mother struggled hard, and got together a little booth, not much larger than a pea-saloon, and managed, by the assistance of the two elder children, and "Big Ball," a tumbler, to keep from starvation. As soon as she heard that Sam and Tom had been sent to the workhouse, she set herself to get the money together to fetch them away, and by hook and by crook she succeeded. When Old Jemmy Wild came out of prison, he rejoined his family, and things began to look up a bit. They had a clarionet for the outside of the show, and a fiddle for the inside, both being played by one performer, Jemmy Wild : and with Jemmy's conjuring tricks and ventriloquism, the children's acrobatic and rope performances, and the pony's fortune-telling, they contrived to get up a taking entertainment. In this way they travelled about from place to place, acquiring more experience than money, but keeping their spirits up amidst it all. James, the eldest son, had by this time come to be a very clever performer, and thinking that he might mend his fortunes if he went into the world on his own account, he left the paternal booth, and engaged himself to Henry Adams, the circus proprietor, as clown and vaulter. This was a serious loss to Jemmy Wild's concern, and with the view of compensating for it in some way, they began to introduce ballet dancing and circus farces into their entertainment. From this they gradually crept on to more ambitious representations, and in 1838 or 1839, at the suggestion of an old actor named Henry Douglas, they launched into the theatrical business entirely, giving their first dramatic performance in the town of Halifax. Three scenes—a street, a parlour, and a shady grove—comprised the whole of their scenic resources at that period, and their *corps dramatique* consisted of the Wild family and Henry Douglas.

Their first piece was *The Village Lawyer*. Douglas was the lawyer, Tom Wild appeared as Sheepface, and old Jemmy Wild was pressed into the service, much against his will, as the Judge. Jemmy was so impressed with the solemnity of the occasion, that when his turn came to sum np he forgot the words of the part entirely, and in this dilemma had to invent a speech of his own, which he did, to the following effect :—" After carefully considering the facts of this case (he said) and the testimony of all parties concerned, I can only see one course before me, and that is to send you all to Wakefield House of Correction for one calendar month," a decision which was received with great laughter and applause.

"We, the younger branches of the family," said Sam, "were pressed into stage service whenever an opportunity offered. I should only be ten or eleven when I appeared behind the footlights, but I had performed as tumbler and posturer from the time when I was only five years old. At that early age I could stand on my head at the top of a ladder balanced by my father—it is as much as I could now do to keep well on my feet, through my infirmity— and made a sort of serpentine descent, by threading my way downwards through the staves. My father was a man of extraordinary strength. He could bear eight persons on his body at one time, and as for us little chaps, he threw us about like ninepins. So, with our Star Company of theatricals, we attended all the feasts, fairs, and races far and wide; sometimes staying three or four weeks at one place, at others as many months. In this way we travelled through Yorkshire, Lancashire, Derbyshire, Leicestershire, and, indeed, through almost all the other shires in England. I believe my first character was one of the farmers in *Cherry Bounce*, whose misfortune it was to take a copious draught of horse medicine under the delusion that we were imbibing a delicious potation. All our family, including my mother, played in one piece or another. But Elizabeth, woman grown, married and left us. So, besides our parents, and any strollers we might hire, there were only Tom, Sarah Ann (Sally, we usually called her), and myself to sustain the minor parts, Selina being as yet too young to appear. We were considered tall children for our years, and being excellently trained by our parents, were soon enabled to take parts usually sustained by adults.

T

As I grew up to be a young man I took an affection for nautical characters, such as Harry Helm, Jack Junk, &c. I practised fencing, and was counted one of the best swordsmen in the profession. I used to fight against six men at one time, using two swords, one in each hand. At the age of eighteen or nineteen I was a leading man, and could do almost anything. Yet I never aspired much to tragedy. Shakspearian characters, such as Richard III., Macbeth, Othello, I rarely attempted, though I have several times played Macduff, the Ghost in *Hamlet*, and similar characters."

In course of time Jemmy Wild took a circus proprietor named Anthony Powell into partnership. Powell had some half-dozen horses, and with this union of the dramatic and equestrian elements, a "grand combination of talent" was formed. While travelling with this establishment, Old Wild had several people with him who afterwards attained considerable eminence as public performers. He gave lessons in conjuring to Anderson, who afterwards styled himself "Professor" and "Wizard of the North;" brought out the famous Joe Morton, otherwise "Curly Joe," who soon surpassed his teacher; and had in his employment for a time Malabar, the equilibrist, who balanced coach wheels, a 21ft. plank, and a live donkey on a ladder. "After leaving our place," says Sam, "Malabar became a 'pitcher' in the streets. 'How much have you got?' he would ask of his wife and the youth who went round 'nobbing' amongst the spectators. 'Ah! we must just have another shilling, ladies and gentlemen, and then up goes the donkey.'"

Wallett became a member of Wild's establishment about this time. He thus refers to the circumstance in his auto-biography:—"I started for Leeds. There I joined a theatrical booth belonging to Mr. Wild, better known as 'Old Jemmy.' This concern was a sort of amphitheatre, being made up of a fortune-telling pony, a tight-rope dancer, and a slight theatrical entertainment. A very severe winter was just over, and matters were not then very brilliant, yet I received a warm reception. I instantly set to work to remodel the establishment, and get it in order for the coming fairs. Towards the end of the first week, the band, consisting of the manager, his sons, and myself promoted to the rank of drum-major, promenaded the district, to acquaint His Majesty's lieges of the great and intellectual treat in store for them at the moderate charge of threepence. Though very poor I was always proud, though not of my poverty. The day was very cold, with a sharp easterly wind. My outward man was not well protected by pilot cloth or fur, nor the inner man well fortified to resist the relentless foe. I endeavoured to conceal my manifest toes in the snow from the observation of the girls, while beating my drum. The manager, a very old man, with a loud voice, persisted in announcing the performance in the intervals of the music. The piece to be performed was *The Floating Beacon*, which he proclaimed as follows :—' This evening will be represented a drama called *The Floating Bacon ;*' to which a wag replied, in the Yorkshire dialect, ' An' a varry good thing too, Jemmy, wi' a bit o' cabbage to it.' The farce for the evening was *Raising the Wind*, rather an ominous title, for a storm came on after the conclusion of the performance. At four in the morning, I and others were called up to disentangle the wrecked theatre of its sails and tackle. The canvas roof, the new scenery I had painted, were torn to rags. While sitting upon the ridge-pole of the demolished roof, clearing the *debris*, the factory bells rang out the hour for work. Then hundreds of the work-people passed by, and many stopped to look at the ruin. I believe I gave vent to my feelings in emphatic language, for a small urchin called out, ' Eh, Mr. Wallett, don't grumble, ye were raisin' the wind yerselves last night.' Our booth, however, was somewhat dilapidated before, and the rain coming through the roof, rendered it impossible to keep the violins in tune. On one occasion, the leader of the orchestra, a talented but eccentric character called Dr. Down, hearing the manager's daughter sing 'Buy a Broom,' stopped playing and looked up, exclaiming, 'Better tell your father to buy a new tilt to the roof.' We soon recovered from our disaster, owing to the happy disposition of Mr. Wild and the industry of his sons, backed by my judgment and energy, and the establishment became one of the most prosperous in the country. . . During my stay at Gainsborough Mart, I observed a very clever young man, a posturer, advertised as 'The Chinese Nondescript,' whose real name was William Cole. His performance was so attractive that I resolved to acquire the practice. I did so to great perfection while belonging to Mr. Wild's company, which added much to my popularity and my pocket. In fact, I became so celebrated in this line, that at Bingley, Keighley, and Skipton, I sometimes had four or five surgeons on the stage to witness my art. It was considered marvellous at the time, though common enough now. This new acquirement introduced me to another branch of the show trade, namely, playing the man-monkey. An interruption occurred on my first appearance in this character, in *Jack Robinson and his Monkey.* This was at Bradford. The leader of the band, either inebriate or inattentive, played the wrong piece of music at a very tragic moment. I was about to die when he played a lively air. So I stepped down to the foot-lights, and looking him in the face, asked aloud, 'Do you think any monkey in the world could die to such music as that?' My second appearance as monkey had an unfortunate conclusion. Just at the close of the drama, the property man, Jem Farrar, was charging a horse-pistol, when it exploded in his mouth, shattering his jaws frightfully. I saw him fall, and instantly rushed to his assistance. Seeing his state, I took him on my back, and though a heavy man, I carried him to the Dispensary in Darley Street. It was then past eleven o'clock, and the place was closed. I rang at the door, which was opened by a woman with a candle in her hand. Her fright may be imagined when she saw the apparition of a man-monkey, with his tail trailing on the ground, and a half-dead man on his back, with the blood streaming down. One glance sufficed. She fell senseless to the ground, and the candle was extinguished. I strode over her in the dark with my heavy load. Knowing the building well, I ascended the grand staircase, and perceiving a light issuing beneath a door, with one knock I brought out the house-surgeon. As he opened the door, and the blaze of gaslight from inside revealed the horrible figures, he, too, nearly fainted away. A few words convinced him that I was of earthly mould, and he promptly summoned several surgeons. Surrounding the bed of poor Farrar, they had but one opinion, that his case was hopeless. One of them remarked, 'We can do nothing for him.' Farrar shook his fist at him, being unable to speak. A fine old surgeon, Dr. Macturk, seeing this action, said, 'Come, boys, the man has pluck enough to live through anything. Off coats, boys, and let us do the best we can to save him.' They did so. His life was preserved."

As Sam related, Wallett and he were inseparable friends and bedfellows. But, after a while, Wallett was induced to transfer his services to the opposition establishment, conducted by Mr. W. S. Thorne, and for a time he and the Wilds were running counter to each other. Before long, however, the future " Queen's Jester " rejoined Old Jemmy Wild. Sam and Wallett had a happy and prosperous time of it together, and saved a few pounds between them. Wallett one day prevailed upon Sam to go with him to Hull, Wallett's native town. " Being young fellows," says

Wallet, "and fond of life, our funds were soon exhausted.
We did not like to write to Sam's mother for money, as
we had run away and were neglecting our business, and
my mother had none to give us. But there's always balm
in Gilead. It was within three days of Hull fair, and to
our unspeakable joy, old Jones arrived with his booth.
We were immediately engaged as stars in this small firma-
ment, at the princely salary of one guinea each per day.
It was on the evening after we made this engagement,
when Sam and I were seated in the bar at Glover's Hotel,
that an elderly gentleman, with either a very high forehead
or a partially bald head, attracted our attention by his
steadfast gaze upon me. He made himself known to us
as Mr. Gifford, the stage-manager of the old Theatre Royal,
Hull. It appeared that they were producing a pantomime
for the Hull fair, and had engaged artists from London,
Signor Garcia and Young Masoura, as clown and pantaloon.
The pantomime was to be produced on the following night.
The steamboats from London were all in, and there was no
railway at that time. The management had given up all
hope of the party arriving by mail-coach, the journey being
long and expensive. This, then, was my first essay in
management, for I forthwith made a contract to supply the
pantomimic characters for £8 a night. I played the clown
and Sam Wild the pantaloon. We instantly waited upon
old Jones, and told him the nature of our engagements.
We said we would work at his establishment from noon till
nine at night, when we must leave to appear in the pantomime. He said, ' Bless you, my boys ; I have children of
my own. Don't let me be any bar to your preferment.'
So, as Wallett and Wild at the show, and Signor Garcia and
Young Masoura at the Theatre Royal—receiving two
guineas from the show, and eight pounds from the Theatre,
and paying one pound a night to harlequin and colum-
bine, and two pounds to my chum and brother Sam for

his day and night—I was left with a handsome margin of profit. All went on merrily as marriage bells for some time. But my luck again! Old Mother Wild arrived with a policeman from Hull, to snatch us from our prosperity, and drag us back to that theatrical factory where labour was certain and payment rather doubtful. With much ado we persuaded the old lady to allow us to remain till the end of the week, undertaking to return on the following Monday, which we accordingly did."

In the year 1835, Sam Wild took unto himself a wife, being then of the mature age of twenty, and full of high hopes and ambitions. The lady was Louisa, daughter of John Worrall, captain of the *Duke* sloop of war, and "a fine woman, I assure you, both physically and intellectually," added Sam. Sam still kept at his father's establishment, and the young couple found it somewhat difficult to make ends meet, with nothing to rely upon but his scanty earnings. Mrs. Sam therefore resolved, before she had been many months a wife, to take to the stage herself, and Sam reluctantly consented. So well did she acquit herself, that in no very long time she achieved the proud position of becoming Old Wild's leading lady. "She was worth any two women we had," said Sam. "She was at home alike in tragedy and comedy, in Irish and in Scotch characters. As Lady Macbeth she was considered excellent, and she gave a very fine rendering of Desdemona, of the Queen in *Hamlet*, and characters of that description. We were continually having fresh pieces, but she readily adapted herself to every occasion." Domestic cares crowded fast upon the young couple, twelve children being born to them in the course of their wedded life, the eldest being born in 1836, the youngest in 1856.

On the 21st December, 1838, Jemmy Wild died at Bradford. That winter the booth—a wood and canvas establishment—had been located at Bradford, on what afterwards became the site of Mr. Mosley's theatre, in that portion of the Old Fair Ground which joined up to Duke Street. The warehouse of Francis Willey & Co. now occupies the site. Old Jemmy had for a year or two been unable to take any active part in the management of the concern, and had grown very corpulent. His two great pets —Billy, the fortune-telling pony (then, in a sort, pensioned off), and Jerry, his faithful bloodhound—occupied his attention chiefly, and were the constant companions of his walks, sometimes even accompanying him to the public-house, and waiting patiently while the old man refreshed himself with his customary two-pennyworth of gin. Occasionally Billy would be called in to delight the parlour visitors with his old fortune-telling tricks, and although he always ended up by pointing his master out as the biggest rogue in the company, a true affection existed between the animal and Old Jemmy. As for Jerry, the dog, it was always at his side. Well, it was on a December night in 1838 that the old man, accompanied by Jerry, strolled forth from the caravan, while his thrifty wife was engaged "counting out the money," and went on to the Manor House Inn, in Darley Street, for a quiet chat with some of his old friends, who met there. But Mr. Wild was not in his usual spirits, the fog had got into his throat, and he was restless and uncomfortable. About nine o'clock, not feeling any better, he left the Manor House and bent his steps towards the caravan. His wife heard him approaching, and opened the caravan door for him. "Betty, my lass, I think it's about over with me," he said, as she led him in. She put him to bed and sent for a doctor, who ordered the old man to be removed to an hotel, but Jemmy would not hear of such a thing, and begged to be taken forward to Huddersfield, where he expected to meet a very old and dear friend. Sam and Tom, and their assistants, packed up the dresses, scenery, and paraphernalia that night, and next morning, at nine o'clock, Sam started with the vans for Huddersfield, leaving his father behind in the living van, under the care of Tom, his mother, and his sister Selina. Sam had not got beyond Brighouse, however, before a Bradford friend came galloping up on horseback to fetch him back to Bradford, informing him that his father was worse. Sam thereupon handed his wife money to pay all dues and demands at Huddersfield, and, mounting the messenger's horse, returned with all speed to Bradford, but too late to see his father alive. The old showman had breathed his last, and while a crowd of sympathisers gathered round the caravan outside, the widow and children inside were in the deepest anguish. A day or two afterwards the old man's remains were buried in the graveyard attached to Trinity Church, Huddersfield, and a vast concourse of people followed him to the grave.

Mrs. Wild now became sole proprietress of Old Wild's theatrical establishment, being assisted in the management thereof by her sons Sam and Tom. Bradford was for a long time one of their most profitable resting-places, and in 1841 Mrs. Wild determined to have a wooden theatre erected there, with the view of making a prolonged stay in the town. Mr. John Crabtree, landlord of the Market Tavern, and also a master builder, put up a wooden building for them, agreeing to take back the timber at the close of the season. When completed the building was capable of holding from 1200 to 1300 persons, and a good house at the ordinary prices, 3*d.*, 6*d.* and 1*s.*, yielded something like £27. They called their establishment the Liver Theatre, and opened it in November, 1841. Amongst the company were the renowned Jack Holloway and his wife, Mr. and Mrs. Robert Lomas, Mrs. Mansfield, and others. Mr. Liver was the scenic artist, and he and his wife performed with the company. The orchestra numbered five instrumentalists—a first and second violin, cornet, flute, and double bass. Mr. Charles Hengler, who subsequently became famous as a circus proprietor, was one of the violinists, and remained with Old Wild's some ten months. He was beginning to learn to play the trumpet when he left.

Wilds were not permitted to have things all their own way in Bradford, however, for Mr. Parrish, another well-known stroller, came and pitched his tent in the town, erecting his establishment in the Hall Ings, facing Leeds Road. Parrish's place was larger than Wild's, and he had no end of "gorgeous costumes" and "entirely new scenery and effects." Mr. Manners, a Bradford artist, was engaged to do something specially grand, and Mr. Parrish put the drama of *Jack Sheppard* into rehearsal—then having an immense run in London—intending, no doubt, to put Old Wild's into the shade. One day, however, when a number of members of the rival companies were fraternising together at the Bermondsey Hotel, the secret oozed out, and immediate steps were taken to counteract Parrish's machinations. Paddy Hall, the stage-manager at Wild's, got hold of a copy of the play, cast the characters, and divided the book amongst the company to be written out. "Each copied his own part," said Sam, "and then exchanged for other parts, until the whole of it was gone through. I know I sat up all night to transcribe Mrs. Sam's part and my own. Jack Holloway was down for the notorious robber, and I for Jonathan Wild. The only new scene we introduced was a view of the exterior of Newgate, for which view a portion of the outside proscenium did duty, after having been enlivened a little by the introduction of a few pointed laths by way of spikes. On the following day—the second after the news of the enemy's doings had reached us—we had a rehearsal, and on the third day it was performed before the public. Up to this very day Parrish had been going on rehearsing and preparing, quite ignorant of what was being done behind the scenes at Old Wild's.

But when he saw, to his dismay, our flaming posters announcing *Jack Sheppard*, for the first time in Bradford, that evening, he rushed back to his own place, called his manager a sleepy fellow, and accused everybody right and left of having betrayed him. Well, the piece took amazingly. We ran it for four nights, and had crowded houses every night, and hundreds went away unable to obtain admission. The part of Jack Sheppard is a very long one—I should think some thirty lengths without the cues—and I remember the first time we played the piece Jack Holloway hadn't got a line of the last act off, but he gagged it so skilfully that the irregularity was never observed." The Monday following, Parrish produced his version of *Jack Sheppard*, but although it was magnificently got up, it went for nothing."

Amongst the patrons of Old Wild's at this period were a number of gallery frequenters known as the "White Abbey lot." There were thirty or forty of them, and they came nearly every night. They sat in a body in a particular part of the gallery, and generally managed to keep the place lively. "Almost all professions and callings were represented by this lot," said Sam, "and a couple of chimney-sweeps, in good black, I remember, generally occupied a prominent position amongst them. Should any unfortunate individual, not of their company, but within reach of these last-named gentlemen, happen to hazard an observation to a friend upon the merits of a performance, and in so doing raise his voice anything above a whisper, switch came their sooty caps into the face of the critic, with a sort of qualified request that he would return them without delay, and give his thoughts no tongue. Nor did they think anything of propelling an offender from the back of the gallery down into the pit—which joined the gallery, by the way—nor of amusing themselves generally at the expense of others." This pretty "lot" cost Old

Wild's eighteen shillings a week, a constable being to engage at that salary to keep them in order. When one of them was detected in any particular act of mischief, he was forbidden the theatre for at least a week afterwards; and good care was taken, too, that he did not make his way in along with his friends. A good deal of tact was required in dealing with these White Abbey gentlemen. Although the constable was the means of keeping them to a certain extent in subjection, it was not deemed prudent, for his own sake, to saddle him with the sole responsibility of turning any of those noisy offenders out of the booth. When ejection was absolutely necessary, Sam and Tom Wild used to go up into the gallery themselves and hustle out the culprits, retaliation upon the members of the order of the sock and buskin being never dreamt of.

In the year 1847 Mr. Sam Wild had the honour of appearing at Drury Lane Theatre, before Her Majesty the Queen, the Prince Consort, the Queen Dowager, the Royal children, and "a host of the nobility and gentry." What the illustrious personages thought of Sam's performance is not recorded; the only *souvenir* of the circumstance which the old stroller possessed was probably the play-bill announcing the entertainment. The piece in which Sam appeared was entitled *The Desert,* and the company comprised three hundred performers, including two bands of instrumentalists, sixty horses, fourteen camels, ten ponies, and two elephants, together with a gorgeous dragon's chariot, and a Burmese Rath. It was as a humble member of this company of three hundred that Sam Wild made his bow before the Queen. Both he and his brother James were engaged as one of Edwin Hughes' circus company, each in the subordinate part of an Arab chief, whose main duty it was to incite their followers to make attacks upon caravans as they crossed the desert.

Soon after this event, Sam began to appear as a co-performer with dogs. His first dog was a retriever, named Tippoo, which played with him in such pieces as *The Forest of Bondy*, *The Red Indian*, &c. This animal Sam sold to William Batty, the circus proprietor, and it was afterwards promoted to Astley's. After this, Sam bought another dog, Nelson, which was destined to obtain a much greater reputation than had been achieved by Tippoo. "He was a difficult dog to teach," said Sam, "but I succeeded with him at last; nor did I regret any extra labour he had cost me, when I saw him turn out a finished performer. I taught him to vault through hoops; to perform on chairs; to take an egg without breaking it out of a pail of water; to fetch a living canary out of a box, without so much as a feather of the little songster being ruffled; to open a letter-box and take out a letter; to pull off his collar, and at the word of command to put it on again; to go up a forty-feet ladder, fire off at the top of it a twenty-four pound cannon, and come down on the other side; and to simulate death and lameness so cleverly that he rarely failed to draw tears from the eyes of the spectators. Then I taught him also to perform in plays. His first appearance as a stage hero was at Lancaster, in the celebrated drama *Mungo Park*. The original version of this play made no provision for the introduction of a dog, but I adapted it myself for Nelson by writing special parts here and there for him, and by arranging a few dramatic effects. In the original text of the play, the African traveller is released from his confinement by Snowball, the cabin boy. The alteration I made at this point, was, that, while still preserving the character of Snowball, I made Nelson take part in the liberation. This I did by teaching him (a prisoner, and in chains, like myself) to slip off his collar, and go and unbar a door or wicket, to let in Snowball. The first time the cabin boy appeared, however, sounds of someone approaching caused him to beat a hasty retreat, while Nelson, to avoid discovery on his part, put on his collar again, and lay at my feet as though nothing had occurred. This piece, which always went off with *éclat* (as did any piece in which Nelson appeared), remained a favourite one with the public for a great many years."

Mr. Wild was able to shed a flood of light upon the capabilities and tribulations of dramatic authors of the class mentioned. They were generally as poor as crows, he said, and would willingly write a three-act piece for the modest recompense of a couple of guineas. "It was simply necessary to state what talent you had, your scenic resources, and the extent of your wardrobe, and they would get you a new piece out in a couple of days," said the stroller. On one occasion, however, Mr. Wild, being about to make a more than usually vigorous effort, Mr. Somerset, the London dramatist, was engaged to come down to Leeds (where the company were then playing) in order to see Nelson for himself, and fix up something special for him.

On the 10th July, 1849, Nelson and his master appeared at the Leeds Zoological Gardens before 14,000 persons, including the Earl of Carlisle, Earl Fitzwilliam, Lord Wharncliffe, and many other distinguished people. On that occasion, Nelson, in addition to his usual performances, drove four geese round the lake, while a combination of brass bands played "See the conquering hero comes." On the 28th September in the same year, while at Penrith, the Wilds were honoured with the patronage and presence of the Marquis of Douro (afterwards Duke of Wellington), Lord and Lady Brougham, Sir George Musgrave, and other noble people, on which occasion *Every Inch a Sailor* and *Mungo Park* were represented. Hair-seated chairs and sofas were obtained from the Royal Hotel, the Marquis of Douro bearing the expense. The gallery was the only part of the house thrown open to the general public that night, and at double prices. The Marquis, on the following day, presented Mrs. Wild with £10.

About this time Mrs. Wild fell ill, and found it necessary to transfer the management of the concern to Sam, although Tom was the eldest son. It was at first considered desirable that Tom and Sam should enter upon a joint proprietorship, but Tom proving rather intractable, the old lady took upon herself to settle the question in her own way. She sent for Fraser, the scenic artist, and thus addressed Tom, "Now, Tom, I'm going to ask Fraser to alter the names upon my vans. What is to be put in place of 'Elizabeth Wild?'" "Thomas Wild," replied the owner of that name. She gave him yet another chance, and said, "Not 'Thomas and Samuel' Wild, then?" "Certainly not," said Tom, with some emphasis. Then, turning to Fraser, the old lady said, "Rub out the name 'Elizabeth' on each of the vans, and in place of it write only 'Samuel.'" Her word was law. Fraser carried out his instructions, and Sam was made sole proprietor of the establishment.

For a time Old Wild's were bereft of the presence of Mrs. Wild. She went to live in snug retirement in a country cottage, but before many months had elapsed she began to miss the clatter and clamour of the fair-ground, the sound of the gong and the drum, and the many other discords to which she had been so long familiar, and the end of it was that one day, while the booth was at Halifax Fair, the old lady drove up with her boxes and packages, and once more settled down in her house-on-wheels.

In 1850 Sam Wild engaged the Riding School at Huddersfield for three months, at a rent of £20 a month, and while there he drew up a set of rules for the guidance of his company, which, though rather slip-shod as regards grammar, were intelligible and conducive to good order. "Any person being intoxicated in their business," was fined 2s. 6d.; "any person being too late for rehearsal (a quarter of an hour allowed for difference of clocks), 6d."; "any person not wrapping up his dress after using, 6d.";

"any person going in front of the house in their dress, or with paint on their face, 1s."; any person leaving the theatre in their dress, unless covered with a cloak, 1s."; and "any member or members of the company quarrelling during the performance, or in the theatre, so that the audience may hear them, each 1s." The season at Huddersfield was a very profitable one. They produced, amongst other attractions, a Christmas pantomime.

Mrs. Wild again fell ill at Huddersfield, and on the company removing to Cleckheaton, they had to leave her behind, in charge of her daughter Selina. The old lady never rallied, but died a few days afterwards, and was buried in the same vault as her husband. "The funeral was a very large one," said her son. "By some it was said to be the largest that had ever been seen in Huddersfield, but as to that, of course I cannot say. In addition to our relatives and the company, who followed in mourning coaches and in cabs, there were a great number of our friends from other towns, while it appeared to me that all Huddersfield had turned out to see the last of the 'Queen of the Travellers.' Tournaire (I believe it was), a circus proprietor, who had succeeded us at the Riding School, sent his entire company, mounted on horseback, to take part in the procession; and as a proof, I think, that my mother was held in some esteem by the Huddersfield people, all the shops, from the Guildhall to Trinity Church, were closed during the time the funeral. *cortège* was passing." Mrs. Wild was sixty-seven years of age when she died.

Shortly after this mournful event, the portable theatre, conducted by Sam Wild, was removed from Cleckheaton to Keighley, where they met with some powerful opposition. A strolling manager, named Edwards, contrived to seduce John and James Holloway into his service, and pushed forward with his theatre to Keighley, a day or two in advance of the Wilds. But, somehow, the opposition did not succeed; for although Edwards could show one or two powerful names, he could not present anything like so lengthy a cast of characters as the Wilds did. The Wilds included in their company such eminent names as Messrs. Jackson, Jones, Harrison, Green, Smith, Brown, and Walker. "These were very useful men," said Sam, "always ready at a moment's notice to represent any character; and though we paid them no salary (for they never asked for any), still they remained with us year after year, and were never known once to object to the parts given to them, however simple those parts might be."

Occasionally, Sam himself found it convenient to disguise himself as another performer. At Whitehaven, in May, 1851, he represented the Bronze Monitor as Mons. Leon, having previously appeared with Nelson on the same boards that evening as Sam Wild. All this passed unsuspected at Whitehaven, but when he came into Yorkshire, where his figure and voice were more familiar, he found that it would not answer. " Just before my appearance as the talented Mons. Leon, there would be a breathless suspense," he observed; " but it took very little time to discover who that personage was, and a short conversation like the following would sometimes be overheard :—' I say, Bob.' ' I'm hearkenin' on tha, Jim.' ' That's noan a furriner, I tell tha ; that's Sam Wild !' ' Tha'rt reight, Jim; it's nobody else.' And this too, bear in mind, when Sam Wild was endeavouring to look as much like a ' furriner ' as he possibly could."

At the Bradford Summer Fair of 1851, Wild's establishment made its appearance in the most resplendent form. In honour of the Great Exhibition, and by reason of certain new outer embellishments in which Mr. Wild had indulged, " regardless of expense," the place was called " Wild's Crystal Palace of 1851." Six large real gas-lamps,

U .

octagonal in shape, supported by pillars five or six feet in height, were placed at regular intervals along the front, and had a magnificent appearance at night when lit up. In addition to these, a new " folding front " had been painted, giving an exterior view of the Great Exhibition building. All this was done in anticipation of further opposition on the part of Edwards ; and, as luck would have it, Edwards set up his booth on the very next stand to the Wilds.

" We were stirring early in the morning of the first fair day," said Sam, " and fixed and tried our lamps, but the front we still kept down, as we intended that for a surprise by and by. Between one and two o'clock in the afternoon, Edwards' procession on the outer stage commenced ; the members of the company, to judge from their gay appearance, having evidently ransacked their wardrobe for the best dresses. The procession concluded, a long strip of calico, containing an invitation to the people to ' Come and see the Brothers Holloway ' was flaunted about, and the prices, which were the same as ours, were then announced. The moment these proceedings were over, up went the new front at Old Wild's, and our full company, from twenty-five to thirty (but exclusive of Messrs. Jackson, Brown, and others) appeared, bearing the flags of all nations, and attired in a gorgeous medley of Greek, Roman, and old English costumes. The band, consisting of cornets, trombones, clarionets, and drum, heralded the approach of the company; the rear of which was brought up by old Finch as clown. The crowd now made for Old Wild's to see the doings there, and Edwards' place was quite deserted. In vain they shouted the praises of the Brothers Holloway, clanged their cymbals, and smote their drum. In vain they sounded their noisy bell, and groaned defiance from their trombones. The only move the people made was up the steps and in at the side door of Old Wild's, the moment we had finished our parade. Our rivals still kept up their noisy proceedings as the crowd continued to make its way into the theatre. Old Finch, who, without appearing to notice them, had his eye upon our antagonists, and saw to what little purpose they laboured, seized a large flag, and, addressing the members of our company, at the same time pointing to the advancing host of patrons, he exclaimed—

"Hang out our banners on the outward walls;
The cry is still 'They come!'"

This, from old Finch, was relished by the spectators, probably all the more because of his clown's attire; and a merry peal of laughter followed. But the opposition only groaned the louder, and its musicians united in producing unearthly yells, while the noise was made still more deafening by the incessant swinging of a huge bell. These latter sounds seemed to give old Finch a fresh cue. Raising his voice to its highest pitch, he exclaimed—

"Ring the alarum-bell; blow, wind! come, wrack!
At least we'll die with harness on our back."

Being of opinion, in the first place, that Finch was now acknowledging too plainly the doings of the opposition, which was contrary to our custom, and, in the next place, feeling that the members of Old Wild's company would 'never say die,' I advanced towards him with uplifted whip. Quick alike in action as in thought, he threw the flag over his arm for a shield, pointed the staff at me with a swordsmanlike grace, and assumed an attitude of defence.

"Lay on, Macduff!
And damned be he that first cries 'Hold! Enough!'"

shouted the inexhaustible Finch, to the uproarious delight of the spectators. We had nearly finished our first house before our rivals had half-filled theirs, and it did not astonish us to find, on returning to the parade, that they had reduced their prices."

For a few years after this Old Wild's establishment had a steady run of success. The Crimean War suggested to them the idea of a military drama, and the London dramatist was called in and commissioned to write with all speed a drama called *The Battle of the Alma*. This was, in due time, produced at Bury, with the assistance of a genuine British sergeant and twenty-four genuine British soldiers. The Russians were represented by "supers"-in-ordinary. "Loud and prolonged was the cheering," said Sam, "when, having at length scaled those mimic heights, and completely routed the enemy, they planted the standard of victory here. And then—after having availed themselves of the use of gunpowder and fireworks to such an extent that the spectators were lost to each other for at least five minutes after the curtain fell ; not to mention the imminent hazard they nightly encountered of being suffocated into the bargain—when the victors took their seats in the pit, just before the commencement of the farce, it was worth all the money paid at the door to witness the hearty reception that was accorded them."

By way of variety, while at Bury, they played *Black Eyed Susan*, with the principal characters reversed, the male parts being sustained by females, and *vice versa*. Sam would on these occasions appear as Susan, and when she fainted, in the last act, where her William dear (Mrs. Sam) was condemned to be hanged, it took no fewer than six persons to bear the disconsolate one from the stage.

In September, 1856, a very tragic occurrence cast a gloom over Wild's establishment while it was stationed at Armley. They had in their company a Mrs. Banham, whom Sam described as an "equestrienne, dancer, and vocalist, and a recent addition to our dramatic corps in the two latter capacities. She was the daughter of John Hope, the leader of my band. In her youth, Miss Hope, a hand-some, light-hearted girl, was apprenticed to Pablo Fanque to learn the equestrian's art. William Banham (better known as 'Billy Pablo'), Fanque's nephew, and a man of colour, was at that time a tight-rope dancer, vaulter, and bareback rider there. Between these two persons a friend-ship arose, and, in course of time, Miss Hope became Mrs. Banham. With a tendency under all circumstances to be somewhat gay, she gave occasion to her husband to believe he perceived grounds for jealousy, and, under the influence of the 'green-eyed monster,' he left her and went abroad. A young man, John Hannan, a tailor from Man-chester, met with her shortly afterwards; an intimacy was formed, and considering that her husband's desertion amounted to a complete termination of the old love, she unwisely lent her ear to the insinuations of the new. But the new love ere long lost its charms, and it was because of a persistent refusal on her part to entertain proposals of a return to him, that Hannan, at Armley, on the 11th September, 1856, took the poor woman's life, for which dreadful crime he shortly afterwards suffered the extreme penalty of the law."

Mr. Sam Wild engaged "stars" from the ordinary theatrical world every now and again: Mr. George Owen, Mr. Henry Lorraine, Mr. T. H. Glenny, Mr. John Coleman, Mr. Arthur Nelson (the musical clown), Herr Teasdale (the man monkey), and others. Herr Teasdale made a great hit at Wild's theatre at York, Dewsbury, and other towns. One night, when it was Teasdale's benefit, and they were playing *Jack Robinson and his Monkey*, a rather awkward occurrence took place. As Mushapeg, the monkey, Teas-dale attacked a large number of his master's enemies, including an arch-villain named Diego. All these people were thrown upon the ground by the monkey, but on this particular occasion Diego, for private reasons, declined to

submit to the usual humiliation. Diego stood immovable.
The monkey then laid violent hands upon Diego, but the
latter was "too many" for his adversary, and, releasing
himself from the monkey's grasp, he bounded over the
footlights into the pit, Mushapeg following. Diego crept
under the seats, and could not be found; and the monkey, frustrated and chagrined, returned to the stage, and,
standing before the footlights, addressed the audience.
"Ladies and gentlemen," he said, "I have to express my
astonishment at the conduct of that man Diego. It was
his duty to be knocked down by me, and, as you have
seen, he resolutely refuses. He has left the stage, and I
am unable to go on with this scene in consequence; but
should he return again he shall have cause to remember
his conduct." "This was the first monkey I ever heard
speak in public," added Sam, with a laugh. Teasdale has
in later times been before the public in the character of
"The Converted Clown and Man Monkey."

In 1860 it occurred to Sam that as the drama did
not pay so well as of old, it might be advisable to go into
the circus line. Accordingly, he bought at Bradford a stud
of horses, van, and other effects, belonging to Harry
Brown's circus, then stationed at the bottom of Vicar Lane,
for somewhere near £100. At Bury Spring Fair he
purchased more horses. When, at last, all was prepared
for the transformation of the theatre into a circus, Sam
gave his dramatic people notice to quit, and with a new tent
and a very promising show, he opened his amphitheatre at
Accrington. Afterwards, at Preston, the tent was blown
down, and they did very badly at other places. "At Wigan
we did next to nothing," said Sam, "and at St. Helen's
less than that, on account of the opposition we met with
there from Hayes's circus." At Bolton matters were
equally depressing, "worse at Bury, and still worse at
Heywood." Thoroughly disheartened by this continued

run of ill-luck, Sam resolved to make an end of the amphitheatre. The public didn't care for it; it wasn't Old Wild's. "So, though I had only four months of amphitheatre life," said Sam, "I was quite satisfied. Remembering all my serious losses, and in face of more, it was, I thought, high time to clear out; and while at Brighouse Feast, in August, I came to the determination to do this. The tenting business accordingly ended there. I sold off my horses at that town; four of them Pablo bought for far less money than I had previously given for one; and two of them—Jenny and Jerry—he sent to Copenhagen to a circus proprietor there, who paid him £70 each for them, while I did not receive from Pablo more than £10. After duly crediting myself with the receipts of the sale, I estimated that my total losses by the amphitheatre speculation would not be far short of £1,000."

Sam now rigged out his portable theatre again, recalled his company, and resumed the legitimate drama at Hunslet. In 1862 Sam returned to Huddersfield, where he had a wooden theatre erected at a cost of £125, which he agreed to pay by instalments. A succession of "stars"—some of greater, some of lesser magnitude—were engaged this season, and when the last of these luminaries had played out his term, Sam launched into the old broad-sword combats again, and his dog Tiger—successor to Nelson—was brought to the front, and they had a brief flicker of success. It was during this season that Sam entered into negotiations for the appearance at his theatre of Mr. and Mrs. Charles Mathews. When the comedian and his wife arrived in Huddersfield, however, and found that Mr. Wild's theatre was not a permanent building, they declined to appear. The non-appearance of this distinguished couple on the evening of the 5th May, 1863, after the announcement that they would do so, and after the house had been filled to overflowing at double prices, was, Sam thinks, "nothing more nor less than the death blow to Old Wild's."

Business was now so bad that Sam was unable to keep up the payment of the instalments due for the building of the theatre, and he gave the builders a bill of sale, under which document the place was sold and pulled down, and the stroller had to take to the road again with his portable booth, still indebted to the builders in the sum of £54. "I remained at Elland," said Sam, "until Halifax Fair was over, for I hadn't the pluck, somehow, in the then faded condition of things at Old Wild's, to show myself in a town where I had hitherto been able to put on a good appearance. I went to Wakefield Summer Fair, however, but just as I was about to leave that town for Knottingley, I was served with a writ at the suit of the Huddersfield builders. To satisfy the demands of the writ within the limited time was quite beyond my power, for I had just drawn all the money I had, £8 12s. 10d., out of the Skyrack and Morley Savings Bank. I consulted with my friends, and they advised me to sell the establishment as it stood, and the wardrobe and vans belonging to it. Therefore, in lieu of the customary programme on the side of the theatre, appeared one morning, while we were at Knottingley, the announcement that the whole of Wild's Theatrical Establishment, with vans, scenery, dresses, and other effects, would be sold by auction in the theatre on a certain date."

Mr. James Hodskinson, of Blackburn, bought the property for £70 or £80, and Mr. Wild's company, including himself, wife, and family, were kept on to continue the theatrical business, and they travelled from place to place until they came to Keighley, at the beginning of December. While at this town a sheriff's officer arrived from Huddersfield, to demand payment of the £54 still owing to the builders, and Sam, being unable to pay, was taken off a prisoner to York Castle. It was Sam's misfortune that year to have to spend his Christmas holidays in prison, but he tried to make the best of a bad job, and with his fiddle and a few jovial fellow-debtors, managed to keep the festival in rather a merry style. He remained at the Castle a month or five weeks, and, on being released, made his way to Huddersfield, where his wife and family were staying. He then accepted an engagement for himself, wife, and dog Tiger, for six nights, at Pickles's establishment, then at Burnley, and on the 26th January, 1864, they duly appeared. Other engagements followed at Blackburn, Rochdale, and Preston. Meanwhile, Mr. Hughes offered to lend Sam £20 to start again for himself, and this was accepted, and another company was got together. His vans, &c., were removed from Keighley to Shipley, and at the last-named place he opened another establishment, at the old prices of 1s., 6d., and 3d. "The weather was all against us during the Shipley season," said Sam, "and the field in which the booth stood was one pool of water most of the time. As soon as I saw a favourable opportunity I removed to Bradford, where, on April 22nd, I opened my 'Colossal Establishment.' The land in Vicar Lane, upon which it stood, belonged to the late Rev. John Burnet." For a time they did fairly well, Tiger proving a great attraction. In the afternoon of June 1st, however, a sad misfortune occurred. Mr. Hope, the band-master and scenic artist, was engaged in the booth on a new scene, and was using a fire. While in the midst of his work one of the company came in, lighted his pipe, and threw the scrap of paper he had used into the fire. The heat carried it, still blazing, to the tilt, which, dry as tinder, immediately caught, and in a moment the place was in flames. Some masons, who were working near, ran with buckets of water and rendered what service they could,

while those members of the company who happened to be
about cut away the tilt, so as to prevent the flames spreading to the stage and scenery. Several German merchants
came out of their warehouses, and seeing the "living-van"
close to the front of the burning booth, ran towards it,
and laying hold of the shafts, soon placed it beyond the
reach of the fire. Then the fire-engines came, and the
fire was put out, though not until damage had been done
to the extent of £50 or £60. There was now a delay of
four days, but Sam started business again as soon as possible. "By and by I gave presents," observed the veteran,
"cups, time-pieces, and the like, and even in the midst of
hard struggle, I threw open my establishment, on June
16th, and gave my own and company's services on behalf
of the workpeople then suffering from a 'lock-out' at the
Bowling Ironworks."

When, however, the season came to an end, and he had
paid all dues and demands, poor Sam found himself penniless, and if it had not been for Joseph Bentley, the bill-
poster, lending him £4 to help him on his way, he would
probably have been unable to have put in an appearance
at Halifax Fair at all. At Halifax they did moderately
well, and the Bradford bill-poster's loan was gratefully repaid. Dewsbury, Hunslet, and Holbeck were subsequently
visited, and about the middle of May, 1865, they found
themselves at Brighouse. There the booth was blown
completely down. They then contrived to get on to
Halifax, where everything went wrong again, and things
got to be so bad that Old Wild's simply had to be closed.

Sam and his wife and family continued to live in the
van, but the company had left them, and Sam was reduced
to sore straits. "I remember on one occasion," said Sam,
"we had been without food and fire for nearly two days;
we hadn't even the consolation of a half-penny dip. I
had gone out in the morning of the second day to see

what my old fiddle would do for us; to try and make
merry the hearts of others, while sadness possessed my
own; to endeavour to put on a cheerful face, though I
had left my wife with a tearful one in the van. About
noon, and while I was away, a gentleman came to the
door of the caravan. My wife's brother and the two
children were with her. She asked the gentleman in, and
offered him a seat. He had heard, he said, that she and
the little ones were without food, and he felt that he
couldn't sit down to his dinner without ascertaining if
such were the case. It needed but little to satisfy him
on that score, and he generously gave my wife half-a-
sovereign. She, staggered at so unexpected a gift, burst
into tears as he placed it in her hand, and couldn't even
thank him; while the joy of the little fellows at the
prospect of having something to eat was simply uncon-
trollable." This gentleman, a Halifax manufacturer, also
found employment for Sam's two sons, as well as for
Mrs. Wild's brother, at his mills. After this, Sam struggled
on for a year or two, getting an engagement where he
could, but about 1871 he was seized with rheumatism,
and was able to do but little afterwards. The death of
his wife on the 18th of January, 1874, was a heavy blow
to the old stroller. After her decease he got along as
best he could. "My old fiddle earned me a dinner now
and then," he said, "when I was able to go about, and
when I could not, my family were good enough to see
that I didn't want for one." But for his children, the
old man would probably have been an inmate of the
workhouse to the end of his days.

THE STORY OF THE GRASS WOOD MURDER.

SOME few years ago, on a dark winter's night, I found myself seated alongside the driver of the little country coach plying between Skipton and Kettlewell. My destination was Arncliffe, that prettiest of Craven villages, but on that particular night I did not propose to go beyond Kettlewell, having promised myself the pleasure of an hour or two's gossip there with an old Bradfordian, who was living in cultured retirement amongst the dalesmen. Our coach was quite full when we left Skipton, and a cheery good-humoured party we made, laughing and chatting together with the familiarity of old friends, the conversation always keeping in a personal channel, and never dropping off into vague generalities. There were the driver, myself, and my Arncliffe friend—a well-known professor—on the box-seat, and through the open window we were able to join in the humours of the interior without inconvenience. As we advanced upon the various little villages that lie in sleepy silence here and there on the roadside, we lost first one and then another of our passengers—a stalwart Craven yeoman and his portly dame getting out at Rilstone; a rosy-cheeked servant-girl leaving us at Cracoe; and a trio of lead-miners taking their departure at Grassington. By this time the darkness had been intensified, and made more cheerless by a steady relentless rain, which had evidently set in for the night, and was urged upon us all the more forcibly by a fitful wind. We three upon the box-seat, however, were well shrouded in wrappings of various kinds, and I rather enjoyed the elemental excitement than otherwise, the novelty of the experience amply making up for any discomfort by which it was attended. We had a rather long halt at a village inn at Grassington, and for about ten minutes steamed our dripping garments in front of a huge fire. Presently, after the driver had been duly treated, and had received various neighbourly messages to convey free of charge forward to friends at Kilnsey and Kettlewell, we resumed our seats on the coach and soon were dashing forward along the road, with the rain driving in our faces more persistently than ever. There was not much to be seen from our perch on the coach; now and then we came upon a glimmering light which shone from a wayside cottage window, sometimes a shout from the road indicated to us the presence of a passing dalesman, and occasionally we heard the angry bark of a farmer's dog: but all else was shut out by the darkness and the rain. It was not long, however, before we seemed to sink all at once into a darker night and a deeper shadow, and were wrapped in a more profound silence. "Where are we?" I asked of my companion, with some little feeling of alarm. A gust of wind and a shiver of trees drowned my friend's answer; but I saw now that we had entered a large wood. This, the driver explained, as well as the stress of the weather would let him, was Grass Wood, where so-and-so committed suicide and such-another-one was murdered; and the trees shook, and the wind whistled in such a weird and ghastly way as he delivered himself of these legends, that I could feel my heart sensibly increase its speed of beating as he spoke. In a little while we came upon a corner of the wood, to which the driver pointed with his whip, and said, "That's t' place where Tom Lee murdered Dr. Petty, and

I've heard folk say ——" Here the mare gave a start.
" Ho, my lass! wo! steady!" said the driver; and then he
continued, "I've heard 'em say—What the hengmond is
up wi' t' owd mare?—They say 'at his ghost comes ——"
The rest of the sentence was completely lost, for the
mare gave a sudden start and rushed forward with us at
a maddening speed, and for about two minutes we were
in imminent danger of being thrown over; but the driver
was sober and knew his business, and was able to subdue
the animal to a proper sense of its position by the
time we had cleared Grass Wood. By and by we came
to Kilnsey, and there at the village inn, the rendezvous
of one of the chief angling clubs in the North, we had
another long rest. After that, we proceeded forward past
Kilnsey Scar, and on to Kettlewell, to rest at "The Race
Horses," one of the cheeriest and most comfortable
hostelries in Upper Wharfedale. Here we shook our damp-
ness from us, and, in due time, before a warm fire, in a
cosy room, we disposed of one of the heartiest meals that
ever I was partaker of. It was while sitting here that I
asked my companion to tell me all about Tom Lee and
the murder of Dr. Petty, but the story was too long, he
said, to be told just then. I must wait until we had
returned from visiting the old Bradfordian. Later on we
visited the old Bradfordian. The first book that I opened
when I got to his house was, curious to say, Mr. Bailey
Harker's " Rambles in Upper Wharfedale," which gave an
account of this very murder that I had been thinking
about so much. I tried to get my friends to speak on
the subject, but they were too much engrossed with matters
of an antiquarian character to do more than put me off
with a few hurried words, and I did not like to be so rude
as to sit apart from them with Mr. Harker's book. So the
evening passed without further mention of the murder;
and I came to be so interested in the other matters that

we talked about that when we took our leave of the old Bradfordian and went to our inn, I even forgot to ask for the loan of the book containing the story of Tom Lee. The Professor and I sat up until late, talking of one thing and another, and Tom Lee never entered our heads again, and just on the verge of midnight we went to our separate bedrooms. The rain was beating pitlessly against the panes, the wind swept down in fearful gusts from Great Whernside, and the windows rattled at times with deafening noise. I placed my candle down on the table, locked the door, and, walking quietly back, seated myself on a chair near the light. Involuntarily I put my hand upon the table; then, after looking yawningly around, I was just on the point of rising to undress, when I perceived that my hand was resting upon a little book in a dingy red binding. I took it up, and opened it, and the first words that met my eyes were "Tom Lee!" I was startled. The awful shadow of Grass Wood rose before me once more; once again I felt the thrill of fear which had possessed me when the horse took fright: and, under these influences, I set myself there and then to read for the first time the story of the murder of Dr. Petty. I shall never forget that night. The morning was considerably advanced by the time I had finished, and the storm of wind and rain had lashed itself to exhaustion, and when I went to bed there was perfect stillness. How long I remained awake thinking of what I had been reading I cannot say, but I know they had great difficulty in rousing me in the morning. Since then I have heard and read much more about the Grass Wood Murder, and in these pages it is my intention to tell the story for the benefit of such of my readers as may not before have heard it.

Tom Lee, then, is said to have kept one of the Grassington village inns somewhere about a hundred years ago. Grassington was a place of more importance in those days probably than it is now, for in modern times it seems to have been left behind in the march of improvement, so far, at all events, as external appearances go. Tom was known throughout the whole district as a bold and desperate fellow, possessing great physical power and wonderful determination of purpose. Under some circumstances Tom Lee might have won a position for himself in the world, for not only was he more daring than his neighbours generally, but he was of greater mental ability. As things went in those days, Tom was an educated man, but low associations and low desires served to divert him from the better achievements of which he was capable, and in course of time he gave himself up to deeds of dishonesty and mystery. Indolent, quarrelsome, and fearless, he contrived to make those about him extremely uncomfortable, being always ready to tyrannise over those who were weaker than himself, and always courting rather than shunning a trial of strength with his boon companions. Tom drank hard and lived hard, and, one way or another, came to be the terror of the locality. It was whispered about, moreover, that Tom employed himself in nocturnal pursuits of a somewhat questionable nature, and many a farmer who met him in the tap-room during the day suspected him of having made secret visits to his farm at night. Burglaries were, indeed, common in the neighbourhood, and, rightly or wrongly, Tom Lee was generally credited with being concerned in them. Many who actually knew that Tom had been engaged in certain depredations were afraid to speak out against him, knowing well that Tom would revenge himself upon them in some desperate way if they divulged what they knew. In this manner, Tom escaped being brought within the reach of the law for a very long time, and grew bolder and bolder in his designs. Tom was by trade a blacksmith, and had good opportunities for fitting himself up with burglarious instruments. He had an apprentice named John Bowness, whom, it is to be feared, he instructed as much in the arts of villainy and deception as in the art of manipulating iron. This apprentice and Tom's wife were the only persons that he took into his confidence in regard to his midnight expeditions, and, from what subsequently happened, it would appear that the apprentice was accustomed to accompany him occasionally at these times. Tom was suspected and distrusted by everybody, but there was not one who had the pluck openly to denounce him. The local constable did sometimes flatter his soul by planning methods for the capture of Tom Lee, but when it came to the working out of these plans his courage generally failed him, and the robber was left to pursue his evil ways comparatively unmolested. I say "comparatively" advisedly, for it was known that once or twice Tom had met with more than he had bargained for in his maraudings. Farmers kept their guns in those days, and one or two of these deadly instruments, it was said, had been discharged at Tom, and not without effect, in the "stilly night," but those who had taken the law into their own hands in this way valued their existence too well to let it be known that they had scotched the robber.

On one occasion Tom set himself to waylay a man who came down on horseback from Green Hill to Grassington every week with money to pay the wages of the lead-miners employed there. There were a great many miners working at Grassington at that day, and their aggregate wages amounted to a considerable sum. The trusty cash-bearer was not unaware of the risks he ran by travelling alone with a large amount of money, but he always contrived to make the journey by daylight, so that the danger of being robbed was greatly reduced. But, daylight or not daylight, Tom Lee determined to make the attempt to ease him of

v

his load, so mounting his own horse, in the orthodox high-wayman fashion, Tom started off down the road to meet his victim. Tom had taken the precaution to disguise himself, and with devil-may-care bravery he rode forth, timing himself so as to meet the bearer of the money in one of the most unfrequented parts of the road. As Tom approached this spot he heard the noise of hoofs, and in another minute the two had met, and Tom had made a dash at the man. Tom's opponent, however, was too quick for him, and putting spurs to his horse, he managed to break away. Tom followed in hot pursuit, and overtaking him, dealt him a heavy blow with a bludgeon. The blow did not disable the attacked horseman, fortunately, for he was enabled to draw a pistol from his breast pocket, and firing it at the robber brought him down, and galloped off with his money all safe to Grassington. Tom mean-while was writhing in agony; he had not only missed his object, but had received a wound which, he feared, would be too many for him. In great pain he clung to his horse, and rode slowly along a secluded by-path, until he came to some moorland rocks, where he kept in hiding until night came on. As he lay there, with his faithful steed beside him, he was sorely perplexed as to what he should do. He staunched his bleeding wounds as well as he could, but he felt that they were too serious to be treated with-out the help of the surgeon's art, so with much reluctance he clambered upon his horse once more, and, under cover of the darkness, made his way to the house of Dr. Petty, the Grassington surgeon. Dr. Petty was a man who was highly respected by the villagers, his medical skill being only equalled by his geniality of mind and generosity of disposition. Long before Tom had reached the village surgery, Dr. Petty had heard of the attempt that had been made to rob the mining agent, and when he saw Tom's

wounds he boldly charged him with the affair, and extorted
a confession from the robber. For some time Tom Lee
continued under the doctor's hands, and although the
blacksmith professed to be much indebted to Dr. Petty, for
bringing him round, he was at heart greatly distressed at
the thought that he was at the doctor's mercy—that,
indeed, the doctor had Tom's life in his hands, for in
those days the crime of which Tom had been guilty was
punishable by death. From that time forth Tom conceived
a violent dislike for the doctor, and cursed the day that
had placed him in his power. "Suspicion," it has been
well said, "ever haunts the guilty mind," and so much did
that feeling trouble the mind of Tom Lee, that he felt
sometimes that nothing short of the doctor's death could
ever satisfy him. But the doctor kept the secret as
religiously as if he had been a monk, and it had been
imparted to him under the sacred seal of the confessional.
He took his daily rounds amongst his patients, a cheerful
and contented man, quite unconcerned as to what Tom
Lee might be thinking or doing.

Thus matters went on for a time, and Tom Lee carried
on his midnight depredations and his daily carousals with
impunity. On a certain autumn afternoon, however,
Dr. Petty and Tom met under rather peculiar circumstances,
and words were exchanged which stirred a terrible fury in
Tom's heart, and led to the most fearful consequences.
Tom had wandered over to Kilnsey, and was deep in his
potations at the Angler's Inn there. A young farmer,
named Dick Linton, happened to be taking his glass there
at the same time, and Tom and he got to high words,
the uncouthness of the blacksmith being almost matched
by the unmincing utterances of the farmer, who was rather
inclined to accuse Tom to his face of the things which
his neighbours only spoke about with bated breath in

secret. Tom was enraged beyond endurance at the farmer's taunts, and at last he rose to his feet with the intention of striking at his accuser, and in another moment the two would have been in a hand-to-hand struggle on the floor had not Dr. Petty happened to alight from his horse at the door, and come in and ask the cause of all the disturbance. Tom's countenance fell as he caught sight of the doctor, and the farmer took advantage of this to repeat his charges against Tom. Again Tom fired up, and again he threatened to do something dreadful to the farmer, but Dr. Petty told him he had better be quiet, as the accusations which Dick was making were but a small matter compared with certain other things which Tom and he would keep to themselves. This remark stung Tom to the heart, and, unable to control himself, he began to threaten the doctor. The doctor was now irritated, and retorted with the remark that if Tom didn't mind what he was saying it would be worse for him. With that, Dr. Petty left Tom and the farmer to settle their quarrel as best they could, and the innkeeper and his dame followed him to the door and watched him mount his nag. When the doctor had got into the saddle the landlady brought him the usual stirrup-cup, and the doctor drained it at a draught. Just as he was returning the glass to the landlady, the horse gave a start, and the glass fell upon the floor, but, to their astonishment, did not break. Such a circumstance as this was considered an omen of evil, and after the doctor had departed, the innkeeper and his wife shook their heads sorrowfully, and feared that something lamentable was about to happen. This glass, connected, as it afterwards seemed to be, with a terrible crime, came to be treasured as a relic, and until a comparatively recent period was preserved at Grassington. So precious was the relic, indeed, that on the owner of the glass going to America some years ago he took it with him, and there it is probably extant to this day.

How Tom Lee and Dick Linton ultimately settled their dispute has not been recorded, but Tom probably calmed down under the weight of a still darker design than any he had previously entered on. He called for more drink, and swallowed the liquid with a sort of frantic eagerness. He then settled down into a morose and sullen brooding, and the aspect of his face became dark and lowering, indicating the working of some strong passion within him. After a time he rose to his feet, with the air of a man who had made a desperate resolution, and left the house, heedless alike of the friendly admonitions of the landlady and the good-humoured chaff of her husband. The sun was just dipping below the western horizon as he betook himself to the highroad, and slowly and moodily walked in the direction of Grassington. Any stray pedestrian who met and recognised him, would presume that he was simply wending his way homeward; but Tom had made up his mind to be even with Dr. Petty, come what might, before seeking home again; so instead of going forward to his own house, and ceasing to trouble himself about what the doctor had said, he made direct for Grass Wood, and, as the darkness of night fell upon the autumn leaves, secreted himself in the wood, ready for the doctor's return from his round.

In the meantime, Dr. Petty was journeying calmly homeward, enjoying the beauty of the scene, and feeling in no way apprehensive of harm. He called at the Angler's Inn again at Kilnsey on his way home, dismounted, and drank another glass of liquor before continuing his journey, the landlady remarking to him that he had better not repeat his previous experience of letting the glass fall. The doctor made a good-humoured rejoinder, and then went his way, letting his nag take its own time. By the time he had neared Grass Wood darkness had fully set in, and a solemn repose had settled over the landscape. It was a beautiful starlight night, and, to all outward seeming, there was not a single sight or sound that was out of harmony with the general picture. Presently, however, the doctor found himself within the shadow of the wood, and, almost unconsciously, he urged his horse to a more rapid pace, but the animal suddenly shied, and showed an unwillingness to proceed, and, as it turned out, not without cause, for the next moment a heavy hand had seized Dr. Petty, and dragged him down into the wood beneath the trees. A blow with a heavy stick sent him reeling to the ground, but did not deprive him altogether of the power to grapple with his assailant, whom the doctor had at once recognised as the desperate Tom Lee. The doctor must have known that it was to be a struggle for life or death, and he bravely turned to meet the robber, and for a long time they strove together for mastery, but in the end Tom proved too powerful for the doctor, who was forced to the ground, and Tom, drawing a clasp-knife from his pocket, plunged it into his victim's side. The doctor uttered an agonised cry, and rolled over apparently lifeless, while the murderer, to make sure of his dreadful work, drove the knife once again into the prostrate body. That done, the guilty wretch dragged the doctor's bleeding form beneath the shadow of the wall, and covering it up with grass and weeds, fled from the scene, feeling not only that he had silenced Dr. Petty's tongue for ever, but that he had created a fresh horror for himself, that was far greater than the mere fear of Dr. Petty's publication of the secret concerning the attack on the mining agent.

Long before Tom Lee had reached Grassington, the doctor's riderless horse had arrived at home, much to the

astonishment of the doctor's wife and servants. After the
first surprise had passed, however, they came to the conclusion that the doctor must have been detained at the house
of some patient, and that the animal had simply broken
away from its moorings and come straight home. But the
night went by, and still the doctor came not, and his poor
wife waited up for him in vain.

Tom Lee walked—nay, almost ran—straight home from
the scene of his crime. His wife was the only person
waiting up, the apprentice was in bed upstairs, and all the
customers had retired to their rustic homes some time
before, for "early to bed and early to rise" was a motto
that was generally acted upon in the country districts in
those days. Tom gave a tap at the kitchen window, and
his wife, who always waited up for her husband, quickly
let him in. Accustomed as she was to open the door to
Tom in the night time, and to witness his return to the
domestic hearth under circumstances of varying excitement,
she had never before seen him in such a state of pertur-
bation as he was in this night. She questioned him eagerly
as to what had happened, and at first he only answered
her with short, meaningless sentences. He could not keep
the secret to himself, however, for he felt that there was
work to do, in keeping the business from discovery, that
he could not do without assistance. So he told his wife
all, and a deep-rooted terror took possession of them both
as they discussed one project after another for putting the
body of Dr. Petty out of sight. In the midst of their
excited consultation, it suddenly occurred to the wife that
Bowness, the apprentice, might not have been sleeping
quite as soundly as was advisable, and might have overheard their conversation. She imparted her suspicion to
her husband, and Tom at once proceeded stealthily upstairs to ascertain whether the youth was asleep or not;

Bowness had heard every word, and was paralysed with fear. He pretended to be asleep when his master, knife in hand, came to his bedside, but the terror of the moment was too strong for him, and he could not for his life preserve the placid appearance of sleep. He leapt from his bed with a shriek, and Tom seized him by the throat. "Oh, spare my life, Tom!" implored the lad. "What has thoo heerd?" hissed Tom. "I've not heerd at all, Tom; I'm suar I hevvant," gasped the lad. Tom fixed his gaze strangely upon the lad's face, and for an instant appeared on the point of committing a second murder that night. "Oh, don't tak' my life, Tom, don't!" cried the trembling lad. Tom relaxed his hold, and commanded his apprentice to put on his clothes. Bowness obeyed, marvelling much what it was that Tom was going to do with him. When the lad was dressed, Tom obtained a large sack, put it over his arm, and the two were soon on their way to Grass Wood. Tom's idea, as he afterwards confessed, was to hide the doctor's remains away among some rocks, hoping that they would there lie undiscovered. It was with no little trepidation that Tom approached the spot where he had covered up Dr. Petty's body with grass and leaves, while the terror of the apprentice was as great as if he himself had been the murderer. Arriving at the place, they found, to their amazement, that the doctor was not dead; he had crawled a few yards from the spot where Tom had left him, and was feebly endeavouring to call for help. Tom, like the cruel wretch that he was, now hit upon the horrible plan of making the poor frightened lad he had brought with him complete the murder, thinking thereby to implicate Bowness, and thus bind him to secrecy, and at the same time exculpate himself in some measure. Threatened with murder if he refused, the lad was compelled to do his master's bidding, and, procuring a stake

from the adjoining hedge, he soon deprived the helpless
doctor of such little remnant of life as had remained to
him. When this horrible business had been done, they
lost no time in putting the body into the sack, and
then they carried it up to the rocky ground above, and,
after much labour, succeeded, as they thought, in burying
the murdered doctor away out of sight. Then the two
guilty beings stole away in the darkness of the early morning towards that home which should have been a place of
rest for them, but in which they would never be able to
find rest any more as long as they lived.

The next morning nothing was talked of in the village
but the disappearance of Dr. Petty. Inquiries had been
set on foot in all directions, and it was impossible to trace
him beyond the Angler's Inn, at Kilnsey, where he called
on his way home. The next link in the chain of evidence
was the return of the riderless horse, with broken reins,
and bespattered with mire. All the rest was conjecture of
the most unsatisfactory description. Foul play was suggested
by some one, and searching parties were organised. For
several hours their investigations were unattended by success,
but at length one party came upon a spot in Grass Wood,
where there were strong evidences of a struggle having
recently taken place. Subsequently it was bruited about
that Tom Lee and the doctor had been heard to threaten
each other at Kilnsey the day before, and this, added to
what was already known of the bad character of the
blacksmith-innkeeper, made Tom's name to be turned over
more often amongst the villagers during the next few days
than Tom altogether liked. Indeed, before twenty-four
hours had elapsed after the murder, Tom felt that something more must be done to make sure of the body of the
doctor being thoroughly put beyond the possibility of
discovery; and when night came again, and the villagers

w

had once more retired to rest, he compelled his apprentice to go with him to the wood again, in order to remove the body to what he considered would be a place of greater safety. This time they took Tom's pony with them, and leading it into the wood, fastened it to a tree until they had recovered the body. After much painful labour, they succeeded in getting the sack and its horrible contents out of its hiding-place and on to the back of the pony, and then they proceeded to a boggy part of the moorlands above the wood, and there they buried Dr. Petty's body. In this place, Tom thought it would be secure from discovery for ever.

Several weeks elapsed before anything further was done. Meanwhile the villagers talked more and more of Tom Lee and Dr. Petty, coupling their names in a way that made Tom wretched. It came to be whispered about that an old farmer had seen Tom and his pony in the dead of the night wandering in the neighbourhood of the moorland bog. On this coming to Tom's ears he was much disturbed in his mind, and intimated to his wife that Dr. Petty's body would have to be moved once more. Thus it came about that on another dark night Tom Lee, accompanied this time by his wife, set out for the purpose of effecting a further removal of the murdered body. They took the pony with them. Having dug the body up, they put it on the back of the pony, and advanced over the moor in the direction of Hebden, and forward to Burnsall, where, tying a stone on to the sack, they threw their deadly burden into the river. There was a sudden plash heard in the water, and then Tom heaved a sigh of relief, and taking their pony they hastily left the place and hurried home.

That dark night's work, however, had not altogether escaped notice. A young man returning from a visit to his sweetheart had heard the plash in the water, and had seen Tom Lee and his wife and pony near the spot. He told his neighbours what he had heard; and shortly afterwards the sack and its contents were found in the river, and there was such an excitement and commotion in the district as had never been known before.

In due time an inquest was held at the Bridge Tavern, and Tom Lee was taken into custody on suspicion. All the evidence that could be procured, however, did not amount to proof that Tom Lee had committed the murder, and the coroner's jury acquitted him. Tom was just on the point of hurrying back to Grassington to inform his wife of the fortunate turn the matters had taken, when an officer arrived with a warrant signed by a Skipton magistrate, Mr. Tobias Sedgwick; and Tom was taken into custody and conveyed to Skipton. He was brought up before the magistrates on the following day, and remanded for a week, at the expiration of which time he was again brought up, and a long and trying investigation took place, ending, however, in Tom being acquitted a second time.

It now seemed as if Tom Lee was for ever exculpated from further connection with the murder of Dr. Petty. Three years passed away, and Tom Lee still remained the terror and disgrace of the district. But in course of time Tom's apprentice lad felt the stings of conscience so keenly that he at last, forced thereto partly by Tom's cruelty to him, turned King's evidence against his master, and confessed all he knew. This resulted in Tom being committed to York Castle, where he was duly tried and sentenced to death, the sentence being that he was to be hanged by the neck until he was dead, and that his body should then be gibbeted on the spot where the murder was committed. This sentence was duly carried into effect, and Tom Lee's remains hung suspended on the gibbet in Grass Wood as long as they could hold together. For four years, it is said, that sad spectacle was to be seen on the gibbet-post, a terror to all passers. The gibbet-irons were ultimately thrown into the Wharfe, and being found many years afterwards were buried under Grassington bridge. The irons were dug up again a few years ago while some farm labourers were digging the grave of a cow, and some one then got possession of them, and has, it is presumed, kept them stowed away ever since.

PRINTED BY RICHARD JACKSON, COMMERCIAL STREET, LEEDS.